Postcolonialism Revisited

Writing Wales in English

CREW

CREW series of Critical and Scholarly Studies
General Editor: Professor M. Wynn Thomas
(CREW, Swansea University)

This *CREW* series is dedicated to Emyr Humphreys, a major figure in the literary culture of modern Wales, a founding patron of the *Centre for Research into the English Literature and Language of Wales*, and, along with Gillian Clarke and Seamus Heaney, one of *CREW*'s Honorary Associates. Grateful thanks are due to the late Richard Dynevor for making this series possible.

Other titles in the series
Stephen Knight, *A Hundred Years of Fiction* (978-0-7083-1846-1)
Barbara Prys-Williams, *Twentieth-Century Autobiography* (978-0-7083-1891-1)
Kirsti Bohata, *Postcolonialism Revisited* (978-0-7083-1892-8)
Linden Peach, *Contemporary Irish and Welsh Women's Fiction* (978-0-7083-1998-7)
Chris Wiggington, *Modernism from the Margins* (978-0-7083-1927-7)
Sarah Prescott, *Eighteenth-Century Writing from Wales* (978-0-7083-2053-2)
Hywel Dix, *After Raymond Williams: Cultural Materialism and the Break-Up of Britain* (978-0-7083-2153-9)
Matthew Jarvis, *Welsh Environments in Contemporary Poetry* (978-0-7083-2152-2)
Harri Roberts, *Embodying Identity: Representations of the Body in Welsh Literature* (978-0-7083-2169-0)

Postcolonialism Revisited

Writing Wales in English

KIRSTI BOHATA

UNIVERSITY OF WALES PRESS
CARDIFF
2004

First published in 2004 by the University of Wales Press.
Reprinted 2009.

British Library Cataloguing-in-Publication Data
A catalogue record for this book is available from the British Library.

ISBN 978-0-7083-1892-8
e-ISBN 978-0-7083-2236-9

THE *A*SSOCIATION FOR
*W*ELSH *W*RITING IN *E*NGLISH
*C*YMDEITHAS *L*LÊN *S*AESNEG *C*YMRU

Printed in Wales by Dinefwr Press, Llandybïe.

For Bren and Vlad

CONTENTS

General Editor's Preface

The aim of this series is to produce a body of scholarly and critical work that reflects the richness and variety of the English-language literature of modern Wales. Drawing upon the expertise both of established specialists and of younger scholars, it will seek to take advantage of the concepts, models and discourses current in the best contemporary studies to promote a better understanding of the literature's significance, viewed not only as an expression of Welsh culture but also as an instance of modern literatures in English world-wide. In addition, it will seek to make available the scholarly materials (such as bibliographies) necessary for this kind of advanced, informed study.

M. Wynn Thomas
CREW *(Centre for Research into the English Literature of Wales)*
Swansea University

ACKNOWLEDGEMENTS

Many people have helped me over the course of the research and writing of this book, and I would like to thank friends and colleagues who have offered welcome encouragement and invaluable advice. I am indebted to Professor M. Wynn Thomas for his expertise, generosity and for his ability to inspire and without whom this book would not have been written. I would also like to thank Jane Aaron, Tony Brown, Ann Heilmann, Ursula Masson, Christopher Meredith and Jeni Williams for their help over the last few years. I am grateful to Tim Chamberlain, at Exisle Press, Auckland, for help in locating some New Zealand texts and to Eddie Morgan and Rhys Huwyn for help with translation. Most of all, however, my love and thanks to Ian Jones, for his support and tolerance.

I would like to acknowledge the support of the University of Wales, in the form of a bursary, which enabled me to carry out the bulk of this research. Parts of this book have previously appeared, in an earlier form, in the following publications: *Welsh Writing in English: A Yearbook of Critical Essays* 6 (2000); *Nations and Relations: Writing Across the British Isles*, edited by Tony Brown and Russell Stephens (Cardiff: New Welsh Review, 2000); *Rhys Davies: Decoding the Hare*, edited by Meic Stephens (Cardiff: University of Wales Press, 2001); *Women's History Review* 11, 4 (2002); *A Tolerant Nation?: Exploring Ethnic Diversity in Wales*, edited by Charlotte Williams, Neil Evans and Paul O'Leary (Cardiff: University of Wales Press, 2003); *The Journal of New Zealand Literature* (2003). I am grateful to the editors and publishers for permission to incorporate those materials into this study.

I would like to thank Gwydion Thomas for allowing me to quote from a number of R. S. Thomas's poems (© 2001 Kunjana Thomas) including: 'Out of the Hills', 'A Peasant', 'A Priest to His People', 'The Airy Tomb', and 'A Labourer', from *The Stones of the Field* (Carmarthen: The Druid Press, 1946); 'Valediction' from *An Acre of Land* (Carmarthen: The Druid Press, 1952); 'The Last of the Peasantry', from *Song at the Year's Turning* (London: Rupert Hart-Davis, 1955); 'Green Categories', 'Absolution', 'On Hearing a Welshman Speak' and 'Meet the Family' from *Poetry for Supper* (London: Rupert Hart-Davis, 1958); 'A Welsh Testament', 'Those Others', 'Too Late', and 'Portrait' from *Tares* (London: Rupert Hart-Davis, 1961); 'Afforestation' from *The Bread of Truth* (London: Rupert Hart-Davis, 1963); 'Reservoirs' from *Not That He Brought Flowers* (London: Rupert Hart-Davis, 1968). All these poems are reproduced in *Collected Poems 1945–1990* (J. M. Dent, 1993). I am also grateful to Meic Stephens for permission to quote from Harri Webb's 'Above Tregaron', from *The Green Desert: Collected Poems 1950–1969* (Llandysul: Gomer, 1969), © Meic Stephens.

1

Theoretical Contexts

Postcolonial criticism bears witness to the unequal and uneven forces of cultural representation involved in the contest for political and social authority within the modern world order. Postcolonial perspectives emerge from the colonial testimony of Third World countries and the discourses of 'minorities' within the geopolitical divisions of East and West, North and South.

Homi Bhabha, *The Location of Culture*[1]

Postcolonial perspectives emerge, Homi Bhabha declares in the quotation above, from the colonial testimony of 'Third World countries'. Bhabha's use of terminology such as 'Third World' and especially his references to geopolitical binaries of East and West, North and South now seem dated. Within the mainstream of postcolonial studies these simplistic categories have long since been challenged. Furthermore, from wherever postcolonial perspectives first emerged they have been quickly recognized, and postcolonial theory embraced, in quarters that have sometimes surprised and even angered 'orthodox' postcolonialists. But if the second part of Bhabha's quotation highlights how far postcolonial studies have travelled in the past decade, then the first sentence (which places an examination of the 'unequal and uneven forces of cultural representation' at the centre of postcolonialism) is testimony to the enduring and pressing relevance of such perspectives today.

What postcolonialism offers, in addition to a collection of complex theoretical tools, is a network of thematic concerns to which post-colonial writers return again and again. These are often bound up with specific anti-colonial struggles, the articulation of structures of domination (internal and external), the decolonization of the mind (to use Ngugi's phrase), and so on. In its engagement with cultural, geographical, political, gendered, sexual and temporal specificities, postcolonial writing (be it creative, academic or political) may be read as forming complex discourses which deconstruct and reimagine personal, cultural and national identities. The wide appeal of postcolonialism is surely due in no small part to this concern with shifting identity, with 're-membering' the self, and is of immediate relevance to and for a nation such as Wales, which has relied in recent centuries on a fairly self-conscious imagining of nation. It is therefore not surprising that the concerns of postcolonial writers and theorists from elsewhere chime so resonantly with the concerns of a significant number of writers from Wales. Before going on to engage with some examples of Welsh writing in English more closely, this chapter offers a brief introduction to some of the ways in which we might approach the notion of a 'postcolonial' Wales and offers some preliminary observations on the way the Welsh 'model' might be seen to challenge some postcolonial orthodoxies.

Postcolonialism refers, primarily, to the study of colonial/postcolonial (that is, post-independence)[2] situations. Postcolonial studies encompass history, economics, colonial and imperial discourses, the condition of colonized peoples, strategies of decolonization, and so on; literary criticism directly engaged with post-colonial writing in any language, but most commonly in a European language; and revisionist projects which force a reassessment of the literature of colonialism and the metropolitan 'centre'. The term 'postcolonialism' itself has been viewed as problematic, not least since it suggests that colonialism is over, thus ignoring 'neo-colonialism'. R. Shome has argued that, in the context of academic investigations, 'the prefix "post" does not mean a final closure, nor does it announce the "end" of that to which it is appended; rather it suggests a thinking through and beyond the problematics of that to which it is appended'.[3] Anne McClintock has famously attacked the tendency of the term to universalize a single colonial/post-colonial condition, thereby replicating the binary between colonizer and colonial other;[4] she thus draws attention to the problem of the prefix 'post', which suggests an adherence to the very idea of progressive linearity that postcolonial theory has tried to undermine. The problems of any such postcolonial model are evident in the case of Wales, whose history and literature in no way conform to the progressive-linear model of moving from colonization (and colonial literature) to decolonization (and postcolonial literature).

The unhyphenated term 'postcolonialism' is used here to refer to a broad field of academic research, literary theory and creative writing, as well as in an attempt to distance it from any temporal or political implication that colonialism is ended and to emphasize the word's reference to a definable field of academic study; its inadequacy, however, is glaring. The label has become so all encompassing that under its umbrella the politico-historical and sociocultural situations to which it is applied range into paradox. If settler colonies are 'post-colonial', what are the native 'First Nations' of these same territories? Once an imperial and colonial overlord, surely Britain is in some sense 'post-colonial' too, and what about the case of North America? How does colonial or post-independence India compare with South Africa? This is not to suggest that the experiences of settler colonies or former imperial powers are not usefully explored within postcolonial studies, or that comparative studies of diverse geo-historical entities are not productive, but rather to demonstrate that there is no possibility of talking in terms of 'the' colonial, post-colonial or even 'postcolonial' model, against which Wales should be measured in order to determine the validity of adopting and adapting postcolonial paradigms in the study of its history or literature. The sheer diversity of ethnicities, places and literatures which might be addressed through postcolonial paradigms means that, while the term may serve as a shorthand to refer to the academic discourses which engage with or make use of postcolonial theory, the subdivision (and perhaps renaming) of the field(s) is long overdue. Within such subdivision there is most certainly space for the use and expansion of postcolonial theory in the context of those countries not normally recognized as colonial or post-colonial. These are countries whose early histories include conquest and colonization prior to the period traditionally addressed by postcolonialism, and whose subjugation or marginalization may indeed continue right through and beyond the eras of overseas mercantilism, colonization and imperialism. In these cases we find a long history of cultural assimilation and/or political co-option, yet also a persistent, self-defined sense of cultural difference and, later, of nationhood. Countries such as Wales and Ireland spring to mind, but outside the British Empire, Slovakia and the Czech Republic, along with other ethnicities and nations of the former Habsburg Empire, for instance, might also be productively examined in this category.[5] The results of ongoing and new studies should complicate our understandings of regions and cultures too often glossed over and dismissed as 'western' or 'white' or 'first world', and demand a reappraisal of certain postcolonial positionings.

If reading Anglophone Welsh writing in the light of postcolonial paradigms may be contentious within the field of Welsh writing in English, making a space for Wales in postcolonial studies is itself not without difficulties. The authors of *The Empire Writes Back* (1989), an early, seminal survey of postcolonialism, suggest that the 'complicity [of Wales and Scotland] in the British imperial enterprise makes it difficult for colonized peoples outside Britain to accept their identity as postcolonial'.[6] Disqualification on the grounds of complicity and the concomitant valorization of a form of victimology have, however, been questioned by more sophisticated readings of colonization and imperialism. Yet something of this attitude persists, and Ken Goodwin has attacked the hierarchical victimology permeating some areas of postcolonialism:

> There is a sense in which the theory of postcoloniality ought to encourage the view that we are all colonial, imperialist, and postcolonial in various proportions. It generally doesn't however. It tends more towards the view that my postcoloniality is more suffused with suffering and unfairness than yours; it is a species of victimology.[7]

If Wales has been regarded by some as an inseparable part of the imperial metropole of the British Empire, as suggested by Ashcroft et al., then at the other extreme there are those who have sought to deny any Welsh involvement in the so-called British Empire. Working from the position that Wales was England's first colony, and that Wales has since been subject to political, economic and cultural imperialism, Wales is exonerated from involvement in the British Empire, its moral purity intact, by the assertion that any manifestations of imperialist tendencies in Wales were necessarily manifestations of Anglicization – and therefore not actually Welsh at all. This view has been articulated by Ned Thomas in *The Welsh Extremist* (1971) (although it should be noted that, elsewhere, Thomas offers much more sophisticated and subtle discussions of a 'postcolonial' Wales).

> I am not exonerating Welshmen from having participated in British imperialism. It is merely that when they did so they did so as Britishers, not

as Welshmen. The Welsh language was not part of that imperialism, and as Welsh speakers in their own country the Welsh were themselves the victim of a kind of imperialism.[8]

Appealing though this proposition may be, it is entirely inadequate and thoroughly misleading. Ned Thomas's statement makes a convenient but flawed and simplistic division between 'Welshmen' and 'Britishers', which ignores Welsh involvement in imperial missionary work throughout the Empire (a role which was, indeed, visualized as something that only the uniquely moral Welsh might fulfil, a project closely followed in the Welsh-language press), as well as Welsh colonization of Patagonia, not to mention of North America, Australia, and so on.[9] It is neither helpful nor acceptable to divide desirable and undesirable attitudes to imperialism into Welsh and British (read English) perspectives respectively, nor do such divisions aid our understanding of the complex experience of Welsh-British-English hybridity. Yet, the fact remains that the position of Wales within the British Empire and the United Kingdom was not, and is not, coterminous with that of England. In Wales we may find that the proportions in which we have been and are colonial, imperialist and post-colonial, to paraphrase Goodwin, are subtly and sometimes significantly different from those of other countries of the UK and the rest of Empire.

The categories of colonizer and colonized are, of course, far more complex than the simple binary suggested by these two labels might suggest. As the present study argues, the case of Wales is an excellent example of how postcolonial paradigms may be employed, as Goodwin suggests, to reveal the ways in which the Welsh have been subjected to a form of imperialism over a long period of time, while also acknowledging the way the Welsh have been complicit in their own subjugation and in the colonization of others.[10] Over-reliance on simplistic, if convenient, binaries is at the root of some of the principal objections which might be raised in the use of postcolonial theory in a Welsh context, such as the binary between (Christian) Europe and the rest of the world, which seems to be inherent in the vast majority of postcolonial studies. Said and others have been criticized for their reliance on binary categories, yet that between a grossly simplified and homogenized Europe (or the west) and other parts of the world remains a persistent one, and many postcolonial discussions thus ironically 'orientalize' Europe, and especially Britain, even as they aim to deconstruct such discourses in former colonies. Indeed, in many postcolonial studies, the existence of

Wales is elided altogether. It is not unusual for England and Britain to be used interchangeably in postcolonial studies – 'England' is even described as a 'nation-state' in *Post-Colonial Studies: The Key Concepts* – and while this slip is a common one, it is none the less significant.[11]

Infuriating though it is when 'England' is used to refer to Britain, or even the whole United Kingdom (with its resulting effacement of Wales, Scotland and, in different periods, Ireland or Northern Ireland), Robert Young points out that this usage is also a fairly accurate expression of the Anglocentricity of Britain. The studied use of the word 'Britain' may in fact, he argues, work to obscure Anglocentric hegemony rather than to expose or undermine it.

> British [is] a cunning word of apparent political correctness invoked in order to mask the metonymic extension of English dominance over the other kingdoms with which England has constructed illicit acts of union, countries that now survive in the international arena only in the realm of football and rugby. The dutiful use of the term 'British' rather than 'English', as Gargi Bhattacharya observes, misses the point that in terms of power relations there is no difference between them: 'British' is the name imposed by the English on the non-English.[12]

The postcolonial idea that 'British' is a misleading label that disguises English cultural hegemony and a project of assimilation is a very interesting one, and was raised by J. R. Jones in *Prydeindod* (1966), where he emphasized the importance of understanding Britishness as an *ideology*. Dewi Z. Phillips explains that, according to Jones, the ideology of Britishness 'tempts the Welsh to believe they can participate on equal terms within the framework of Britishness, and yet they are also aware of the unreality of this hope'.[13] This awareness in turn, Jones argues, causes much of the tension and bitterness found in Wales.

These points, however, need not necessarily undermine an attempt to *decentre* the Anglocentricity of Britain – to give the island and its peoples their 'proper names', to recall Seamus Heaney's poem.[14] Britain is a slippery – and versatile – appellation that is invested with a variety of meanings.[15] 'British' may well be a label 'imposed' on the non-English by the English, but it is also one *chosen* by those wishing to claim they belong to the island without identifying themselves as English, or for that matter as Welsh, Scottish or Irish. It is also an identity that is claimed in addition to these identities. Extricating Britain from hegemonic Anglocentricity is part of a larger project which, in postcolonial terms, might be described as the 'dehomo-genization of whiteness', where the category of 'Europe' constructed by postcolonial discourses is enlarged and complicated, a project to which this book contributes.[16] In this book, every effort is made to use 'Britain' to refer to the island only, although 'British' refers to all citizens of the United Kingdom. The meaning of 'Britishness', where this is used, should be clear from the context, although this is inescapably a shifting and relational term.

The proximity of Wales to England, their geographic union within the island of Britain, is another factor in the reluctance of some to consider Wales in postcolonial terms. Definitions of a colony often place considerable emphasis on distance between colony and mother country. Indeed, the distinction between colonization and 'national' expansionism and annexation generally relies upon whether or not there is a sea separating the two territories. According to this argument, Ireland was colonized by the Anglo-Normans (later the English and British), while Wales was conquered and assimilated into the nation-state. While it is of course correct to draw distinctions between the attempt to assimilate a territory and the mercantile, imperial or colonial exploitation of other lands, the absence of sea-space dividing Wales from the rest of Britain should not undermine the case of considering Wales through the prism of postcolonial theory. The lack of a dividing sea certainly makes the situation more complex in Wales, where the borderland becomes imbued with enormous significance. On a simplistic level, borders can be reduced to a set of binaries characteristic of frontier imagery; however, the permeability and instability of the extensive borderlands between Wales and England seem especially suited to be interpreted according to postcolonial paradigms of hybridity, which emphasize constantly shifting transcultural production.[17] Jeffrey Jerome Cohen makes use of a similar argument in his discussion of the Welsh Marches in the Middle Ages as a hybrid space. Indeed, he suggests that with the colonization of Ireland the whole of Wales becomes a border, or liminal, territory between colonizers and colonized.[18] Cohen's book is evidence not only of the usefulness of postcolonial theory to a wide spectrum of Welsh writing (he looks at Giraldus Cambrensis' *Itinerarium Kambriae* and *Descriptio Kambriae* in some detail), but also of how postcolonial theories are being adopted and adapted in areas which have been excluded by traditionalist demarcations of postcolonialism.

Apart from the lack of sea-space and Wales's location within Europe, the argument that Wales is neither a colonized nor post-colonial country rests on a definition of colonialism which posits the colonial era as beginning with the 'Great Discoveries' of the sixteenth century. According to this argument, by the time the era of colonialism proper begins, Wales has ceased to exist as a country and is, politically and economically at least, one with England. The idea that colonialism somehow came into being only in this period of European exploration has been challenged by studies which show that the material, political, emotional and ideological motives that powered these expeditions have a much longer and wider provenance. The Crusades, for example, are viewed by some as the beginning of European expansionism,[19] while in a Welsh context medievalists have long described the period of Anglo-Norman conquests, from the eleventh and especially the thirteenth century, up to the political assimilation of Wales in the sixteenth century, as an era of colonialism in Wales.[20] This colonization included violent displacement of peoples from fertile land, the planting of foreign peasantry as well as alien overlords, and attempts to wipe out difference even while maintaining racial hierarchies and racially differentiated laws. Neil Evans describes how, 'As colonial rule took over from a looser sense of lordship, so colonial resistance stiffened', yet at the same time there was a certain degree of acculturation, as the Welsh adopted Anglo-Norman inheritance laws and adapted to a money economy.[21] Even earlier, of course, there was Anglo-Saxon invasion and settlement and it is arguable that, in terms of Welsh memory at least, discourses of domination and loss, of cultural imperialism, resistance and complicity may be traced from Aneurin's poem about the defeat at Catraeth, 'The Treason of the Long Knives', through Arthur and Giraldus Cambrensis to nineteenth-century works such as T. J. Llewelyn Prichard's *The Adventures and Vagaries of Twm Shon Catti* (1828), and up to the present day.

The use of postcolonial paradigms to inform a study of Welsh writing in English, however, does not in fact rest upon proving that Wales is 'post-colonial' in the same way that India or Zimbabwe are 'post-colonial'. For, of course, India and Zimbabwe were not colonial and are not post-colonial in the same way at all. Wales, as already observed, does not fit neatly into a linear-progressive model of colonization, anti-colonialism and decolonization/independence; but, as postcolonialism has the capacity to recognize, structures of influence and subjugation are not necessarily coterminous with formal colonization or decolonization. The realization that formal independence may make little difference to the structures of cultural and economic domination (or neo-colonialism) has resulted in much more thought being given to cultural imperialism and hegemony (along with economic exploitation and dependency, especially globalization in the present day). Significantly, Welsh nationalism has focused on resisting the *cultural* imperialism of England, with political autonomy regarded as a means to securing and protecting Welsh cultural difference. It is this cultural imperialism and the resistance to its organizing principles that form the main axes of a postcolonial study of the literature and/or history of the Welsh. Having moved away from a reductive, linear model of conquest, colonization, resistance, independence and post-coloniality, it is possible to focus on the discourse of Anglocentric cultural imperialism over Wales's long and complex history, with its close geographical proximity to England and its participation in British domestic and imperial government.

Going beyond the linear model makes it possible to see instances of devastating cultural imperialism centuries after the Acts of Union (described by Gwyn A. Williams as an attempt to make Wales 'invisible'[22]) were passed. The nineteenth century is of particular interest here, not least because the imperialism of the British Empire, exemplified perhaps in the discourse of the 'civilizing mission', finds expression and parallels within the United Kingdom itself. The influential ideas of Matthew Arnold, who considered the Welsh language to be an impediment to the Welsh and to the unity of Britain (beliefs echoed in a wider public debate) may be understood in this context. Arnold's championing of the Celtic genius and his creation of the Chair of Celtic Studies at Oxford echoes other imperial discourses, which exoticized and coveted the artistic and material treasures of colonized territories at the same time as the native peoples were constructed as uneducated and uncivilized. As Robert Young puts it: 'Never was the colonial relation to other cultures in the nineteenth century more clearly stated: the force of "modern civilization" destroys the last vestiges of a vanquished culture to turn it into an object of academic study with its own chair.'[23]

The belief that the Welsh were a backward people in need of the enlightening influences of the English language or, in a slightly different interpretation, that the Welsh were an unruly bunch who needed to be brought under control, was not, of course, unique to Arnold. The most infamous and by far the most enduring example of this was the inherently imperialist 1847 *Report into the State of Education in Wales*, better known as 'Brad y Llyfrau Gleision' or the 'Treachery of the Blue

Books'. Gwyneth Tyson Roberts's book, *The Language of the Blue Books: The Perfect Instrument of Empire*, offers an excellent discussion of the language and ideology of the report itself as well as of the prevailing attitudes of the English towards the Welsh at the time. She also discusses the civil unrest in Wales which led to the report's being commissioned and the impact of the report in England and Wales.[24] Her book demonstrates how the Commissioners produced a document, based on inadequate research, which belied their imperialist attitudes and depicted the Welsh language, Nonconformity and Welsh women in particular, as degenerate. Responses to this cultural denigration were various, ranging from attempts to rectify the perceived inadequacies of the Welsh as described in the report, to the defiant refutation of these accusations – some pursuing both courses simultaneously. All these responses, however, worked to interpellate the Welsh in a discourse which constructed them in binary opposition to Englishness – as other.[25]

In addition to such historical and cultural evidence, Welsh writing itself seems positively to invite a postcolonial consideration, bearing witness, as it does, 'to the unequal and uneven forces of cultural representation involved in the contest for political and social [and cultural] authority within the modern world order'.[26] Furthermore, it is not difficult to find numerous examples of Welsh writers, poets, novelists, short-story writers and academics who make use of the language of colonial or imperial domination in describing the cultural (and even the politico-economic) status of Wales: from Rhys Davies to Gwyn Thomas, from Emyr Humphreys to Owen Sheers. Moreover, the plethora of literary depictions of Welsh experience that might be interpreted in postcolonial terms seems to suggest that these parallels are based on more than the strategic co-option of such tropes. Even in the work of writers overtly committed to internationalist, leftist politics, for example, we may find tropes that are fairly common in postcolonial writing and which work to support a postcolonial reading of Welsh cultural history.

In Lewis Jones's socialist novel, *Cwmardy* (1937), Big Jim (who has himself aided British imperialism as a soldier in the Boer War) is introduced in the opening sentence of the novel. He is given two names, the name he uses and is known by in his local community, Big Jim, and his official name, James Roberts, by which he is 'known to civil servants and army authorities'.[27] This division of course illustrates, in accordance with the book's communist agenda, the alienation of the workers from the structures of state power, but the emphasis on naming recurs later in the book in ways which might equally be interpreted according to postcolonial paradigms. The power to name oneself and one's landscape is crucial to the sovereignty of the individual or nation, and the renaming of colonized territories, like America and Australia, and people, such as African slaves, played an important part in the domination of these territories and people. Big Jim finds himself caught up in an inquest to discover the cause of a pit explosion and during this the issue of official and community names again comes to the fore. Big Jim, whose 'poor grasp of English', coupled with nervousness, undermines his ability to follow the inquest, fails even to recognize his 'own' name being called: 'He heard a far-away voice call for "Mr James Roberts", but it did not occur to him that the name was his until Ezra nudged him sharply'.[28] Shoni Cap-du, the man blamed for the explosion, which is in fact due to the pit managers' negligence, is repeatedly referred to thus by Big Jim, while the clerks persist in their use of 'John Jones': 'Did you know John Jones?' 'Yes. We did call him Shoni Cap-du.' 'Never mind what you call him'.[29]

This scene, in which the name used by Shoni and his friends is arrogantly dismissed by the state, represented here by the English-speaking court, has its roots in a much older imperialist, or perhaps more properly, colonialist act when the Welsh were 'given' surnames by the English. Gwyn A. Williams describes the origins of the ubiquitous Welsh 'John Jones' in pre-Union Wales.

Bishop Rowland Lee, with no great love for the Welsh, moved into the middle March as a hanging judge, cluttering the landscape with gallows and his reports with a jovially racist contempt. In the process he started to give the Welsh surnames. He wearied of the long strings of *ap* (son of) in the legal presentments of their kindred-trained memory and ordered their deletion. It is from this time that surnames spread from the border region to reach western Wales by the eighteenth century. In the process many of the Welsh got surnames much as Jews got theirs at Ellis Island.[30]

The inquest in *Cwmardy* serves to demonstrate the power and irresponsibility of the ruling classes, and it does so by playing on the tension between legal name and the given 'nicknames' which, as Williams points out, 'became a necessity when eight out of ten were saddled with a handful of English or Anglicized Christian names as surnames'.[31] Indeed, *Cwmardy* might repay a much more detailed postcolonial reading than is possible here, not only in the sense that there are clear similarities between postcolonial and communist/ socialist constructions of subalternity. The ambivalent treatment of the idea of national identity might repay further exploration, as would the sometimes bizarre use of language in the attempt to convey a Welsh-speaking community.

The *status* of the body of writing of which *Cwmardy* is a part offers another perspective on how the Welsh situation may be seen as post-colonial and another example of how postcolonial paradigms may offer a useful approach to Welsh writing in English. Even within Wales itself, the status of Welsh writing in English is generally very low: it makes little or no appearance in secondary or further education. The lack of prestige accorded to the academic research of this body of writing further marginalizes this literature, and courses on Welsh writing in English are far from universally available in universities in Wales, let alone in the rest of Britain (although seminars on Irish, Scottish and other world literatures in English are relatively commonplace). Indeed, it would seem to be quite possible for a Welsh child to leave school or university without ever having been introduced to Anglophone Welsh writing. The protestations that Welsh writing in English is not of a high enough standard to be studied at university will be recognized as expressions of ignorance by anyone familiar with the best of this literature, but such objections are also based upon a traditional approach to literature which ignores the vast array of cultural and literary theory that may, along with learning to appreciate literary accomplishment, inform our study of literature and other forms of writing. Such protestations and exclusion from the 'English canon', as taught at universities and protected by a complicit publishing industry, will, moreover, be a familiar echo from the recent history (and indeed the ongoing situation for many) of colonial and post-colonial writing from across the globe.[32]

Having left school or university, our hypothetical, yet all too representative, graduate is unlikely to come across contemporary or 'classic' books from Wales without making a deliberate effort to seek out such texts. There is minimal coverage of such books in the Welsh or British media, and most bookshops in Wales are part of major, centralized and Anglocentric chains which have neither the interest in stocking nor the expertise to select and promote contemporary Welsh writing in English – tending inexplicably to relegate all books from Welsh publishers or books of Welsh interest to small, obscure shelves marked 'local interest'. 'Classic' texts from Wales are more often out of print than in, available only through the second-hand book trade, if at all. Until the 1960s, moreover, there were no English-language publishing houses in Wales, forcing Welsh writers to publish elsewhere, mostly in London. Such writers were subject to conditions of implicit censorship not too dissimilar to those constraining writers such as the Nigerian, Chinua Achebe, and others from colonized places where no indigenous infrastructure of literary production was available.

The creation of Poetry Wales Press, which receives considerable subsidy, and the extension of such subsidies to a few other small Welsh imprints, along with grants to help publish individual literary titles, have allowed Welsh authors to publish in Wales and, more importantly, to address a Welsh audience without having to have their work 'filtered' through London publishers. But the publishing industry in Wales remains very fragile and dependent on inadequate subsidy. Many Welsh writers still 'choose' to publish outside Wales, in order to achieve the sales and financial remuneration that are simply not on offer through Welsh publishers, who have limited resources, inadequate marketing budgets and small print-runs. The devolved National Assembly, at the time of writing, is conducting a policy review of 'English-medium writing in Wales' to try to alleviate some of the effects of the historical disadvantages with which Welsh writers and publishers are struggling. Yet it remains the case that – positioned between Welsh-language literature and the power of London publishers and Anglocentric booksellers, with a weak publishing and bookselling infrastructure and academically institutionalized denigration – Welsh writing in English remains in a precarious and persistently marginal position within Wales and beyond.

POSTCOLONIAL PARADIGMS AND WELSH WRITING IN ENGLISH

The late Edward Said (1935–2003) is acknowledged as the founder of postcolonialism, but there are a number of significant 'postcolonial' figures whose writing pre-dates Said's *Orientalism* (1978) and who are, of course, labelled 'postcolonial' retrospectively. One such writer and activist was Frantz Fanon (1925–61), whose work has been so important to Homi Bhabha and others. Albert Memmi (b. 1920) is another key figure, and is particularly interesting since, as a Jew in Tunisia, he found

himself belonging neither to the colonized Arabs nor the colonial
French, but sitting uncomfortably (yet rather productively) between the
two.[33] Closer to home, Raymond Williams (1921–88), along with other
Welsh commentators, seems to have regarded Wales as – to use the term
loosely – a colonized nation. In one dramatic and moving BBC radio
talk (1975) Williams describes the Welsh thus: 'To the extent to which
we are a people, we have been defeated, colonized, penetrated,
incorporated.'[34] Interestingly, in the same talk Raymond Williams uses
the term 'post-colonial' with reference to Welsh culture. Williams's use
of 'post-colonial' appears to refer to a self-confident and decolonized
(in Ngugi wa Thiong'o's sense of decolonizing the mind[35]) people:
'There are some signs [in Wales] of a post-colonial culture, conscious all
the time of its own real strengths and potentials, longing only to be
itself, to become its own world but with so much, too much, on its back
to be able, consistently, to face its real future.'[36] One of postcolonialism's central aims is the recovery, interrogation, deconstruction
and coming to terms with all the 'baggage' that, Williams suggests, is
preventing the Welsh from engaging fully in the present and looking
forward to the future. Thus, we may see how writers not normally, or
self-consciously, labelled postcolonial may actually contribute to the
construction and understanding of Wales as a colonized or 'postcolonial' nation. The central themes of the following chapters include
issues of alterity, gender, imperialism and nationalism, place and exile,
language and hybridity and assimilation. Each chapter explores various
Welsh texts in the light of postcolonial theory, but it is worth briefly
exploring a number of related theoretical issues here, along with some
of the key issues which must be borne in mind when discussing postcolonialism in a Welsh context.

Creating a 'Usable Past'
Interrogating the past is not, of course, a politically disinterested or
neutral act. In *Devolving English Literature*, Robert Crawford argues
that it is not enough simply to deconstruct the rhetorics of authority
and imperialism. In addition, it is essential that 'a "usable past", an
awareness of a cultural tradition [is (re)constructed] which will allow
them [small/vulnerable regions] to develop a sense of their own
distinctive identity, their constituting difference'.[37] The emphasis here
on strategic re-memory will be familiar from a wide range of postcolonial writing: postcolonialism itself has been described as working
towards a similar goal. Leela Gandhi has articulated the central project

of postcolonialism as an act of recovery (in all the senses of this word). She writes that 'postcolonialism can be seen as a theoretical response to the mystifying amnesia of the colonial aftermath. It is a disciplinary project devoted to revisiting, remembering and, crucially, interrogating the colonial past.'[38] The act of recovering histories of colonialism is intimately connected with understanding the present, as Homi Bhabha suggests: 'Remembering is never a quiet act of introspection or retro-spection. It is a painful re-membering, a putting together of the dis-membered past to make sense of the trauma of the present.'[39]

Postcolonialism, then, offers a structure within which the past can be interrogated with the aim of (re)constructing the present. It is a strategic methodology, a self-conscious act of cultural and historical imagination and, as such, is rich with possibilities for peoples whose stories and histories have been suppressed, neglected, untaught. Yet, equally, such projects are full of dangers and must be subject to continual contest-ation. Take the concept of nativism, for example. Nativist constructions of cultural authenticity look back to the pre-colonial past in order to salvage what is conceived to be an essential or pure culture, which existed prior to the moment of colonization. In European communities, a version of this kind of nativism is discernible in a variety of nation-alist movements. In Bohemia, for instance, nineteenth-century national-ists looked to the non-industrialized rural peasantry as somehow conserving an essential Czech culture, which had been eroded in the Germanized towns and cities. This romanticization of the national role of rural 'peasantry' can be seen in turn-of-the-century Ireland and also in some Welsh nationalist conceptions of Welsh identity. While such (re)invention of traditions as a revivifying cultural force can be a vital method for (re)affirming identity, as the work of Prys Morgan[40] and others has shown, postcolonial critics, such as Gayatri Chakravorty Spivak, have rightly warned that 'a nostalgia for lost origins can be detrimental to the exploration of social realities within the critique of imperialism'.[41] Given the extraordinary length of time since Wales was colonized, the notion of a reinstitution of pre-colonial or 'nativist' Welsh culture seems absurd, and this example should surely also alert us to the fallacy of designating some other, arbitrarily selected period as an era somehow essentially Welsh.

There are many examples of Welsh writers constructing usable pasts, with Emyr Humphreys, perhaps, prominent among them. Yet, equally, Spivak's critique, quoted above, is one which might be adapted easily to refer to some of the most problematic examples of Welsh writing in

English, and, indeed, to aspects of some of the better examples. The honeyed nostalgia of Richard Llywellyn's *How Green Was My Valley* produces romanticized ideas of an essentially Welsh Wales where heroic and moral men fight oppressive overlords while yet being undermined by alien and immoral incomers to the valley. Set in a conveniently distant past, Llywellyn's novel elides the contemporary struggles that other writers of the 1930s were exploring Yet much more gifted and committed Welsh writers may be guilty of similar constructions. R. S. Thomas's reliance on the timeless figure of Iago Prytherch and other images of a rural Welsh peasantry raises some interesting questions. While his focus on the depopulation of the hills was nothing if not topical at the time, the way he made these figures into national heroes, who seem to stand outside of time, appearing as iconic figures throughout his evocation of Welsh history, is problematic. What is revealed by a postcolonial reading of Thomas's depiction of a heroic but impoverished indigenous people under constant siege, slowly losing a battle of attrition, is the way this essentialized, timeless perspective conforms to the kinds of histories of colonized peoples encouraged by imperial discourse. The past is glorified but is always a picture of defeat. In this way the conquered people may retain some sort of nationalist pride in former heroism, but the ultimate effect is to strengthen the notion of the inevitability of their defeat. An elegiac sense of doom and lament is central to R. S. Thomas's depiction of the hill country of Wales and the farmers who struggle to survive there. His poem 'Welsh History' offers the image of a people at home in the land, prepared to fight heroically, but always facing defeat.

> We fought, and were always in retreat,
> Like snow thawing upon the slopes
> Of Mynydd Mawr;[42]

In one sense this is an optimistic poem. While it refers to the internal struggles which prevented a united Welsh opposition to the Anglo-Norman invaders, it ends with the assertion 'We were a people, and are so yet'; but it is the pervading tone of lament which makes this poem so moving. The 'new dawn' promised at the end of the poem is vague and insubstantial. In contrast, poverty and defeat are vividly realized and placed at the centre of Welsh history. The choice of diction for the expression of perpetual retreat is of great significance here. It is not 'We fought, *but* were always in retreat', the structure of which implies a challenge, an attempt at victory at least. Instead the poem reads 'We fought, *and* were always in retreat' (my italics). This 'and' implies inevitability; it is suggestive not of resistance but resignation, thus reinforcing Welsh defeat and subordination. Postcolonialism, then, offers rich possibilities as well as a means of highlighting the pitfalls of remembering the past.

Colonial discourse
The tendency to draw spurious parallels between different experiences of subjugation, thereby disregarding or belittling the atrocities committed in so many colonial arenas, while collapsing historical and cultural specificity, is partly the cause of some of the hostility towards western countries claiming the condition of (post)coloniality. While drawing *rhetorical* parallels between varying types of oppression may have strategic value in specific instances of protest and resistance – middle-class western women comparing their situation to Negro slavery, or the Welsh empathizing with the struggles of various oppressed groups around the world – it is, of course, crucial that differences in the forms and experiences of oppression, resistance and complicity in different colonial, imperial, post-colonial and neo-colonial situations be observed.[43] At their best, these rhetorical alliances may forge mutually supportive links between various resistance movements, but in an academic context it is essential that spurious parallels and reductive universalizing are eschewed. This does not, however, mean that *comparative* studies ought to be avoided – quite the contrary. Gareth Griffiths has rightly challenged such a simplistic position: 'Why should comparison across and between the different periods of colonization "collapse" historical difference? . . . Specificity can be a function of comparison just as much as specific studies.'[44] Nor do I mean to suggest that there are not striking similarities between systems of domination, as alluded to by a variety of colonial and postcolonial writers, including Fanon and Memmi.

In the 1965 preface of Albert Memmi's book, *The Colonizer and the Colonized*, he writes: 'I discovered all colonized people have much in common, I was led to the conclusion that all oppressed are alike in some ways'.[45] A perusal of the rest of the book makes it clear that the colonized in this context are non-European (Europeans are the colonizers) and this situates colonization, as Memmi describes it, in a particular, if lengthy, historical period. Nevertheless, it is interesting to note that much of what Memmi has to say about the condition of the colonized will be familiar to Europeans who have experienced forms of colonization or imperialism. As Liam O'Dowd's discussion of Memmi's work in relation to the situation in Ireland testifies, a variety of different ethnic groups suffering various forms of oppression have felt a sense of affinity and discovered great relevance in the oppression and resistance of others.[46] We may find parallels, for instance, between sixteenth-century colonial policies in Ireland and Wales, designed to undermine their indigenous languages and cultures, and the policies of nineteenth-century British governments in colonies across the globe – including, of course, these first colonies, by then subsumed into the United Kingdom of Great Britain and Ireland.

A great deal of postcolonial theory, from Said's *Orientalism* to Bhabha's theories of hybridity, has been criticized for its homogenizing and universalizing tendencies. Yet, equally, one of the strengths of colonial discourse theory, for instance (of which Said and Bhabha are principal exponents), is that it exposes some of the common assumptions and mechanics of imperial hegemony, drawing attention to the plethora of interpenetrating ideologies which find expression in common tropes and, indeed, in imperial policy within both the metropole and its colonies. While there is a danger that limiting binaries will be set up in place of multifaceted and geographically, temporally and culturally shifting colonial and post-colonial realities, this is not an inevitability. The study of colonial discourse and the forms of knowledge-as-power which such discourses produce comprise a large, diverse, multi- and interdisciplinary field, encompassing a wide range of writing, cultural artefacts and so on, from disparate sources. Colonial discourse theory itself offers a range of very useful tools for deconstructing and demystifying categories of knowledge produced by orientalizing discourses, and specifically by *textual* contributions to such discourses.

The study of colonial discourse has given rise to perhaps the best-known and possibly the most overused concept in postcolonial studies: 'the colonial other'. 'Otherness' or 'the other' are, at their most basic, simply signifiers of difference, but the postcolonial understanding of the term – derived from psychoanalytic theory – is more complex, with a distinction between the 'other' and 'Other', after Lacan. The non-capitalized form is most commonly used in postcolonial studies. This 'other' is a recognizable but different entity, against which the 'I' or 'self' or 'norm' can be defined. In colonial discourse, the qualities despised, feared and covertly desired can be projected on to such others. The capitalized 'Other' refers to the '*grande-autre*', in whose gaze the subject *gains* identity: the symbolic Other is a 'transcendent or absolute pole of address summoned each time the subject speaks to another subject'.[47] In postcolonial terms, the Other can be described as the imperial centre of Empire itself since it 'provides the terms in which the colonized subject gains a sense of his or her identity as somehow "other", [and] it becomes . . . the ideological framework in which the colonized may come to understand the world'.[48] In this study otherness generally refers to the non-capitalized concept, but the idea of the Other described here is implicit in discussions of hegemony, Anglocentricity, interpellation and self-alienation (see chapter 6).

One disadvantage to the concepts of 'the other' – or even 'the Other' – is that such discussion tends inevitably towards the homogenization of *the* other. In terms of constructing, coherent sentences – and perhaps theories, too – using the definite article is much easier than talking about 'others' or 'an other' to signify that there are many forms of colonial other. It is important, however, to remember that, while theories of 'the' colonial other may offer a model applicable to a wide range of postcolonial situations, there is great diversity among different historical examples of colonial others: describing the Welsh as 'others' of the English, for example, is neither intentionally nor inevitably to imply that such otherness is coterminous with the otherness of Irish, Kenyans or Indians, for example. We must be wary, in using such theories, not to engage in reductive universalization. That said, however, colonial discourse theory and associated studies have highlighted some very interesting interpenetrations and correspondences in discourses of otherness. In *Difference and Pathology* (1985), Sander Gilman explores how ideas of class, gender, sexuality and sexual behaviour, race, culture, physiology, sanity and sickness interpenetrate and inform one another. Thus the various forms of 'otherness' against which a ruling class of upper- and middle-class white men defined themselves clearly have much in common. In the next chapter, we explore how such interpenetrating discourses of the nineteenth and twentieth centuries find their way into Welsh writing in English and inform representations of the Welsh themselves.

Hegemony and interpellation
Perhaps among the most pressing issues for a postcolonial study of Welsh writing in English are how writers address issues of acculturation and assimilation and how far they might be seen to contest, resist or

simply expose structures of hegemony and interpellation. Gramsci's
theory of hegemony describes how the oppressed tolerate and are even
complicit in their oppression when the ideology of the dominant class is
perceived to be natural and normal to the exclusion of all others.
Ashcroft et al., in *The Empire Writes Back*, define this process in
explicitly colonial terms as 'the conscious or unconscious oppression of
the indigenous personality and culture by a supposedly superior racial
or cultural model'.[49] Althusser refers to the process by which 'subjects
collude with ideology by allowing it to provide social meaning' as
interpellation.[50] Hegemony and interpellation rely on the apparatus of
the state: police, Church and especially education. The history of
education in nineteenth- and twentieth-century Wales is central to any
postcolonial interpretation of national history and has a significant
bearing on Welsh writing in English – from the Blue Books to the fight
to teach a curriculum which reflects Welsh issues, the still contentious
matter of teaching all subjects through the medium of Welsh and the
lack of Anglophone Welsh literature in schools. The man who called for
the setting up of a commission to investigate the state of education in
Wales in the mid-nineteenth century (the MP for Coventry, William
Williams, originally of Llanpumsaint) was explicit about using education as an instrument of control, just as Babington Macaulay had been
in his 1835 Minute of Education, which set out his ideas for education
in India. William Williams

> quoted from the official reports of a previous decade which argued that
> education was a cheaper and easier way of creating an obedient population
> than the use of force, and added his own gloss that the 'moral power of the
> schoolmaster was a more economical and effectual instrument for
> governing this people than the bayonet'.[51]

As one might expect, the Welsh colluded in the demise of the language
and there was no shortage of commentators, including many of the
Welsh themselves, who saw the key to the progress of Wales and individual Welshmen as being to learn English and, increasingly, to forget
Welsh. Although government policy was not always explicitly anti-
Welsh, and while the industrialization of and attendant in-migration to
nineteenth-century Wales were certainly the most influential factors in
the loss of Welsh in areas of south-east Wales, schools continued to play
a vital role in the Anglicization of Welsh children. Despite a shift in
government policy to 'a fairly sympathetic attitude towards the Welsh

language' from the 1880s, Gwyn A. Williams notes that 'a significant number of Welsh school-teachers . . . saw it their duty not simply to introduce their students to the world of the English language, but to eradicate every trace of Welshness they could get their self-justifying hands on'.[52] The significance of schooling in a colonized country is described by Albert Memmi, and it is a description which is applicable to late nineteenth- and early twentieth-century Wales. 'The teacher and the school represent a world which is too different from his [*sic*] family environment . . . [F]ar from preparing the adolescent to find himself completely, school creates a permanent duality in him.'[53] In Wales, the legacy of centuries of denigration and institutional exclusion, of concerted attempts to render the language obsolete and a less-than-sympathetic education policy during much of the twentieth century, was compounded by the widespread decisions of parents not to pass on the language to new generations for fear of it hindering their progress. The effects of this cultural imperialism remain clearly visible today, and the linguistic fracture which occurred in Wales as a result of inward and outward migration, as well as deliberate policy, is a recurring theme in Anglophone Welsh writing. The construction of the Welsh language as inferior resulted in writers such as Dylan Thomas and Emyr Humphreys and, in a different way, R. S. Thomas, being 'protected' from the language; consequently, like Achebe and others, these writers found themselves writing in a 'colonial' language and yet one which was undeniably their own.

For many contemporary writers, the Blue Books remain a potent icon of this linguistic fracture and of the Anglocentric cultural imperialism which lay behind them. Alun Rees's poem, 'Anglo-Taffy', presents the Blue Books as directly implicated in the creation of English-speaking, culturally impoverished, hyphenated 'natives' (in the derogatory, imperialist sense of the word):

> Brad y llyfrau gleision [the treachery of the blue books] had unbloomed
> the gardens of Dafydd ap Gwilym, Iolo Goch,
> Siôn Cent and Saunders Lewis...
>
> . . . I am the empire's saddest prize,
> a mission-educated native.[54]

Here the dual identity suggested by the satirical hyphenated title refers not to a productive hybridity, but to a reductive fracture and a sense of self-alienation and dislocation. More recently, Owen Sheers has high-lighted a new linguistic 'fracture' in Wales, as younger generations benefit from a new appreciation of the importance of the Welsh language and the provision of Welsh-medium education. In a poem called 'The Blue Book' (2000) Sheers depicts the Commissioners' report as an instrument of empire, before turning to 'another blue book', the exercise book of his younger brother, who attends a Welsh-medium school:

> It has fallen open on a half-written page,
> the space beneath his work shot across with red pen:
> '*Pam nad yw hyn wedi ei orffen?*'
> 'Why is this not finished?'
>
> Well, maybe it is now, if not in me, then in him,
> my brother, ten years younger,
> but a hundred and fifty years and one tongue apart.[55]

If one effect of this linguistic fracture upon the Anglophone Welsh has been the self-conscious subject of much Welsh fiction in English, the ghost of a lost language also haunts the work of writers who may be less than sympathetic to this language. The Welsh language is as great a presence in Alun Richards's short stories, for instance, with their resent-ful references to 'jabbering' Welsh-speakers, as it is in the work of more sympathetic writers. A more theorized and textual discussion of the manifestations of the dual linguistic heritage of Wales is explored in chapter 5, when the focus is on the postcolonial concept of code-switching. Other ways in which this might have been explored include Bakhtinian notions of hybridity and heteroglossia (as used by Cairns Craig and Robert Crawford, among others, in a Scottish context), which have proved so useful for postcolonial readings of colonial and post-colonial texts.[56]

Self-alienation and hybridity

Frantz Fanon and Albert Memmi both identified an inferiority complex associated with colonized peoples, where one learns to evaluate oneself according to the values of the colonizer or, to express it differently, a sense of inferiority derives from to the internalization of the perspec-tive, values and ideology of the colonial or imperial hegemony. Describ-ing the 'myth of the colonized' which is perpetuated by the colonizer as an implement of colonial power, Memmi writes:

He [sic] ends up recognising it as one would a detested nickname which has become a familiar description. The accusation disturbs him and worries him even more because he admires and fears his powerful accuser. 'Is he not partially right?' he mutters. 'Are we not all a little guilty after all? Lazy, because we have so many idlers? Timid, because we let ourselves be oppressed.' Wilfully created and spread by the colonizer, this mythical and degrading portrait ends up by being accepted and lived with to a certain extent by the colonized. It thus acquires a certain amount of reality and contributes to the true portrait of the colonized.[57]

Fanon delineated the psychological condition of self-alienation, which results from the internalization of the colonizer's perspective (or the production of the subject in the gaze of the Other, to put it in post-colonial, Lacanian terms, as pp. 18–19 above) in *Black Skin, White Masks* (1967). He describes the paradox of a sense of identity that issues from identification with the colonizer (or dominant group) in terms of the racial, or rather epidermal, realities of his experience of colonization: 'For the black man there is only one destiny. And it is white.'[58] Fanon's statement about the impetus for the black Antillean to become white becomes more obviously helpful in understanding self-alienation and the inferiority attendant on such self-division, when one remembers the way he describes blackness and whiteness. Having previously described how 'The Negro of the Antilles will become proportionately whiter – that is he will become *closer to being a real human being* – in direct ratio to his mastery of the French language',[59] Fanon goes on, in a later chapter, to emphasize the association of virtue and vice with white and black respectively, and he describes the difficulties associated with the dawning self-awareness of the black Antillean:

the Antillean has recognised himself as a Negro, but by virtue of an ethical transit, he also feels (collective unconscious) that one is a Negro to the degree to which one is wicked, sloppy, malicious, instinctual. Everything that is the opposite of these Negro modes of behaviour is white.[60]

While being 'literal' descriptions of skin colour, then, Fanon's constructions of whiteness and blackness are also signifiers of cultural attributes and the dynamics of power. Indeed, Fanon himself writes: 'Furthermore, I will broaden the field of this description and through the Negro of the Antilles include every colonised man [sic].'[61]

Writing from a Welsh perspective, Ned Thomas has described some Welsh people as having 'an ambivalence in the personality'. He suggests that:

> Welshmen [*sic*] are often fighting something in themselves. Since deference to the English language, and to English people in Wales, has for centuries been inseparable from deference to the higher class, there is some plausibility in the theory that Welshmen do not grow up with full confidence in their identity as Welshmen but to different degrees awaken to it, and that process of gaining confidence, straightening the back and holding the head up high is a painful one, and one that meets with some internal resistance, as with the awakening of a suppressed class or group anywhere.[62]

Raymond Williams also discusses a Welsh sense of inferiority in 'Welsh Culture', where he interprets what might sometimes be mistaken for pride and confidence as a defensive exuberance.

> Who has not heard . . . of the fluent, quicksilver Celt, making rings around the dumb English? The energy of the talk is indeed not in doubt, but we have to listen more carefully to what it is really saying. It is often a lively exuberance. It is just as often an unmitigated flow to prevent other things being said. And what those other things are we hear more often among ourselves, an extraordinary sadness, which is indeed not surprising, and at the edges, lately, an implacable bitterness, even a soured cynicism which can jerk into life – this is what makes it hard to hear – as a fantastic comic edge, or a wild self-deprecation, as a form of pride: a wall of words, anyway, so that we do not have to look, steadily and soberly, at what has happened to us.[63]

The exuberant, sometimes verbose, fantastical humour mentioned by Williams, as well as the sadness and bitterness, would reward further postcolonial investigation. However, the point I am trying to make here (without wishing to go so far as to draw a parallel between the situation of black Antilleans and the Welsh in historical terms) is that the psychological analysis of the colonial situation offered by Fanon, Memmi and others is useful in understanding the Welsh experience, where the Welsh sense of inferiority described by Thomas and Williams is instilled (in part) by the internalization of negative English/British perceptions and constructions of the Welsh, as well as by a version of history which shows Welsh defeat as an inevitable phase in the progressive march of civilization. As we might expect from Thomas's and Williams's statements above, fracture and a sense of dislocation have been central to the work and lives of many Welsh writers in English. In *Welsh Writing in English* (2003), edited by M. Wynn Thomas, duality and fracture are themes which emerge again and again in many of the essays. The various contributors make frequent use of a lexicon of fragmentation, dislocation, loss, exile, distortion, displacement, borders, frontiers, alienation, translation, fracture, wholeness, division and so on.[64] (In chapter 6 of the present study, the idea of cultural dislocation and self-alienation is explored more closely in a novella by Bertha Thomas, 'The Way He Went' (1912).) But, while 'fracture' and 'self-alienation' may evoke ideas of a divided, or broken whole, postcolonial theories of hybridity are in fact much more positive and productive concepts.

Hybridity arises from cultural contact and interchange. While for the individual this may be a painfully divisive experience, in terms of cultural production the hybrid, liminal space becomes an exciting and fertile arena of cultural production. In some senses the state(s) of cultural hybridity, as described by postcolonialism, offer an outline of any and all living cultures, as evidenced by the adoption of the versatile term across literary and cultural studies. Bhabha's foregrounding of interstitial cultural production is clearly of great interest to a country such as Wales, which is nothing if not culturally hybrid, and of special interest to Welsh writing in English. The details of various theories of hybridity offer a variety of avenues of exploration of Welsh writing in English – from the possibility of a hybrid, heteroglossic text issuing from the bilingual inheritance of Wales, to the sort of autobiography recently written by Charlotte Williams in *Sugar and Slate* (2002). This melds a variety of textual forms, and geographical, historical and cultural perspectives to create a rich, interpenetrating work, which embodies and performs a postcolonial concept of hybridity – or rather, of synergy. Its choice of a liminal, in-between space (an airport lounge) reveals its self-conscious debt to theories of hybridity, while its relentless search for and construction of identity – its project to make a space for Williams's Welsh identity – can be described as a 'quintessentially' Welsh project ('where are you from?' being a perennial question of everyday life as well as academic research) which yet finds many commonalities with other postcolonial cultures.

Charlotte Williams's engagement with hybridity offers another important insight into the significance of this concept – ideology, even – for Welsh writing in English, since her use of hybridity in her project to make a space for black and mixed-race Welsh identities in Wales emphasizes its strategic value. Williams has joined other writers in drawing attention to the 'fragility of many of the exclusionary markers of Welsh ethnicity – the language, accent, locality, name – and the ways in which these categories are constructed to create smaller and smaller sites of authentic identity'.[65] She and others are exploding these 'sites of authenticity' to offer a more invigorating and expansive space to explore and remake Wales. Other academics and writers have also emphasized – explicitly or implicitly – the strategic possibilities of 'postcolonial' hybridity – from Christopher Meredith (in *Griffri* (1991), discussed in chapter 6) through the recuperative feminist work of Jane Aaron and others, to M. Wynn Thomas's emphasis on the 'correspondences' between Welsh writing in English and Welsh-language writing and culture (also briefly discussed in chapter 6).

Hybridity, like postcolonialism itself, is not a term without drawbacks. Its colonial history is difficult to shake off, and there is a tendency to start talking in terms of blood, race and breeding, mixture and purity, or the cultural equivalents of borrowings and authenticity, and quickly to descend into an essentialist and limiting concept of cultural purity versus a contaminatory process of cultural miscegenation. Indeed, the bipolar relationship of postcolonial constructions of authenticity and hybridity is emphasized by Neil ten Kortenaar in his essay 'Beyond Authenticity and Creolization: Reading Achebe Writing Culture':

> When conceived as a peculiarly postcolonial condition . . . creolization is open to the same objection that is levied against authenticity: that cultures have always been characterized by fluidity and exchange. Hybridization, like authenticity, is unintelligible without a notion of cultural purity.[66]

Nevertheless, postcolonial concepts of hybridity are rather more versatile than these etymological spectres might suggest. Hybridity lends itself variously to a delineation of colonial discourse, the experience of individuals including the privileging of the hybrid perspective and a wider assessment of ethnicity and culture. If the individual's experience of 'self-division', of a certain cultural duality, if not cultural hybridity, can be unsettling at times, perhaps giving rise to a sense of being perpetually 'out of place', as the title of Edward Said's autobiography suggests, then it can also be an enabling and creative position.

The writing of Alun Lewis has begun to be explored in the light of postcolonial ideas of hybridity and duality, where Lewis's Welsh-British identity, his education and his experiences as a member of the British imperial forces in India during the Second World War are seen as inflecting his writing and providing him with a complex, uncomfortable yet privileged perspective.[67] It is an approach that clearly has potential beyond the work of this one writer, as evidenced by the contribution of Tony Brown and M. Wynn Thomas to *Welsh Writing in English*, entitled 'The Problems of Belonging'.

The positioning of cultural production in liminal hybrid spaces and a move towards synergistic cultural models, which go beyond ideas of multiculturalism, may include a *strategic* use of hybridity. This last is explored in greater detail in chapter 6, with special reference to Christopher Meredith's *Griffri*. It may also be observed in academic and critical discussions of Welsh writing in English. This is, perhaps, especially relevant for recuperative projects which aim to make a space for some of the more marginalized voices in Wales. Most of all, then, the concept of cultural hybridity or synergy offers the possibility of a supremely fluid sense of cultural identity – as Charlotte Williams puts it, the 'idea of moving away and moving back as [a] continual process of border crossing allows for a recognition of multiple points of identification'.[68] Hybridity opens up exclusive sites of authenticity, offering a permeable but containing space for the making and remaking of Wales.

CONCLUSIONS AND BEGINNINGS

This book does not try to propose a totalizing, final model of post-colonialism which may be *applied* to Welsh writing in English – indeed, any single book-length study which attempted to do so would inevitably offer only a reductive or overly simplistic survey. In Wales, with an increasing number of academics showing an interest in a variety of postcolonial models, we need to begin to explore further some of the recurrent motifs of self-division and fracture, for example, as well as more subversive ideas of mimicry. It should also be interesting to delineate the formal and stylistic ways in which Welsh writers have addressed and expressed their 'postcolonial condition', such as through attempts to create a distinctively Welsh 'english'.[69] Beyond this scholarly debate there is a need to engage with other European explorations of postcolonialism, as well as engaging reciprocally with other inter-national discourses of postcolonial studies, in order to reveal further how the experiences of one of the oldest 'colonies' of Europe, with a still-young literature in English, can highlight some of the fallacies as well as the usefulness of some of the more universalizing features of postcolonial theory.

2

Stereotypes of Alterity: Race, Sexuality and Gender

The interpenetrating constructions of race, gender and sexuality, as engendered through scientific and colonial discourse, were among the central organizing ideas of post-Enlightenment Europe and Empire. The nineteenth century was a particularly fertile era in the production of knowledge that sought to categorize, define and delimit the different peoples of the world. Fundamental to the project of ethnological cartography were the supposedly empirical sciences of anthropology, such as physiology, phrenology and craniology, which produced a powerful hierarchy of ethnic stereotypes. These continued to inform popular and literary images of otherness far beyond the reign of Victoria (remaining in many respects meaningful signifiers into the present) and writers have often consciously or unconsciously drawn upon them when portraying fearful or threatening characters or scenarios.[1]

It is the aim of this chapter to consider how Welsh writing in English is informed by such stereotypes of alterity, with special emphasis on racial, gendered and sexual otherness. While it is not difficult to find abundant examples of Welsh writers participating in and perpetuating the dominant images of pathological alterity in their work – Arthur Machen's work, discussed below, clearly reflects *fin de siècle* anxieties about social, racial, sexual and cultural degeneration, for example – this discussion will also attempt to illustrate how these wider imperial discourses have informed constructions of the Welsh themselves as other. As we shall see, the anomalous position of the Welsh (located well within the imperial metropole, yet as a nation within the United Kingdom which is marginal to the Anglocentric centre) gives rise to a series of ambiguities and contradictions. Welsh readers, and indeed writers, can find themselves simultaneously inside and yet outside the implied British audience who, collectively, can relate to constructions of non-European racial otherness while yet being internally divided, since the Welsh themselves may be constructed as marginal or threatening others to an Anglocentric norm, in terms that are common to racist colonial discourse. The first part of this chapter considers the various perspectives offered in some short stories by Arthur Machen (1863–1947) and Bertha Thomas (1845–1912), so as to draw out some of the ambiguities suggested above. It ends with a consideration of the use of the anthropological rhetoric of primitivism in the poems of R. S. Thomas (1913–2000). Of course, for many writers or readers the dual or split perspective of being simultaneously both insiders and outsiders adds a welcome complexity to certain texts; of the writers discussed here, both Rhys Davies and R. S. Thomas make deliberate and occasionally ironic use of atavistic imagery, while Davies and Margiad Evans (also included in this chapter) make use as well of established stereotypes of racial and gendered otherness in order to explore interlinked taboos of female sexuality.

Stereotypes of alterity, and racist tropes in particular, have been explored elsewhere in reasonable depth, so it is not necessary to rehearse the more common expressions of racial alterity at this point. Sander L. Gilman, for example, has demonstrated the power of the medical model of pathology in the management of gender, sanity, sexuality, race/ethnicity, criminality, class and other related social constructions of alterity (sickness) and normality (health).[2] While H. L. Malchow's *Gothic Images of Race in Nineteenth Century Britain* is typically Anglocentric in its scope, his work illustrates how Gothic fictions from Mary Shelley's *Frankenstein* (1818) onwards, consciously or unconsciously, draw upon stereotypes of race when portraying fearful or threatening characters or scenarios.[3] We begin here, then, with a brief look at how the greatest Welsh writer of Gothic horror, Arthur Machen, employs mystical and primitive Welsh settings in his stories, and a consideration of the ambiguous identity of the inhabitants of this landscape.

Machen's most successful fiction concerns itself with ancient evils that pre-date known history and perhaps even time itself, but, as Mark Valentine observes, 'he was tapping deep sources of unconscious dread for Victorians – the threat to their civilisation from an underclass of sordid, violent, secret, and subterranean terrorists, or from frighteningly alien races'.[4] Valentine points out that contemporary fiction vividly expressed Victorian fears of 'the Yellow Peril' and similar perceived threats of empire by way of an example, but might elements of Machen's writing construct *Wales* as the home of equally strange and potentially threatening races? Machen's native Gwent is the setting for some of his most disturbing tales, perhaps the most successful being 'The Novel of the Black Seal' (1895).[5] In 'The Novel of the Black Seal' Machen uses the Welsh landscape and a largely Celtic folklore to evoke images of a mystical borderland between the contemporary world of Victorian rationality and scientific investigation and the dark, sinister realm of an atavistic, supernatural past. The descriptions of the surrounding countryside are central to the creation of a suitably oppressive, ominous and mysterious atmosphere, and this area of Wales is represented in terms reminiscent not just of Gothic literature but of colonial texts, which produce the otherness of foreign landscapes[6] and peoples: the hills are repeatedly referred to as 'wild' and 'savage'; rocks are of 'fantastic form'.

The Professor himself, the central character of 'The Novel of the Black Seal', is a scientist-explorer, a common enough figure in nineteenth-century literature and history and, significantly, he is 'an authority of ethnology and kindred subjects'.[7] The Professor's investigations are couched in the language of territorial exploration and discovery. He confesses 'I covet the renown of Columbus; you will, I hope, see me play the part of an explorer'[8] and later his quest is described metaphorically as an attempt to find 'the undiscovered continent'. The ancient Welsh Border hills, littered with megalithic stones and burial mounds, become peopled by the 'tylwyth têg', or 'fair folk', whom the Professor believes to be 'a race which had fallen out of the grand march of evolution'.[9] The identity of this 'lost' race, while not coterminous with the modern Welsh, is clearly closely linked to an atavistic Wales, the Professor avowing that 'I became convinced that much of the folk lore of the world is but an exaggerated account of events that really happened, and I was especially drawn to consider the stories of the fairies, the good folk of the Celtic races'.[10] In this story the equating of the scientist with explorer or discoverer, as well as the fact that the text suggests that the mythology of the Celts may provide a link with the forgotten people or powers sought by the scientist, works to produce a picture of the professor-explorer as an imperial English (Saxon) rationalist risking all amongst a dark, forbidding and thoroughly *other* race who, if not Welsh, are intimately linked to Celtic Wales.

In the context of the late nineteenth-century discourse of degeneration, the most threatening aspect of the racial other was perceived in terms of contamination, or miscegenation. Thus, the womb (which in other discourses of pathology was viewed as a cause of illness, at the same time as it was central to defining traits of femininity[11]) becomes a potentially dangerous site of the corruption of the perceived purity of the races, particularly with reference to fears of 'black blood' going unnoticed in white society; of 'passing'. The fear of such covert contamination is expressed regularly in Gothic fiction, but has a much longer history. Thomas Jefferson, whilst noting the detrimental effects of slavery upon both slaves and slavers, justified its continuation thus:

> Among the Romans, emancipation required but one effort. The slave, when made free, might *mix* with, without *staining* the blood of his master. But with us a second is necessary, unknown to history. When freed, he is to be removed beyond the reach of *mixture*.[12]

This fear of 'mixture' is forcefully expressed in Machen's writing. In *The Great God Pan* (1894), evil is visited upon society in the form of an apparently beautiful woman, Helen Vaughan. Helen is the offspring of a supernatural coupling between a young girl and Pan, which has been brought about by a scientist. Although suspicions of Helen's dangerous nature have made themselves noticed during her childhood in the Welsh Borders, her power and her threat lie in her great beauty, which masks her diabolic hybridity: she *passes*. 'The Novel of the Black Seal' also makes use of a hybrid child, after a woman found in a distressed state alone on a mysterious Welsh hill gives birth, eight months later, to a boy who is living evidence for the Professor's belief in

> stories of mothers who have left a child quietly sleeping, with the cottage door rudely barred with a piece of wood, and have returned, not to find the plump and rosy little Saxon, but a thin and wizened creature, with sallow skin and black piercing eyes, *the child of another race*. Then, again, there were myths darker still; the . . . hint of demons who *mingled* with the daughters of men.[13]

The sallow skin is suggestive of the unhealthy, but also hints at racial ambiguity through connotations of non-whiteness; the piercing eyes, on the other hand, are signifiers of the demonic in Gothic literature, and here, combined with the non-white skin, work to suggest that races different from (other than) this idealized image of a healthy *Saxon* are themselves demonic. It seems clear that the reader is supposed to identify with the rosy Saxon, rather than 'the child of another race', which may be problematic for Welsh readers who find themselves excluded from the implied audience, or who are forced to 'read white'.[14]

The descriptions of the hybrid child, of whom the Professor makes an ongoing study, are also suggestive of ambiguous links with the Welsh, or at least the Welsh as atavistically related to an otherworldly past. The boy is subject to fits during which his face becomes 'swollen and blackened to a hideous mask of humanity' and he speaks in an unintelligible tongue.[15] This strange language is connected with the primitive, with a lack of evolutionary 'progress'; the boy uses 'words . . . that might have belonged to a tongue dead since untold ages and buried deep beneath Nilotic mud, or in the inmost recesses of the Mexican forest'.[16] The affinity between the primitive and the colonial exotic evoked here is reinforced and associated with the ancient race sought by the Professor, who surmises that, 'on my hypothesis of a race which had lagged far behind the rest, I could easily conceive that such a folk would speak a jargon but little removed from the inarticulate noises of brute beasts'.[17] It is interesting, then, that a word the boy uses whilst speaking this 'primitive language' is repeated to the local Welsh-speaking parson, with the aim of obtaining a translation. While the Professor chooses to put his question during a conversation which highlights the exoticism of the Welsh language, he is not surprised to hear that there is no such word in Welsh. The parson whimsically suggests instead that, 'if it belongs to any language, I would say that it must be that of the fairies – the Tylwydth Têg [*sic*], as we call them'.[18] Thus, again, although the local Welsh people are clearly not the same as the race the Professor is seeking (the *tylwyth teg* of the Welsh hills, who are described in the folklore of the Celts), certain connections are repeatedly hinted at.

The idea that the *tylwyth teg* were the vestiges of an aboriginal British race was not new in the 1890s. In *British Goblins* (1880), Wirt Sikes refers back to Revd Peter Roberts's 'Collectanea Cambria' of 1811, where Roberts espoused the thesis that the Fair Folk were 'the Druids, in hiding from their enemies, or if not they, other persons who had such cause for living concealed in subterraneous places, and venturing forth only at night'.[19] Sikes also cites a 'Dr Guthrie' who believed they were 'some conquered aborigines'.[20] Other theories of Roberts included one in which hostile Irish invaders had found themselves stuck in Britain and, 'fearing discovery, had hid themselves in caverns during the day and sent their children out at night fantastically dressed, for food and exercise'.[21] Sikes, and others, assert the mythological rather than actual material connections between the ancient Britons and the *tylwyth teg*, but, in his 1911 study of *Folk-lore of West and Mid Wales*, Jonathan Ceredig Davies still gives some credence to the 'realistic origin of the fairies' as being the ancient aborigines, living in hiding from their oppressors, who may in fact have survived in a sparsely populated and heavily forested Wales for much longer than generally imagined.[22] In support of this thesis, Davies draws the reader's attention to the existence of newly 'discovered' tribes on the banks of the Congo,

> whose existence, until Sir Henry Johnston's recent discovery, had been regarded as a myth, though they must have lived there from time immemorial. They exist in caves and in their way recall the fairies. 'Undoubtedly,' says Sir Harry, 'to my thinking most fairy myths arose from the contemplation of the mysterious habits of dwarf troglodyte races lingering on in the crannies, caverns, forests and mountains of Europe, after the invasion of neolithic man.'[23]

Thus, Machen's not-quite-Welsh fairies have interesting antecedents both in Wales (or ancient Britain) and on the peripheries of colonial explorations, just as the Professor in 'The Novel of the Black Seal' suggests. It is also worth remembering that, while Machen plays on the exoticism of the Welsh, he is careful to make some distinction between the Welsh and this ancient and sinister 'race'.

In a short story by Bertha Thomas, published in 1912, any distinction between the *tylwyth teg*, or 'Pixies', as she calls them, and the Welsh is much more blurred. Her story echoes wider discourses, which paint peasants as romanticized and elusive creatures and the Welsh as sly or secretive people, although her treatment of the Welsh farming family at the centre of the novel is very sympathetic. 'The Only Girl' begins with a description of 'Pixies' and links them with an unmodernized, remote and rural Wales.

> It is my firm belief – corroborated by the most recent prehistoric research – that the original Pixyland was Wales. The landsmen – the little men, the tricksy men, the unaccountable, elusive, secret people of the hills – mighty for mischief, or for kindness, according as they choose – dark, quaint-

headed, quaintly clad – you may call them Welsh, or Picts, or Ibero-Silurian, or the ten tribes, or what you please – I call them Pixies.[24]

The narrator goes on to remark on how they are vanishing, in the wake of county school education and the destruction of their rural hideouts, but she asserts that 'everywhere on the Black Mountain . . . their spirit is present yet' and 'You may surprise the little folk themselves by sudden chance, hurrying furtively along, cleverly disguised as miners or quarrymen, dark-faced, with dogs of some unknown breed in their wake, coming you know not whence and bound you wonder whither.'[25]

'The Only Girl' of the title is an epileptic young woman, whose extreme superstitious beliefs and use of an unknown language in addition to her native Welsh, along with the fact that her death heralds the demise of the family farm, place her on the border between the outlandish and the supernatural. The narrator of the story is in no doubt about her status after hearing what turns out to be this girl's unearthly voice, in a thick mist which has suddenly descended upon the Black Mountains:

Then, in that wild and lightless wild a sound arose . . . meaningless, a whisper, an utterance; low, continuous, and though dimly articulate utterly unintelligible. It wasn't even Welsh! Anything so uncanny never broke upon my ears . . . it sounded human and yet non human at once. Spirit-talk – Pixy-talk.[26]

Thus, albeit in a rather less sinister form, Thomas echoes Machen's construction of the Welsh as intimately, if always ambiguously, associated with the strange and prehistoric folk who have survived in the mysterious wild uplands of Wales. This view of the hills as uncanny and potentially threatening places is of course diametrically opposed to the view of mountainous retreats as places of refuge, which is a powerful motif in much Welsh writing, in both languages. This story, like many of the others in this collection, is written from the perspective of the privileged explorer or tourist (and there is no evidence that Thomas herself was any more than a visitor at the home of her Welsh family near Llandeilo). That is, the narrator is familiar with and well informed about the scenes depicted in the story, but the perspective is nevertheless that of an outsider. Yet, for all that they indulge in fairly stereotypical presentations of the countryside as providing a suitably romantic and remote backdrop for some fairly fantastic tales, and for all that they follow the form of colonial writing in offering up descriptions of exotic locations for a metropolitan readership, Thomas's stories are never simplistic constructions of Welsh otherness as discussed later.[27]

It is not hard, then, to find (especially in the nineteenth century) numerous examples of Wales being constructed as a place of mystical landscapes, a land which is home to strange and atavistic peoples (supernatural or simply foreign) in texts which are ultimately addressed to a London, or Anglocentric, audience. There are clear parallels between these 'domestic' constructions of otherness and those oriental-izing discourses which produced the binary others of the wider Empire. The rest of this chapter will consider how Welsh writing in English participates in or is influenced by these wider colonial discourses, and it will be specifically concerned with the central anthropological and/or ethnological representations of race. But, before attending to these discourses as they are present in Welsh texts, we need first briefly to consider their wider provenance in the nineteenth-century world of Empire and race.

It has become customary to draw attention to the similarities between patriarchy and imperialism, yet the uncomfortable premise that these two discourses unite firmly on the site of the black female body is less well documented. Here one may see the discourses of racism taken to their extremes, for black women were considered to be the lowest humans in the hierarchy of creation known as the 'great chain of being'.[28] The (crudely conceived) Black Woman became a highly sexualized construct, and racial distinctness was asserted through the (mis)construction of black female genitalia and secondary sexual parts, particularly the buttocks, as pathological, as grotesque *deviations* from the white norm. The case of Saartje Baartman (later known as Sarah Bartmann, although her original name is not recorded) is paradigmatic. Baartman, who came from South Africa, was exhibited as the 'Hottentot Venus' in London and Paris between 1810 and her death in 1815. She wore various costumes including a traditional apron which covered her genitals but allowed the audience to view the large buttocks and breasts that generated interest amongst scientists and the public alike. Saartje Baartman was dissected in Paris after her death by the anatomist Georges Cuvier who found an 'overdevelopment' of the labia minora which he described as the Hottentot Apron (while also commenting on the supposed similarity of her genitals to those of orang-utans). This genital formation was pathologized, in that it was seen to be abnormal and undesirable, yet it was also believed to be common to the racial group to which Baartman belonged and, therefore, this whole group could be considered to be pathological. Furthermore, this signifier of racial difference/pathology was linked to supposedly deviant manifestations of female sexuality, in particular those associated with an excessive female libido, such as prostitution. Later in the nineteenth century, another variety of supposedly pathological female sexuality, lesbianism, came to be associated with Baartman's genitalia. Sander Gilman observes:

> The author, H. Hildebrandt [writing in 1877[29]], links this malformation [the 'Hottentot Apron'] with the overdevelopment of the clitoris, which he sees as leading to those 'excesses' which 'are called "lesbian love"'. The concupiscence of the black is thus associated with the sexuality of the lesbian.[30]

Interestingly, Lisa Moore suggests that the 'overdevelopment' of the clitoris, which Hildebrant associates with lesbianism, was a common feature in 'the discursive representation of the [lesbian] body that came back from voyages of colonial exploration'.[31] Moore describes how the supposedly pathological sexuality of the lesbian was portrayed as a common characteristic of the 'Hindoo'. In an 1811 court case, in which two women brought a libel case against the guardian of a former pupil of theirs who claimed she had witnessed the two teachers indulging in 'indecent and criminal practices',[32] the judgement finally rested on a belief that race was a primary factor in determining the sexuality of an individual. That is, a belief that the girl was lying necessitated a convincing explanation of how such a young girl might have *imagined* her story, a problem solved by asserting that the '"Hindoo" background', or mixed race, of the witness (she was born in India to an Indian mother and a British father) was the cause of her vivid imagination and false testimony.[33] Thus we may see how the ostensibly unrelated discourses of race and sexuality inform and influence each other. The recognition of the interrelation of such discourses in our re-reading of 'white' texts has been one of the most significant contributions of postcolonial studies. For example, the discourses which construct upper- and middle-class white Victorian women as prone to madness, hysteria and irrationality are now understood to be entwined with those that pathologized the non-white. It makes little sense, therefore, to discuss the construction of one manifestation of otherness, be this based on sexuality, race, class or gender, without simultaneously recognizing the influence of a variety of interrelated discourses of otherness.

The interaction of the various images of cannibalism, witchcraft and lesbianism in constructions of white women as other may be seen, for instance, in Margiad Evans's short story, 'A Modest Adornment' (1948), and such interaction illustrates how racialized discourses intrude into areas which might formerly have been read in solely 'white', gendered or gay terms. The story is about the death of an elderly woman, a lesbian, in a state of apparent neglect, and the way her lifelong partner deals with her demise. Miss Allensmore's reaction (or lack of it) to the slow death of Miss Plant is in sharp juxtaposition to the response of an elderly widow in the village who has begun to idolize Miss Plant – an affection that hints at the possibility of a less destructive homosexual, or at least homoerotic, relationship. Despite a moving ending, which testifies to the old love between Miss Allensmore and Miss Plant, it is difficult for the reader to sanction Miss Allensmore's apparent selfishness during the last days of her partner's life. Indeed, Miss Allensmore might easily be read as a typical representation of a witch, so drawing on old European constructions of female others. She lives without male company, outside the village. She is described as a 'fat black cauldron of a woman'.[34] She keeps a hoard of black cats, and even Miss Plant takes on some resemblance to a cat, with her 'great silky green eyes' in which 'there was a curious sort of threat'.[35] Suggestive of another traditional witch's familiar are Miss Allensmore's bare feet, 'as dark as toads'.[36] The chips she makes are 'long and warped and as gaunt as talons' and her house is festooned with 'sagging black cobwebs'.[37] Miss Allensmore's home is also described as housing a 'prowling smell', the adjective conjuring animalistic and predatory images.[38] Yet the interpretation of these features in terms of popular conceptions of the witch are complicated by the subtle but persistent images of cannibalism and racial otherness in the story, and these are not divorced from the fact of Miss Allensmore's sexual orientation.

Black cauldrons may be typical of witches, but large, people-sized cauldrons are also the staple of popular portrayals of (black) cannibals. Miss Allensmore's cooking habits suggest the fabled savagery of cannibals: from the kitchen comes the perpetual sound of 'furious frying or the grumpy sound of some pudding in the pot, bouncing and grunting like a goblin locked in a cupboard'.[39] Miss Allensmore's appetite for food is emphasized at every opportunity – even her letters are sent by the baker – and our first glimpse of her sees her eating sweets. Elsewhere, Miss Allensmore drops grease on her naked, blackened feet (which are suggestive of the black 'savage' as well as of edible flesh); an inappropriate half-smile, she 'lick[s] away with the point of her tongue';[40] she regularly squats or sits in front of a 'great fire', almost cooking her own body, her 'fat, soft flesh that looked as if it had been mixed with yeast, all naked and flushing';[41] even more explicitly, she is described by a villager as 'sit[ting] on top of a great fire a-frying [her]self'.[42] There is the continual suggestion that Miss Allensmore has somehow devoured Miss Plant – Miss Allensmore is fat, in contrast to the emaciated Miss Plant – although it is Miss Allensmore's body that is more obviously edible. The cannibalistic overtones are clear: this is a woman whose appetite is so voracious that she seems to have eaten her partner, a notion reminiscent of the purported behaviour of some South American women, who were supposed to eat their lovers after sex, rather like some species of mantis.[43] The association of appetite and sexuality and the perceived excesses of these is clear, while the link between ambiguous sexuality, gender and food is established in the opening line of the story: ' "Bull's eyes are boys' sweets", said Miss Allensmore and popped one in her mouth.'[44]

Yet, if the stereotypes of lesbianism, cannibalism, race and witchcraft may be seen to converge in this story, the 'authenticity' of such constructions is challenged. Miss Allensmore *is* constructed as thoroughly other, and her refusal to conform to recognized feminine norms is accentuated by the contrast provided by Mrs Webb (Miss Plant's caring admirer), as well as by the nurse who attends Miss Plant. However, such dichotomies are problematized, and the image of Miss Allensmore as other is questioned not only by the romantic 'sub-plot' (which describes the young, sensually alert Miss Plant making a slow pilgrimage, on foot, to London 'just to say to her [Miss Allensmore], "I can no longer bear to live away from you." '[45]) but also in the way the reader is subtly encouraged to reassess the nature of Miss Allensmore's appetites. For example, the disapproval of the nurse when Miss Allensmore makes chips as Miss Plant lies dying upstairs apparently links her appetite for food with 'unnatural' feelings. She seems uncaring, and cooking and eating at such a time is certainly a rejection of the customs surrounding a death; however, there is also a strong suggestion that it is the *way* in which Miss Allensmore cares that is unacceptable. After Miss Plant has died, Miss Allensmore sits alone in her cottage and plays her clarinet through the night – a form of music she knows has never been understood and of which, hearing it drifting from her cottage, the villagers sternly disapprove. The painful conclusion of the story confirms Miss Allensmore's love and not only reveals the unreliability of the narrative perspective, which may have encouraged the reader to condemn Miss Allensmore's apparently heartless behaviour, but also challenges the distorting gloss of the language of stereotype. The reader is forced to recognize that we have glimpsed Miss Allensmore only as she is characterized by village gossip – she remains throughout the story a distant, problematic and rather intangible figure. This is emphasized when Miss Allensmore returns to her cottage after Miss Plant's funeral at the end of the story; she papers over her windows and shuts herself off completely from the world, significantly excluding the reader, too.

The racialized images of otherness (here expressed in terms of cannibalism and witchcraft) which are associated with 'deviant' sexuality are also to be found in an almost contemporaneous novel by Rhys Davies. *The Black Venus* (1944) draws on gender-specific constructions of racial otherness in an exploration of female sexuality (both heterosexual and lesbian), but, although Davies employs many stereotypical images of the black female body, his manipulation of them is often 'double-edged' and rather sophisticated. The black female body, as the sexualized emblem of 'dark' passions, is explicitly present in Davies's novel. Furthermore, sexual desire is conceived of in atavistic terms, using the vocabulary of race and purity, bloodlines and miscegenation, savagery and civilization, and so linking sexuality to dark, primitive impulses which are relics of humankind's barbarous and even bestial origins.[46] Although it is not known whether Davies was aware of the original 'Black Venus' (the 'Hottentot Venus' described above) or whether he had simply come across later versions of what T. Denean Sharpley-Whiting describes as 'the narrative of the Black Venus'[47] – that is, the inscription of the black female body by white Europeans as libidinous to the point of pathology – it is difficult to read *The Black Venus* without hearing echoes of this older narrative.

The plot revolves around Olwen Price, the beautiful young heiress of Tŷ Rhosyn, the wealthiest and most fecund farm in 'ancient Ayron'[48] during the reign of Edward VII, 1901–10, with the third part of the novel spilling over into the years leading up to the First World War. It is a comedy about the old custom of *caru yn y gwely* (courting in bed), and the bulk of the novel is taken up with Olwen's exacting search for a husband and the mounting frustration and disapproval of the community, but, although the novel is for the most part a comic and light-hearted story, its portrayal of social desires and inhibitions, of sexuality and restraint, is complex. Sex, or the possibility of sex, is suggested in the text through references to the black Venus. In fact, there are two black Venuses in the novel. One is a life-sized, nude, ebony statue of the classical European goddess, which takes pride of place in the cluttered cottage of the fiercely independent, idiosyncratic hunchback, Lizzie Pugh. The other is an embroidered picture of 'a buxom young negress', which forms the centrepiece of the canopy of Olwen's bed: 'The bed was a large four-poster with a design of fishes and shells, boats and anchors, with, as a centrepiece, for no reason at all, a buxom young negress holding up a large key.'[49] Both these figures can be associated with the Roman goddess, Venus, or her Greek precursor, Aphrodite, as can Olwen herself. The 'buxom young negress' seems to be pictured in a version of the birth of Venus – Aphrodite was supposed to have been created from 'the "foaming" remains of Uranus [that were] scattered in the sea by Chronos'.[50] In a comic version of this watery creation story, the ebony statue is (re)born when, after being pitched into a river because it had become a costly embarrassment to Lizzie, the black Venus is washed ashore on to a beach full of holidaymakers: 'the tide cast it up out of the *pearly foam*'.[51]

Nevertheless, despite the clever classical intertextuality of Rhys Davies's Venuses, their more exotic as well as their erotic credentials are firmly established. The embroidered negress, centrepiece of a tapestry of fish, ships and the sea, and holding up a key, is as evocative of slavery as it is of the birth of Venus. Olwen uses the chains of slavery as a simile for the condition of women, bound by conventions of sexuality, marriage and domesticity, in a speech to the chapel elders and thus the key held up by the negress might be read as an appeal for release from such chains. There are, of course, connotations here of shackles of a different kind – the chastity belt – and it is not insignificant that the proffered key is again highlighted in the text just as the sexually alluring Rhisiart Hughes is about to get into Olwen's bed (minus the bolster normally used to separate Olwen from her suitors) for the first time: 'Among the rainbow fishes of the bed canopy, the negress held up her key.'[52]

The body of the black woman as a symbol of female sexuality is taken still further in the form of the ebony statue of Venus – the black Venus of the title. Originally the property of Moesen Rowlands, a man who had travelled extensively and had 'used the world's countries for the full benefit of his mind, his heart, and his loins', Lizzie associates the statue with these exotic (and erotic) travels.[53] The sexual suggestiveness of the statue itself is acknowledged by both Olwen and Lizzie, in different ways. For Olwen, the figure is perceived in reductive physical terms (which are typical of the wider 'narrative of the Black Venus'):

Smooth and undisturbed her limbs, and the meek face was empty of all woe. Whatever stained it that body would come up shining. But, Olwen thought, it was clear from her aimless face that she had no brains to trouble her. Flesh she was, flesh's dark beauty, and no more.[54]

When Lizzie moves into Olwen's house it is on the condition that she does not bring her statue, which is banished to an outbuilding. At the close of the novel the readmission of the statue into the house coincides with the suggested revival of Olwen's sex life after thirteen years of celibate marriage.

Lizzie recognizes the sexual suggestiveness of the statue, seeing a direct relationship between a tramp's attempts to court her and the black Venus: ' "Know they do I got a naked black statue", Lizzie scowled. "No doubt she do draw them." '[55] She is also in the habit of covering the black Venus's nakedness on the Sabbath: 'On Sundays, and in deference to possible visitors, Lizzie always tied a muslin apron about its smooth thighs.'[56] This apron is of great significance as a symbol which not only functions within the confines of the text itself but resonates far beyond. T. Denean Sharpley-Whiting has drawn attention to the way in which the traditional apron worn by Saartje Baartman, the 'Hottentot Venus', when she was exhibited 'became a highly eroticized article of clothing'.[57] The apron covered Baartmann's genitalia and onlookers were consequently forced to 'imagine what [was] behind the "veil" (apron) . . . to discern the sexual mysteries of Africa'.[58] The apron became a tool of trade for nineteenth-century prostitutes and, while (according to Sharpley-Whiting) Alan Corbin sees the fetishization of aprons as being a result of their association with domestic servants and the way the garment is suggestive of women's underwear, Sharpley-Whiting contests that the apron became 'a highly charged sexual article' through earlier association with Baartmann.[59] This extended 'narrative of the Black Venus' was still being played out well into the twentieth century in French colonial cinema as well as a multiplicity of other racialized/racist discourses. Josephine Baker, an African-American actress and star of the French theatre and film during the 1920s and 1930s, appropriated this narrative, which constructed black women in corporeal terms as exotic, licentious and lascivious, using 'various costumes, ranging from feathers to bananas to a pink muslin *apron* . . . [and dancing] topless and buttock-accentuating dances'.[60] As Sharpley-Whiting points out, Baker knew little of Africa or African women, but created a highly sexualized performance that would conform to, as well as titillate, white imaginings of black women.

The erotic suggestiveness of Saartje Baartman's apron is echoed in the sexual subtext of Lizzie's ritual of veiling and unveiling her statue. Lizzie covers her statue on Sundays, the traditional night for courting men to visit the bedrooms of their lovers, although, since it is the sabbath, they cannot get into bed until the clock strikes midnight. In two parallel chapters in the novel, Olwen receives a suitor into her bedroom while Lizzie opens her house to some of the village women. In one chapter Olwen talks to her suitor until midnight, and then:

> Olwen looked at the clock. She went to the bed, pulled back the covers, drew the long bolster from under the pillows and placed it down the bed, so that the space was halved. Then she lifted her arm and took the prong out of her hair.
> For it was midnight and Sunday was over.[61]

Lizzie's actions in her parallel scene emphasize the sexual symbolism of both the statue and the events in Olwen's room, for 'as midnight struck from the church clock she rose, climbed on a stool, and removed the muslin apron from the black Venus. It was Monday now.'[62]

Lizzie herself is a fairly exotic character, whose garish clothing finds an echo in the 'garish dressed negress' of Olwen's bed canopy, and whose cross-dressing reminds one character of a 'Turkish custom'.[63] She is sometimes associated with the bestial, always croaking, screeching, bleating or spitting rather than speaking, while she is also associated with witchcraft, with her figurines and potions. This fascinating figure is closely linked to Olwen in the text, although it would be a misleading simplification to describe Lizzie as Olwen's alter ego, for the relationship between the two is far more complicated. Olwen is fascinated by Lizzie's flouting of social convention, while Lizzie's attraction to Olwen is partly avaricious but also sexual.

Lizzie is a passionate creature, even though we are told that her deformed body is 'squeezed clean of the juices that vex others'.[64] Her passion is often malignant, perverted, and, furthermore, her gender and sexuality are ambiguous: her black hair is 'cut like a boy's',[65] she reads *Gentleman's Magazine*, and by the end of the novel she is wearing 'a crimson cloak flung back over her shoulders like a Roman toga. Beneath it were white cabin boy's trousers and a tunic of green linen. It was not the first time she had worn trousers in Tŷ Rhosyn.'[66] Her first articulated fantasy about cross-dressing comes in the form of a plot to discover Olwen's 'tricks', when Lizzie suggests that the village women find a woman prepared to dress as a man in order to court Olwen in bed. When they demur, she turns angrily upon them:

> 'Well find your own ways. A witch I am not. Let Miss Olwen grow fat in her pleasurings. Worth the whole pack of you she is. . . . Poo', she added with a spit of rage, 'dress up as a man I wish I could, after her I would go.'[67]

Lizzie's feelings for Olwen are 'at once jeering and admiring',[68] but the sexual attraction is undeniable and, at one point, Lizzie exclaims 'If a man I was! I'd give that Olwen a courting in bed!'[69] The confused suggestion of violence and sexual conquest are typical of Lizzie's attitude towards Olwen.[70] Lizzie acts as both confidante and agent in Olwen's search for a husband, but at times Lizzie seems to act in the role of suitor, or perhaps rather the courted, herself. Olwen brings Lizzie gifts and, when she is invited into her cottage, a performance which echoes the courting scenes in Olwen's bedroom is played out. The black Venus is, of course, prominent in this scene: 'Reigning over the room the statue glowed darkly'; and Lizzie informs Olwen that she 'did her all over with beeswax yesterday . . . even her backside behind'.[71] Paralleling Olwen's bedroom routine of providing wine and delicate cakes for her suitors,

> Lizzie brought [from her cupboard] a bottle of home-made wine, glasses and small honey cakes. Her wine was of a good taste and colour, thick and purple with a red under-tinge. They ate and drank under the statue's mild but dark smile . . . Lizzie said insidiously: 'You and me only two women of nice mind in Ayron. Oh there's love and hate your body I do, Miss Olwen! Better than my black statue you are. There's pleasure it would be for me to bathe you. A faithful servant I would be.'
> 'Some day perhaps – ' Olwen smiled.
> 'Curd and honey in your flesh!' Lizzie chanted in admiration. 'A darning needle I could rip in it and dip a piece of bread in the juice . . . Someone to live for I want!' she bleated.[72]

Here then, under the 'dark smile' of the black Venus, cannibalistic fantasies are articulated along with suggestions of lesbian sexual desire.

As we have seen, the black female body has been constructed as the epitome of (pathological) excess, and a voracious sexual appetite has been linked to other perceived pathologies, including lesbianism and cannibalism, but in Davies's novel, when the two black Venuses are nowhere to be seen, sex is still conceived of in terms of darkness and some kind of primitive, residual instinctive urge. Interestingly, Rhisiart Hughes, the only man to whom Olwen is sexually attracted, is described as 'a throwback to savage times. Such beings swim up now and again from the deep pool of the past.'[73] Our psychological or, rather, subconscious links with the past are suggested by Noah Watts's assertion that all the trappings of polite civilization are but a flimsy cover for the baser, sexual instincts of humankind, where again cannibalism and sex are associated: 'Tongues wag pretty . . . tongues wag in fashionable clothes, and upstairs is a different family sitting naked like a lot of wicked cannibals.'[74]

Rhys Davies's use of images of black women's bodies, and of the vocabulary and ideologies of racial purity and degeneration, is far from disingenuous. His manipulation of the themes of savagery and civilization, and the playful echoes which resonate and rebound through the novel, make any simple analysis of his use of these contentious images impossible.[75] Although Davies makes very deliberate and self-conscious use of the black Venus as a sexual signifier, playing with themes of lesbianism and feminism, tradition and rebellion, the construction of the body of the black woman in terms of libidinous excess does not seem to be subverted, unless the very sexual and social rebellion which Olwen attempts and which Lizzie takes much further – and with which the black Venus is associated – can be read as a disruption of the racist discourse which constructed the sexualized black female body as pathological. Despite Olwen's refusal to be trapped by the sexual and gendered codes of the day, as well as the lesbian subtext of Lizzie's relationship with Olwen, it is difficult to see how this might in turn work to disrupt the discourses which constructed the black female body as silent sexual signifier. This is a story about white, western sexuality, not the black body used to signify it; in this sense, Davies's novel, for all its other accomplishments, seems to reinforce the reductive racist discourse which inscribed the body of Saartje Baartman and all other black women with a white, European fantasy of sexual voracity.

The figures of the two black Venuses, however, are not the only elements of this novel, or indeed of Davies's other works, which make use of the language and theories of colonial ethnology. Nineteenth-century physiological anthropology has offered literature potent and enduring signifiers which are nevertheless easily overlooked as constituting merely descriptive detail. The remainder of this chapter aims to draw attention to the way such descriptions of facial features, skull shapes and so on, which are informed by such anthropological discourses, appear in the work of some Welsh writers in English. The now infamous image of the anthropologist, equipped with callipers, taking cranial measurements in order to assert a hierarchical evaluation of intellectual capabilities, based on skull shape and size, might be seen as the epitome of scientist as imperialist and patriarch; both non-whites and women were 'proven' to be intellectually inferior to white men in this way. Yet brain size and intellect were not the only features anthropologists felt qualified to comment upon, based on their physiological observations, and it is in the obviously subjective values which are stated as objective scientific truths that we may find an important aspect of the construction of otherness.

In *The Races of Britain* (1885), John Beddoe attempts to describe the racial elements which exist on the island through the cranial statistics and the colours of eyes and hair of its inhabitants. Robert Young notes that Beddoe's work was influenced and encouraged by Robert Knox, who believed that, while Britain had been settled by many different peoples, it did not follow that the British were a hybrid race. Rather, as Young describes Beddoe's idea of the racial make-up of Britain,

> Though the races may now be intermingled, they remain distinct, and it is still possible to distinguish between them. The races do not fuse but live on separately, in a kind of natural apartheid – an idea that in fact first occurred to Knox while serving in South Africa.[76]

Such anthropological studies were not restricted to physical traits, and anthropologists' comments about the 'character' as well as the appearance of the groups studied were not unusual: indeed, the seamless ease with which they pass from hair colour to descriptions of obstinacy or rudeness would be startling, if it were not so common.[77] On the subject of people from 'Shetland and the Lewis', Beddoe 'cannot refrain from quoting [Hector] Maclean':

> Eyes blue and bluish-gray; occasionally hazel or brown . . . Hair flaxen and sand-colour . . . passing into various shades of brown. Gait firm, often awkward; little bending of knee, calf and foot not so well formed. Strong digestive organs. 'Doubts numerous, convictions few.' Accurate and impartial observers. Powerful local memory, which gives a talent for

geometry, astronomy, navigation. Firm, self-reliant, truthful; less irritable than the Celt and less ready to forgive.[78]

Again, there is a progression from observable physical characteristics to descriptions of temperament and behaviour, which finds innumerable echoes in descriptions of Africans, for example, as both bestial and intrinsically lazy or savage. It was perhaps a natural progression, then, from the racial context of this use of physiology to suggest temperament to the attempt to employ physiological observations to predict the potential for undesirable behaviour in individuals. Could the others amongst us – those who 'passed', such as the criminal, the insane, the prostitute – be identified by physical traits before any obvious signs of degenerate behaviour became manifest?

Cesare Lombroso is probably the most well known of those Victorian scientists who investigated supposed links between physiology and behaviour or temperament, but there were many more who were engaged in similar investigations of insanity, criminality and other kinds of social and sexual deviance, including Pauline Tarnowsky, who in 1893 published her study of Russian prostitutes.[79] Tarnowsky's study is typical in its reliance on ideas about physiological attributes offering identifiable signs of degeneration. As Gilman explains, in *Difference and Pathology*, Tarnowsky claimed to be able *scientifically* to detect 'stigmata of criminal degeneration' in women, hidden to the untrained eye by a superficial beauty. In her observations of some prostitutes she draws models of badness together with madness, claiming that these women's faces show the ' "wild eyes and perturbed countenance along with [the] facial asymmetry" of the insane'.[80] Significantly, as Gilman notes, it is only the scientist who may detect the hidden faults and, of course, the nature of these physical signs is revealing, as Gilman remarks: 'All of the signs [which were interpreted as signifiers of deviance] belong to the lower end of the scale of beauty, the end dominated by the Hottentot. All of the signs point to the "primitive" nature of the prostitute's physiognomy'.[81] Tarnowsky states that, with age, the prostitute's 'strong jaws and cheek-bones, and their masculine aspect . . . hidden by adipose tissue, emerge, salient angles stand out, and the face grows virile, uglier than a man's'.[82] The 'strong jaws' suggest the prognathous jaws understood in anthropological terms as signs of 'backwardness' or 'degeneracy' and linked to the 'Africanoid' skull,[83] while the ambiguity of secondary sex-traits may be seen to refer back to stereotypes of lesbianism, as well as to images of the insane.

Thus, discourse which constructed black women as sexually pathological was part of a wider anthropological and ethnological discourse
of race, gender, sex and sanity, which engaged with ideas of primitivism,
atavism, degeneration and pathology. Rhys Davies regularly refers to
racial atavism in his fiction, and this is a recurring idea in *The Black
Venus*, while the methods and theories of the physiological anthropologists are the focus of a later story called 'The Chosen One' (1967).
In *The Black Venus*, the village of Ayron is portrayed as an ancient,
unchanging place with its 'antique foothills' and 'dales where streams
ran pellucid as in the dawn of time'.[84] Here, antiquity is associated with
timelessness, just as the pristine African jungle was regarded as
representing both an ancient period, far back in European humanity's
development, and yet simultaneously as a timeless, almost prelapsarian
world. The inhabitants of Ayron themselves are closely associated with
the primitive, even to the point of suggesting humanity's bestial origins.
The most respected figure in the area, Moesen Rowlands (in whose
veins 'the blood of old traditional princes flowed'[85]), is described thus:
'In the olden days it was such as he who would have been the leader of
the horde to whose side all the tribe's women came, until a younger man
challenged his failing powers.'[86]

Throughout the text there are racial references, from the 'Iberian-
headed' maidservant at Tŷ Rhosyn,[87] to the 'Saxon-faced' Anglican,
Mrs Drizzle.[88] These descriptions recall scientific practices, such as
craniology, that purported to be able to distinguish the supposedly
distinct 'races' of Britain.[89] Although such 'knowledge' had been largely
discredited by the time Davies was writing his novel, as already noted,
racial stereotypes informed by such discourses nevertheless endured as
meaningful signifiers for much longer.[90] Davies's descriptions of other
characters are also informed by discourses of racial breeding as well as
by the concept of racial degeneration. Interestingly, the language of
Victorian discourses of race, of savagery versus civilization, is used
against the people of Ayron by Ayron's arch enemy, Mrs Drizzle, the
English incomer, who campaigns against the custom of courting in bed.
She maintains that 'courting in bed is an entirely barbarous habit left
over from the dark ages'.[91] Ayron's antiquity is proof of its backwardness to this woman, who, startled by gravel being thrown at her
own bedroom window, thinks to herself:

Savages, savages. Secret and sly, they were prowling about in the night,
come down from the mountains with their dark crafty faces. This ancient

land was not civilised; it had the feel, particularly at night, of being a thousand miles from the railway station.[92]

But Mrs Drizzle herself is not immune from equally insulting stereotypes couched in exactly the same language of race. We, as readers, are told that 'The divinely appointed Anglo-Saxon race [represented by Mrs Drizzle] is known for its invading, missionary and exploring energies.'[93] Indeed, aspects of characterization are regularly dependent upon the reader's accepting that certain traits are inherited as a result of the character's racial or familial origins, and thus we must assume that the authorial voice, if not the author himself, takes such notions of racial heredity and breeding at face value. While the world-view implied by the narrative is, of course, not necessarily synonymous with the author's own ideology, the lack of a distinct narrative voice can make it difficult to find the boundary between narrative, narrator and author.

In 'The Chosen One', Davies makes much more explicit use of anthropological language and ideas of atavism in a story in which one of the two central characters is actually an anthropologist. In the story, Rufus, a Welsh, working-class tenant of a cottage his family have inhabited for many generations, is fighting to renew the lease with the Anglicized (or possibly English?) lady of the manor who, while seeming to share Mrs Drizzle's opinion of the natives, is a far more enigmatic and frightening figure. It is quite clear that this lady not only enjoys observing Rufus with a professional eye – she is the (retired) anthropologist – she is also able to predict and therefore manipulate his behaviour at will; she is thus able to commit suicide by using Rufus as her unwitting instrument of death. For the purposes of this chapter, however, the disturbing, if somewhat baffling, ending of the story is of less consequence than the way the relationship between landlady and tenant is sketched. The 'othering' of the working classes by the upper classes is highlighted by Davies, but the significance of the 'racial' or, rather, national implications of the story ought not to be overlooked. The historical relationship between Wales and England seems to be echoed in the details we are given about the way the cottage, with some land, was obtained, rather deceitfully by the owners of the larger estate from the old Welsh family to whom it had originally belonged. That the aristocratic family made money through this small-scale empire-building, because of the expansion of the railways (which elsewhere were a vital component of the colonial project, not to mention the symbol of safety imagined by Mrs Drizzle, above) and that they underpaid for this land while making misleading promises about the cottage lease, places the story in an implicitly colonial context. Rufus himself, as a representative of an old race, is a fascinating figure. The dark curly hair, low brow and stocky build sound as if they come from a description of a Welshman in Beddoe's *Races of Britain*, while the lady of the big house lives as remotely cut off from her neighbours as if she was a white settler in an African or Indian colony.

In 'The Chosen One', the Welshness of the simian man is contrasted with the apparent 'non-Welshness' of the anthropologist, whose class and culture are shown as distancing her from her Welsh surroundings. Indeed, the anthropological associations of the story are explicit; Mrs Vines has 'lived among African savages, studying their ways with her first husband',[94] has African masks adorning her walls, keeps a sheep's skull because of the 'purity' of its breeding and views her tenant as a fascinating specimen, intensely observing his movements through binoculars. What are particularly fascinating are the descriptions of the tenant and his girlfriend in terms so familiar from studies of African or African-American people. Rufus 'prowls' around his garden, he has 'full-fleshed lips', and lives in a house Mrs Vines declares to be unfit for human habitation. She tells him 'You are almost as hairy as an ape' and shows the obligatory interest in his genitals, commenting that 'your organs are exceptionally pronounced'.[95] His girlfriend is distinguished by her tendency to shriek, while she is referred to by Mrs Vines as a 'jazz-dancing slut' with 'bare feet'.[96] The combined reference to sexual promiscuity and the style of music and dancing which originated in black America evokes familiar images of both the degeneracy of the working-class prostitute and the sensual black. The connotations are of the primitive, even the degenerate, and are described in the terms of physiological anthropology:

> To her eye, the prognathous jaw, broad nose, and gypsy-black hair of this heavy-bodied but personable young man bore distinct atavistic elements. He possessed, too, a primitive bloom, which often lingered for years beyond adolescence with persons of tardy mental development.[97]

The prognathous jaw is associated with the mentally, racially and socially inferior; the broad nose draws parallels with Negroes, and racial otherness is also suggested in the description of his 'gypsy-black hair'. That these are racial rather than accidental is emphasized by the description of his traits as 'distinct atavistic elements'.[98] In using an authorial narrative voice to describe what are effectively the anthropologist's observations, which typically run from physical appearance to assumptions of character and mental capacity, Davies draws attention to the complicity of literature with such constructions and parodies the self-referential academic/scientific language used in such discourses to assert and maintain authority (Mrs Vines's letter giving notice of eviction to her tenant is deliberately, provocatively obtuse). The story becomes almost a deconstruction of the methods of suggestion employed by some forms of literature, particularly, but by no means exclusively, the Gothic. By this I mean to suggest that the anthropologist reads physical 'signs' much in the same way as a reader interprets 'literary' signs littered about the text, signs which are interpreted according to fixed conventions such as, to give a simplistic example, the association of the colour black with evil, or rural isolation with an 'uncivilized' or 'savage' threat – references which are not innocently contained within an arbitrary literary convention but which continually refer back to social and cultural discourses.

It is illuminating to reconsider R. S. Thomas's peasant figures in the light of this understanding of the significance of anthropological markers, since Thomas consistently makes use of such imagery to describe his hill farmers. In 'Out of the Hills', we are introduced to a prototype of the figure that would later become Iago Prytherch. This slightly Neanderthal form, which emerges from the mysterious hills, does not have a head, but rather a skull – and a 'sallow' one at that. His 'Dreams' are 'Dark as curls',[99] suggesting a certain impenetrability of intellect and, therefore, a lack of intelligence, while firmly registering him as a 'typical' dark-haired Welshman. The shape and size of the skulls of Thomas's Prytherch figures are often commented upon. They have 'savage skulls', suggesting the uncivilized, the degenerate. The 'wide skull' of 'The Hill Farmer Speaks' hints at a vacant mind; and in 'The Figure', the unnamed man has a 'thick skull' around which his thoughts lift and fall in a 'dark wrack'. As already mentioned, anthropologists who based their study of race upon cranial measurements have placed the skull firmly within a racist discourse of primitivism.

The primitive or atavistic qualities of the Prytherch figures are established explicitly in 'A Peasant', where Iago Prytherch is described as 'your prototype'.[100] In the context of the poem, this assertion forms part of an attack upon the reader (or a castigation of the poet himself) for his or her 'refined, / But affected, sense' which is horrified by this apparently subhuman peasant.[101] However, it is impossible to get away from the connotations of the evolutionally challenged in the word 'prototype', connotations which echo the anthropological and colonial discourses that constructed colonized peoples as representing a stage in the development of humankind, which had been surpassed by the colonizers long ago. *The New Oxford Dictionary of English* defines the word 'prototype' as the 'first or preliminary model of something . . . from which other forms are developed or copied'.[102] The emphasis tends to be on the development from the first model, and a look at the meaning of the stem 'proto-', which the dictionary defines as 'original; primitive', bears out this semantic overtone.

If the 'something frightening in the vacancy of his mind'[103] is not enough to create an unbridgeable distance between the reader and Prytherch, then his subhumanity is further suggested by a muteness that is often described in terms associated with stereotypes of idiocy or insanity. The Welsh hill farmers are drooling, inarticulate wretches, like John Three, in 'Meet the Family', '. . . still outside / Drooling where the daylight died';[104] in 'Portrait' Prytherch's eyes are 'So shrill they would not permit the ear / To hear what the lips' slobber intended';[105] and, in 'A Peasant', Prytherch is capable only of 'spittled mirth';[106] while in 'Valediction' the farmer is distinguished from his animals only by his smile, a sign of humanity: '. . . I saw you loitering with the cows, / Yourself one of them but for the smile'.[107] The association of the bestial with the primitive is well established, particularly in the anthropological discourses of race which saw Negroes as so closely related to apes that there could be sexual contact between the two species.[108] R. S. Thomas's descriptions of the animalistic qualities of his 'peasants' can be equally demeaning, and it is interesting that the most hostile or derogatory comparisons tend to involve women and sex. In 'A Priest to His People' where the poet addresses the '*men* of Wales', the women are closely associated with the animals which belong to the farmers: 'With your sheep and your pigs and your ponies, your sweaty females'.[109] Again, in 'The Airy Tomb', women form the link between the farmer and his animals, so that in coupling with them his bestiality is suggested:

> But surely it happened that one of those supple bitches
> With the sly haunches angled him into her net
> At the male season . . .[110]

Away from the misogynistic imagery, the farmers retain a persistent association with the animals they husband; in 'The Last of the Peasantry', the farmer is described as moving 'With a beast's gait'.[111]

That Thomas is, of course, aware of the anthropological overtones of such language is evident in a powerful poem entitled 'A Welsh Testament'. Here, he mocks the perspective of what is constructed as a tourist-imperialist's concern to conserve supposedly authentic markers of 'race' and culture:

> My high cheek-bones, my length of skull
> Drew them as to a rare portrait
> By a dead master.[112]

The final two stanzas of the same poem pursue this image of the imprisoning gaze of the tourist-imperialist (or perhaps an essentializing nationalist, and Thomas implicitly places himself in the role of the one rebuked by the speaker in this poem).

> And always there was their eyes' strong
> Pressure on me: You are Welsh, they said;
> Speak to us so; keep your fields free
> Of the smell of petrol, the loud roar
> Of hot tractors; we must have peace
> And quietness.
>   Is a museum
> Peace? I asked. Am I the keeper
> Of the heart's relics, blowing the dust
> In my own eyes?[113]

And the farmer rejects

>   . . . the absurd label
> Of birth, of race hanging askew
> About my shoulders.[114]

The image suggested here, of dusty skulls and other specimens hoarded by anthropologists in museums, from which sweeping deductions were made about the nature of the peoples represented on their labels, is strong.

The construction of the farmers as bestial, mindless peasants, is refuted directly by the poet on numerous occasions, perhaps most obviously with the direct statement, 'I am a man', in 'A Welsh Testament'. However, this claim sounds more like a plea than a statement, and the frequency of its occurrence leads one to question just whom the poet is trying to convince. In 'The Hill Farmer Speaks', the poem hinges on the repetition of the line 'Listen, listen, I am a man like you.' The protestations are reminiscent of anti-slavery propaganda, which showed African slaves in chains kneeling in a posture of supplication along with the inscribed question 'Am I not a man and brother?' or, sometimes, 'Am I not a woman and sister?' These pictures were widely and abundantly circulated during the anti-slavery campaign and, although well intentioned, had the effect of firmly connecting the image of Negroes with slavery, establishing them as servile and pitiable creatures, certainly not as equals. Jennifer DeVere Brody describes their posture of supplication as one which suggested a certain nobility in the endurance of suffering, and points to the Christian associations of such iconography.[115] It is sometimes difficult to see Prytherch as a human being and, when he does emerge as a man, we are asked at once to sympathize with the probable imminence of his demise and yet to admire his uncomplaining endurance of physical hardships.

If Thomas constructs these Welshmen as dark and primitive, as thoroughly and often repulsively other, then he also constructs a more palatable, although no less problematic representation of Prytherch, which might be described as the 'noble savage'. If Prytherch is a mindless figure, almost an animal, who horrifies and infuriates the poet or reader, then he is also the man who communes with the land, who is at one with nature, as in 'Absolution'.

> . . . the day's end
> Finds you still in the same field
> In which you started, your soul made strong
> By the earth's incense, the wind's song.[116]

I do not, in setting up this dichotomy of noble savage versus uncivilized degenerate, wish to suggest that the two portrayals work in opposition to one another or are mutually exclusive – quite the opposite, for both elements appear in the same poems, and the overall effect is to create a dialectic which elevates Prytherch beyond any narrow, individual existence.

The *New Oxford Dictionary of English* describes the noble savage as 'a representative of primitive mankind as idealised in Romantic literature, symbolising the innate goodness of humanity when free from

the corrupting influence of civilization'.[117] For R. S. Thomas, the
farmers' 'innate goodness' seems to lie in their adherence to a way of life
which is not only ancient, but fundamentally Welsh, in a way that urban
or industrial Wales cannot be, for Thomas. Or, to put it another way,
Prytherch represents an existence which challenges industrial, imperial
and consumer capitalism. Prytherch's nobility is to be found in his
identification with the natural world (which is by implication an
identification with God, the creator), which also signifies an involvement with a cyclical temporal register dominated by the seasons, rather
than a linear timescale dominated by the pernicious forces of 'progress'.
This raises interesting questions about how the Prytherch figures may
function as part of a strategy of resistance, in the Romantic vein, but I
want to concentrate here on how, in constructing Prytherch as an ideal,
if beleaguered, archetype, Thomas reveals an unbridgeable distance
from him. Thomas's gaze emanates from the imperial metropolis, not
from the land of his fathers.

This perspective of the poet as an outsider looking in is consonant
with R. S. Thomas's autobiographical writings.

> While I was at the Theological College in Llandaff, I used to take the train
> home from Cardiff. As you know, the line from Cardiff to Shrewsbury runs
> through the Marches, with the plains of England on one side and the Welsh
> hills on the other. I was often stirred by the sight of these hills rising in the
> west. It sometimes started to get dark before we reached Ludlow. In the
> west, the sky would be aflame, reminding one of ancient battles. Against
> that light, the hills rose dark and threatening as though full of armed men
> waiting for a chance to attack. There was in the west a land of romance and
> danger, a secret land.[118]

Here, Wales is a medieval land of guerrilla fighters, unseen but sensed.
The 'secret land' is still an unknown territory – a subject for the
imagination. In 'Y Llwybrau Gynt 2' R. S. Thomas goes on to say that
he 'set about learning Welsh, so as to get back to the real Wales of my
imagination'. The paradox here is striking, as is the use of the temporal
idiom; he wants to 'get back' to 'the *real* Wales' of his '*imagination*'.
This construction of Wales as a place not only strongly associated with
the past, but also a land which is firmly contained within his own
imagination, would seem to ally Thomas with the gaze of those
Romantic and Victorian imperialists who perpetuated the images of the
mysterious Celtic periphery. This imagined Wales is a nostalgic,
essentialist, and even a nativist construction[119] – consider such a poem

as 'On Hearing a Welshman Speak', where a pre-colonial past is
retrieved, somehow preserved intact in the Welsh language:

> And as he speaks time turns,
> The swift years revolve
> Backwards.[120]

Goronwy returns, the Bible is untranslated, the destruction of Glyndŵr
is repaired.

> Stones to the walls fly back,
> The gay manors are full
> Of music; the poets return
> To feed at the royal tables.
> Who dreams of failure now
> That the oak woods are loud
> With the last hurrying feet
> Seeking the English plain?[121]

Hoping to find an essentialized national(ist) rural population is by no
means unique to R. S. Thomas, to Welsh or other nationalist movements. The *gwerin* (folk) Dewi Emrys evokes in Thomas's epigraph to
'Those Others', '*A gofid gwerin gyfan / Yn fy nghri fel taerni tân*' [And
the pain of all the ordinary folk / In my cry like the relentlessness of
fire],[122] finds a parallel in the German *Volk* and the Czech *lid/národ*,[123]
and these (imagined) rural people, supposed to have preserved some
kind of unawakened but 'pure' and 'authentic' culture, have been sought
by anti-colonial nationalists across the globe. Thomas's imagining of a
rural dark-faced people associated with valour and defeat, yet also with
a heroic survival despite the odds, seems rooted in the imperial
stereotype of the Welsh.

The close relationship between man and the land he farms is pushed
so far in Thomas's Prytherch poems that the boundary between the two
is sometimes blurred. The relegation of the rural inhabitant to an aspect
of landscape is not without significant precedent – most notably,
perhaps, in the Romantic works which are part literature, part travel-
writing, part historical tract. Saree Makdisi, in *Romantic Imperialism:
Universal Empire and the Culture of Modernity*, describing Wordsworth's appropriation of a working countryside for the purposes of
composing a portrait of a landscape in 'An Evening Walk', says that 'It

takes another look [at the poem] to realise that the workers themselves have all but faded into and become part of the landscape'.[124] If Thomas focuses more directly on rural figures, then, at times, he does so in such a way as to cause them to fade in different but comparable ways into the pastoral landscape. Expressing the holistic character of Prytherch's existence in nature, the rather patronizing poem, 'Green Categories', portrays Prytherch as dominated by

> . . . a green calendar
> Your heart observes; how else could you
> Find your way home or know when to die
> With the slow patience of the men who raised
> This landmark in the moor's deep tides?[125]

Prytherch's features are often described in terms borrowed from the upland Welsh landscape. In 'A Labourer', the man's face has been shaped by the elements. The ambiguous agelessness of his face has associations with the endurance of rock.

> Who can tell his years, for the winds have stretched
> So tight the skin on the bare racks of bone
> That his face is smooth, inscrutable as stone?[126]

The merging of man and landscape like this contributes more to the romanticized notion of the 'noble savage' than to any impression of the Prytherch figures as viable human beings.

Welsh writing in English makes use of an array of stereotypes of alterity – be these of racialized, atavistic savagery or more romantic, prelapsarian nobility – but, as this chapter has shown, this literature can also offer subtle and challenging engagements with such imagery. The European colonialist's perception of non-whites is often reflected in horrifying or uncanny Gothic figures, but also in less sensational writing, and such literary images themselves reflect back upon notions of racial and gendered others, influencing our collective 'knowledge' of the non-white. In this chapter I have focused on the way that, in Welsh writing in English, stereotypes of the racial other are used to mobilize (and depend for their success upon) the reader's preconceptions, prejudices and associated fears. To some extent, this use of racial otherness parallels the function such constructions serve in English literature – the racist, imperial images hold sway in both literatures.

Wales was, after all, part of the metropole of the British Empire. Yet, in Welsh writing in English the colonial status of Wales as peripheral nation within the United Kingdom is reflected in the way the Welsh are themselves often cast in the role of the racial other. The Welsh reader, then, is faced with the somewhat dichotomous experience of functioning/responding as the implied (metropolitan) audience usually assumed by the texts – that is, we recognize and respond to the literary motifs of the fearful other – while simultaneously realizing that we are excluded from the implied audience, from the metropolis, and actually *belong* to the group being represented as grotesquely other. Perhaps it is not surprising then, that many of the texts I have discussed here test or contest and problematize any straightforward interpretation of the racial other as literary signifier. Ironically, a non-white Welsh reader must face a further level of 'splitting' or displacement, for the construction of 'the' Welsh other which relies so heavily on racialized discourses nevertheless tends to be a largely homogeneous white other. The status of the Welsh as authors, readers and textual representations is profoundly ambiguous, and their positioning(s) within a variety of discourses of alterity is unstable. It is in these areas of instability, however, that we may begin to understand and negotiate both the indebtedness of Welsh texts to imperialist discourse and the way the Welsh themselves have been 'othered' by such discourses.

3

En-gendering a New Wales: Nationalism, Feminism and Empire in the *Fin de Siècle*

Declan Kiberd describes the Irish as having been 'both imperial and counter imperial, sometimes seemingly in the same gesture',[1] and, as the previous chapter has begun to illustrate, it is an analysis that is equally true of the Welsh, especially during the apogee of British imperialism at the end of the nineteenth century. Viewed from a present where British imperialism is, at best, treated with suspicion but commonly regarded with antipathy, the fact that Welsh writing (along with other forms of cultural expression) could simultaneously champion the causes of Home Rule or cultural nationalism *and* British imperialism may appear to be downright paradoxical. In fact, as the texts examined in this chapter show, cultural nationalism and aspirations for Home Rule could be presented as forces which would improve and strengthen the Empire (albeit in a sometimes thoroughly reformed state). This chapter will explore the confluence and interpenetration of the rhetorics of nationalism, imperialism and feminism[2] in late nineteenth- and early twentieth-century Wales. It was a period in which Wales could be constructed simultaneously as central to the imperial project, with a special contribution to make to the 'progressive' civilizing mission of the British Empire, but also, arguably, as subject to a variety of internal imperialism which hampered as much as it benefited Welsh culture. It was also a fascinating period in the history of the Woman Question[3] in Wales, when Women's Liberal Progressivism was closely allied to the Home Rule movement.

If (anti-colonial) nationalism and imperialism are generally presented as binary opposites in much postcolonial discourse, then feminism and nationalism are often also seen to be in competition rather than in alliance, since anti-colonial nationalism has often proved to be overtly patriarchal while women's rights may be viewed as subordinate to the primary aim of achieving national independence. In most of the texts discussed in this chapter, however, the Woman Question is very deliberately allied to the national question. This reflects, of course, the period from which these texts originate (women's rights were all too briefly enshrined in the constitution of the Cymru Fydd movement in 1895, an event anticipated by my central text in this chapter, 'Lady Gwen', which dates from 1890–1) and it would be misleading to overstate the endurance of this early 'feminist' era of Welsh nationalism.[4] Nevertheless, this alliance, which Ursula Masson suggests 'may have been unique in British politics',[5] offers a fascinating opportunity to explore the ideals, rhetoric and tensions of an alliance of movements which are often perceived in postcolonial, national and feminist studies to be dissenting rivals.

Both male and female writers from Wales emphasized the importance of the role of women in building a new and independent Wales. Similarly, the same writers often argued that, just as liberated women would better serve the Welsh nation, a more autonomous and self-confident Wales would better support and enrich the British Empire. Nora Philipps, for example, writing in *Young Wales* in 1895, argues against the simplistic ideas of social reformers who would have women choosing *either* home *or* public life, stating that there is no reason why women may not balance public and private lives just as national loyalty ought not to exclude imperial patriotism:

> to be truly great is to care with a passionate patriotism for this great empire – great not only in extent, but far more in the intent of her civilization, – and yet with joy and pride and devotion [also] strive for the country, that part of the great whole to which we, by special love and human linking of family, language, and religion, belong.[6]

In this article Philipps draws parallels between the nature of the 'calming influence of advancing civilization' that women promise to bring to politics and the importance of the civilizing mission of Empire in which the Welsh may make a special contribution.[7] She thus rhetorically links the qualities of women, nation and civilization within a Welsh national framework.[8] The causes of emancipation of women and greater autonomy for Wales are also rhetorically linked in a note in the very first issue of *Young Wales*, which declares that 'the day is not far distant when Mrs Philipps and other leaders of the Women's Movement in the Principality will be elected to a duly established Welsh National Assembly'.[9] Of course, given the propagandist nature of the writing in *Young Wales* (a journal of the Liberal Home Rule movement) and other similar writing discussed below, we should be careful not to interpret such texts as simply providing a window on to the actual status of women in Wales and its nationalist movement at the time. Rather, recognizing that nationalism is the enactment, the performance, of an invented community and, as such, 'Nations are situations under constant contest',[10] we should follow Ursula Masson's suggestion that these Welsh declarations should be read as engaged in constructing and contesting nationalist ideology and the place of women.[11]

The role of women as real and also emblematic figures is further complicated by discourses which resonated through cultural and national debate during the second half of the nineteenth century. While it is not possible to enter into a full and detailed discussion of such a broad area, a consideration of how the figure of woman as national allegory functioned, with reference to wider interpenetrating discourses of woman, nation and Empire, offers some interesting insights into the complex status of women as contested icons of nation and national character. The rhetorical association between cultural nationalism, Home Rule and women's emancipation in Wales was inflected by a great variety of factors, but it is worth briefly reminding ourselves of some of the specific politico-cultural contexts within which any discussion of woman and nation in Wales must be framed.[12] It is, of course, well recognized that gender is a social construct, subject to constant regulation and contest, and nowhere more so, perhaps, than in Wales when gender and nationality were conflated by the Commissioners of the Education Report of 1847 (the Blue Books), a conflation then reinforced by the perpetuation of this perspective in Welsh responses to the report. The project of the Blue Books to erase cultural and, specifically, linguistic difference, in a bid to exert control over a nation which had seen significant civil unrest in the first half of the nineteenth century, has been well documented, as have the fundamentally imperialist motives and techniques of the reports. In condemning not only the state of education in Wales, but the morality of the nation as a whole, the report focused on the role of women, in particular, as the (failed) moral guardians of the nation. In Wales, then, as in many colonized countries, women became central to the constructions of national character in the discourse of both 'colonizer' (or hegemonic power) and 'colonized' (or subordinate nation); and, in the attempt to project an image of a pure and peaceable Wales, Welsh women became the focus of a massive national and cultural project to disprove the slurs of the report. Moreover, while responses to the Blue Books tended to focus on real women and their role as wives and mothers, the figure of woman was nevertheless thus transformed into an ideological instrument, an allegory of nation.

The fusion of the goals of the women's and the nationalist movement is presented in a fictional form in a serialized story, 'Lady Gwen; or, the days that are to be, by A Welsh Nationalist', which appeared in the bilingual periodical *Cymru Fydd: Cylchgrawn y Blaid Genedlaethol Gymreig*, from 1890–1.[13] I have been unable to identify 'A Welsh Nationalist', but this anonymous story provides a most fascinating example of an idealized woman who performs an allegorical representation of Wales as a noble, honourable, chaste and pious nation. What is especially interesting about this story, however, is that Lady Gwen Tudor is also the embodiment of radical feminist and Home Rule ideals. As the prime minister of an independent Wales, Gwen is the head of a powerful nation of warriors – Christian soldiers, perhaps – and, as such, she is the representative of a country which has become a leading force in a more equitable and universally bountiful Federated Empire of Greater Britain. This story affords us the opportunity to examine an example of a Welsh writer being both anti-colonial and imperialist in the same gesture and, at the same time, to consider how far this utopian vision or feminist story actually serves the cause of women's emancipation in its use of clearly idealized or allegorical female figures.

It is not easy to summarize the narrative of 'Lady Gwen', ten chapters of which appeared across eight issues of *Cymru Fydd*, from 1890–1. The story was still incomplete when it ended, with the discontinuation of *Cymru Fydd*, in March 1891, and the plot is the most insubstantial element of the writing. 'Lady Gwen' is hardly a major work of fiction, but it is nevertheless a textually rich novel which offers no fewer than thirteen pieces of verse (in English and Welsh) of up to thirteen stanzas each, along with a number of lengthy speeches, demonstrating in form what it declares in prose: that the Welsh are a people who thrive on rhetoric and song, poetry and hymns. Its political message dominates the narrative and, rather than characterization or

plot, the emphasis is on historical and social comment. There is a sub-
stantial commentary on the land question of nineteenth-century Wales,
the cruelty of landlords, the tithe wars and disestablishment, while the
success of Wales is shown to be the result of the influence of uniquely
Welsh Calvinist principles in private and public life. The events of the
novel, as already suggested, are fairly slight, not least because there is no
opportunity for the development of the sub-plots. Briefly, the setting is
Harlech, in 2000 AD, on the last day of the National Eisteddfod, when a
banquet is being held to celebrate the victorious role of Wales in a war
between America and the Empire of Greater Britain. Sir Roland
Wynne-Hughes, a lawyer, opposition politician and the most popular
man in Wales, having just returned a soldier-hero from a war against
America, finds himself drawn into a plot to bring down the government
headed by his fair cousin, Gwen. This is all because of his inappropriate
and unrequited love for Miss Herbert, a woman of 'Saxon' descent, who
is therefore utterly unsuited to Sir Roland's Celtic temperament. Thus
Sir Roland becomes the dupe of a plot to bring the whole of the British
Empire under the sway of the Roman Church. Lady Gwen is further
threatened by the arrival from America of her estranged half-brother,
who appears in disguise, bent on destroying Gwen out of an old enmity
and in revenge for his ruin in America, the result of the recent war.
Unfortunately, however, little of the intrigue elaborately set up in earlier
chapters is given a chance to evolve. What this story offers instead is a
fairly detailed vision of a Wales which is run according to Calvinist
Christian doctrines, which celebrates its literary and historical past and
its nationalist and imperialist present and the freedom and full civic
participation of women.

The purpose of this fiction, as a piece of utopian writing, is to
encourage its Welsh nationalist readers to fight for Home Rule, dis-
establishment, votes for women and Empire; in an important preface to
the story, the author describes 'his' intentions: 'Under the disguise of a
romance, he wishes to offer to his countrymen an ideal which, if they
choose, they can realise for themselves.'[14] Before examining the central
character of Lady Gwen and her role in this future Wales, it is necessary
to consider in a little more detail the social vision presented here, and
the imperial politics of the text in particular. This utopian Wales has
prospered because it rejected 'the dogmas . . . of English economic
reformers, – the Manchester School and the Socialists'.[15] Instead, it has
'Christianis[ed] the relations between rich and poor',[16] instituted
universal suffrage for men and women alike, and created an education

system in which all go to university. Consequently, resentment and bitterness between classes is eliminated and Wales is populated by a *gwerin* that is spiritually and culturally equal with the returned and duly Cymricized aristocracy. Most importantly, in the estimation of the narrative, Wales has recognized the value of empire and the Empire has benefited enormously from 'the influence of the Welsh political originality'.[17]

The Federated Empire described in 'Lady Gwen' was not a new idea. The Imperial Federation League was formed in 1884 and had great support in the Dominions, but the declared source for 'A Welsh Nationalist's' narrative is a novel by the ex-Prime Minister of New Zealand, Sir Julius Vogel. *Anno Domini 2000; or, Woman's Destiny* was published in 1889 and, although it was not the great popular success the author and publisher had hoped for, it has since gained prominence in New Zealand as a radical feminist text and also for its surprisingly accurate prophecies of technological development.[18] 'A Welsh Nationalist' follows Vogel in many aspects of plot – the war with America is acknowledged as lifted straight from Vogel – and he or she also copies Vogel's array of feminist characters. The most appealing feature of Vogel's utopian novel, however, seems to have been that of Imperial Federalism, which offered, as 'A Welsh Nationalist' notes, a world order offering all the benefits of autonomy without the need to sacrifice the advantages of empire. The very success of this Federated Empire, moreover, is dependent on the genius of small nations (New Zealand and Ireland in the case of Vogel), and the position of Wales in 'Lady Gwen' follows Vogel's model of an independent but enthusiastically imperialist Eire, portrayed in a chapter called 'Grateful Ireland'. Vogel depicts the achievement of Irish independence as being a result of 'the intervention of the Colonies'[19] which topple a British government 'puffed up with the pride of old traditions'[20] to give 'Ireland the boon it had long claimed of local government'.[21] Ireland thus becomes a dedicated, valuable and eternally grateful member of the Federated Empire: 'The Irish people, warm-hearted and grateful, felt they could never be sufficiently thankful.'[22] In 'Lady Gwen', Imperial Federation is actually 'effected to no small extent by the votes of the Celtic population in all parts of the Empire', and Wales is no less 'passionate [in its] devotion to the Empire which had so freely recognised the right [of Wales to independence]'.[23]

Although both Vogel and 'A Welsh Nationalist', in their visions of a Federated Empire, are critical of the late nineteenth-century status quo in the United Kingdom, and 'Lady Gwen' explicitly rejects the British Empire of the nineteenth century and its oppressive rule, it is worth examining more closely the kind of Imperial Federation imagined in the Welsh narrative. The new empire is a federation of independent states, more like a commonwealth than an Anglocentric empire, and perhaps not so far from the European federation towards which Wales looks for representation today. It retains the Royal Family at its head and there is an Imperial Parliament, but England is only one member-state amongst many. The nations that make up this new empire are worth noting. New Zealand is mentioned in the preface, and Canada and Australia appear more than once in the main body of the text, and members of all these nations are present at the celebratory banquet in Harlech. However, this utopian federation still reflects its roots in the colonial hierarchies of the nineteenth-century British Empire – it seems that only the white-settler colonies (excluding America) are referred to by the name 'Greater Britain', while all the other (non-white) countries have conveniently disappeared, except for a thoroughly reformed, Christianized India. In Vogel's novel, Africa makes an appearance in the figure of 'Lady Cairo' (although she seems to be of western rather than Egyptian origin), but otherwise here, too, it is just the Dominions rather than all the colonial territories of the British Empire that seem to be represented.

For all the arguments in favour of allowing 'each separate portion of the Empire – whether great or small – the free right to live its own life in its own way',[24] there are also, ironically, echoes of a Welsh cultural imperialism, which emphasize this narrative's championing of the civilizing mission of the British Empire. It is a feature which we would now recognize as being complicit with the very form of empire the story purports to reject. In her Eisteddfod speech, Lady Gwen expounds the Welsh imperial renaissance:

> The Englishman conquered it [the Empire], and he never, until we taught him, managed it on any system. Throughout the nineteenth century, Wales knew little and cared less about the empire. To her Imperialism was but another name for cruelty, for oppression, and for the extinction of the rights of nations. But after a time, she learnt to judge the fact more accurately. She grew to see that a great empire, which admitted the principles of liberty and self government to have fair play in its dominions, gave grander and nobler opportunities to a small state than a proud and barren independence. Wales also saw, with wonder and awe, the gigantic miracle of British rule in India which in our own day has

attained its consummation and engrafted liberty and Christianity on the
old imperishable customs of the sacred east. Wales has served this empire
by the songs of her poets, by the wise administration that she has given to
its various provinces, and lastly by the blood that she has so freely shed for
it.[25]

In this interesting speech, nineteenth-century British imperialism is
condemned as the instrument of the unjust oppression of small nations.
This alignment of Wales with other colonized countries informs the
whole of 'Lady Gwen', which uses similarly uncompromising images of
tyrannical English or Anglicized landlords and an 'alien' Church of
England, ministered by a comprador class who 'jeered at their fellow-
countrymen; but [who] for that very reason . . . were forced to bend the
knee in humble obeisance to the leaders of the English political party
that allowed them for its own ends to tyrannise over their countrymen'.[26] However, the Federated Empire that is championed as allowing
Wales the space and security to express its own national genius is,
perhaps unsurprisingly, not so far removed from nineteenth-century
imperial ideals. While the civilizing mission prominently featured in this
extract was of course regarded as a progressive idea in the late nineteenth century, it has since been recognized in colonial discourse theory
and elsewhere as a fundamentally treacherous ideal, complicit with
wider colonial and imperial exploitation. The civilizing mission of
Empire was evidently an aspect of British imperialism in which the
Welsh themselves invested heavily, as this speech implicitly recognizes.
Thus we find the contemporary Welsh audience of 'Lady Gwen' constructed as anti-colonial, through their sympathy with the oppression of
their own and other small nations of the British Empire. Yet they are
simultaneously supporters of imperialism, through the Christianization
of India, although even here there seems to be some scope for cultural
difference since Christianity has been engrafted on to the 'old imperishable customs of the . . . east'. This may be seen as allowing for the
possibility of a kind of nationally differentiated and culturally sympathetic religion.[27]

    In addition to these echoes of nineteenth-century missionary zeal in
Gwen's speech, another orator, Watkin, the editor of a national paper
based in Cardiff, describes Welsh commitment to the fictional empire of
the twenty-first century, in a manner that recalls the rousing echoes of
much more traditional and jingoistic British imperial rhetoric:

Wales has shed its blood like water for the empire . . . Wales has helped to preserve the empire from disintegration, she has extended its boundaries, and she has made the advance of its banners to mean the progress of liberty, of chivalry and religion. Cymru Fydd called forth the spirit of purity and love that made Wales a nation. The example of Wales rescued the British Empire from selfishness, from materialism, from infidelity, and made her imperial ascendancy a blessing to the world.[28]

Rather than forming a clear challenge to contemporary versions of British imperialism, then, this nationalist view asserts that Wales could do a much better job of civilization than England. Thus we might read this story as staking a claim in nineteenth-century Empire as much as it is clearly trying to assert Welsh claims to nationhood. Nevertheless, in emphasizing the importance of the 'special mission' of the Welsh within the Empire, the author of 'Lady Gwen' is also pleading for the valorization of the cultural difference of Wales. This is a warning to contemporary readers of the story of the dangers of bowing to English cultural hegemony:

> The success of the anti-nationalists would have assimilated Welsh and English political thought. Welshmen would never have ventured to think on any political subject; for their first lesson in politics would have been that they could only become citizens by forgetting they were Welshmen. Reflect for a moment what Britain would have lost if Wales had contributed nothing to her political thought.[29]

There are many more examples of powerful anti-colonialist/nationalist rhetoric to be found in the story, as well as further instances of 'imperial patriotism', and it is worth looking briefly at one more particularly interesting example which articulates both. Recalling eighteenth-century Welsh history, the period of Methodist revival, Lady Gwen highlights its glories, drawing her audience's attention to a picture hanging in the hall of Welsh soldiers who 'may soon have to meet the invading French'.[30] The defence of Welsh soil from foreign incursions establishes the overtly anti-colonial/nationalist scene and the figure of the early Methodist, Howel Harris, appears in the centre of the painting as a Christian soldier. He 'prays from the canvas, and . . . though he wears a sword at his side, wears the features of a saint'.[31] This portrait of the ultimate Christian soldier is associated with colonial triumph and duty:

Was not Howel Harries [*sic*] a soldier, and is he not also a canonised saint in our church[?] The age in which he lived witnessed the foundation of our colonial empire, and no man's heart beat more proudly than his when the news of the glorious victories which the genius of Lord Chatham had planned, reached our Cambrian shores. The ignorant critic has described Welsh Methodism as narrow and provincial. I tell you that Howel Harries was the first man who brought home to the children of Wales their privileges and duties as co-heirs with Englishmen of an Empire on which the sun never sets. When I say to-night of the British race and Empire, -

> 'We sailed wherever ships might sail,
> We founded many a mighty state,
> Pray God our greatness may not fail
> Through craven fears of being great,'-

I know I am saying nothing more than what the great Methodist preacher would have said had he been in your midst.[32]

The founder of Welsh Calvinist Methodism – the creed of Lady Gwen's Wales – is here revealed as an ardent imperial patriot of eighteenth-century Britain.

If the vision of an independent Wales within a Federated Empire is an example of a Welsh nationalism being both imperial and counter-imperial in the same gesture, then equally complex and paradoxical is the figure of Lady Gwen herself, since she functions both as a feminist icon and as a national allegory. Indeed, Gwen may perhaps most helpfully be understood not as a real woman, that is, as an individual, rounded character, the prime minister of a utopian Wales, but as the embodiment of all the supposed virtues of the nation, and she is deliberately presented in this way by the narrative. We are introduced to Gwen at the end of the first chapter, which has sketched the state of Wales and its pivotal role in the empire. Gwen is the leader of the progressive party, 'a second Cymru Fydd',[33] that aims to push through the agenda of a new wave of Welsh radicalism. She is now prime minister of Wales and at the height of her popularity.

The leader of the reforming party was a woman, – and this accounts, to some extent, for the purity of ideals and chivalric behaviour of the party which recognised in her the most perpect [*sic*] example of an *ideal Welsh womanhood*. No one reproached the reforming party for being led by a woman. It had been clearly understood that all great periods in the history of the world had been characterised by the presence of heroic women. Welsh literature is characterised by what one may call a worship of woman; Dafydd ap Gwilym and Dafydd Nanmor and Ceiriog, the popular singers of Wales, are at their best when they describe the influence which woman exercises, – *a modifying, purifying, enobling influence*. In Lady Gwen Tudor the new Welsh movement found an ideal leader, typical of what was best in the past of what would be in the future, – a new Lady of Snowdon or Joan of Navarre.[34]

Here, essentially feminine qualities are linked with Welsh social successes through the form of Gwen. If the link between Gwen and her country is not obvious enough in this passage, then the following chapter (the second instalment of the serial) makes the connection explicit: 'An aristocrat in taste and feeling, but a Calvinist in religion, Gwen seemed to combine in her own person every feature of Welsh nationality.'[35] Gwen's credentials as a representative or embodiment of this particular version of Welsh nationalism are authenticated by her rural origins. She was born and brought up in Merioneth, and her father was the Earl of Y Bala [*sic*]. The ascendancy of the rural Wales she represents over the industrial and urban south is emphasized, although this is not a case of domination but rather of enlightenment. The editor of 'the old Cardiff Tory paper', Mr Watkin, has himself become a friend of Gwen's Cymru Fydd party, since

he had seen what his predecessors had failed to see, that the true fountain of Welsh ideas must lie in the pure Welsh Wales; that, while the commercial cities of the South, of the Northern border, might be the centres of commercial and industrial activity, the soul of Wales lay in the wild mountain land, whose children had brought the people back to Christianity in one age, and won for their country a place among the nations of the earth in the next.[36]

Having conveniently unified rural and industrial Wales in this way, with Watkin worshipping the beautiful Lady Gwen as the embodiment of 'pure Welsh Wales', he proposes a toast 'of *ein gwlad, ein hiaith, ein cenedl* [our country, our language, our people], never so honoured as by its union with the name of Lady Gwen'.[37]

Gwen is the embodiment of radical religious and nationalist ideals (in terms of nineteenth-century Welsh politics). She also symbolizes a feminine ideal, which needs to be considered in the light of her supposed function of promoting female suffrage, and there remains the question of how the prominence of conservative and, perhaps, rather limiting traditional feminine traits might be reconciled with her potential as a feminist character or allegory. Gwen is single, but she is beautiful – although it is interesting to note that while she is described as embodying Welsh womanhood, her beauty is of a distinctly Anglo-Saxon variety: she has blonde hair and blue eyes, rather than dark Welsh features.[38] Gwen's talents do not end with her grasp of politics, but extend to include the more traditional feminine accomplishments, such as music and singing; she even breaks off her busy preparation of an important speech in order to entertain her cousin (a newly returned war hero) with tea, song and the playing of a 'traditional' small Welsh harp.[39] Thus we at once are presented with a feminist ideal – a woman prime minister in a country that has benefited enormously from the input of women – and with a traditional, harp-playing, pious, feminine angel in the Victorian mould. The assumption that this angelic figure was antithetical to the cause of feminist independence would be wrong, however. In terms of Anglo-American New Woman discourse it could be viewed as anticipating a feminist strategy, advocated by Sarah Grand in 1893, of New Women making every effort to appear as feminine and attractive as possible, so as to undermine the efforts of anti-feminists to portray the New Woman as 'unnaturally' mannish and ugly.[40] That is, in portraying Lady Gwen as being ultra-feminine and highly desirable as well as an intelligent and capable politician, 'Lady Gwen' presents an iconic figure who should appeal to as wide an audience as possible – to Welsh nationalists and feminists alike – while undermining the criticism of those who saw professionally active women as de-sexed and dangerous. Gwen's youth – she is just twenty-three – may seem fantastical, but it is consonant with both Vogel's novel and other feminist-nationalist writings of the same period, such as the novel *Gloriana; or, the revolution of 1900*, published in 1890, by the Anglo-Scottish writer, Florence Dixie. In this utopian novel, a cross-dressing woman becomes prime minister of Britain aged just twenty-nine, and such youthful energy is associated with the generally rather young New Woman writers and activists of the 1890s. Moreover, the youth of these always allegorical figures could also be understood as an expression of the vibrancy, freshness and promise of the causes they represent – Cymru Fydd or Young Wales, for example.

Women pictured as upholders of the nation's purity and as pillars of the national culture could be interpreted as a strand of *fin de siècle* constructions of the New Woman as a regenerative (read 'progressive') social force. However, the highly idealized Gwen might equally be read as conforming to rather more conservative pictures of Welsh woman-hood. An article in *Young Wales* in 1898 illustrates the point. 'Patriotism and the Women of Cymru', written by 'Un o'r ddau Wynne' (Mallt Williams), has been interpreted by Ursula Masson as reflecting the drift of the Cymru Fydd movement away from radicalism and towards a more romantic and conservative outlook. Although Ceridwen Lloyd-Morgan has suggested that this article is not particularly typical of Williams's outlook,[41] the text itself does seem to typify a certain element of reactionary and romantic nationalism. The article suggests that Welsh women's patriotism ought to manifest itself in the revival and preservation of 'the most picturesque and graceful of all occupations for women': spinning – preferably whilst wearing the Welsh national costume![42] Mallt Williams also urges women to rediscover and pass on to their children the language, poetry, history and legends of Wales. The apparently reactionary tone of the article is complicated, however, by Williams's comment about the importance of passing on the '*mother*-tongue' of Wales (the emphasis is in the original), since here the language is claimed as a matriarchal gift to be bestowed by women.

The importance of the mother tends to be undermined by·some western models of feminism, which can devalue maternity (although New Women could often represent motherhood as a positive regen-erative force within the discourses of degeneration and regeneration of the *fin de siècle*). Advocating that women find their national role through motherhood could consequently all too easily be dismissed as reactionary. Significant strands of postcolonial feminism, however, while not ignoring the restrictions which may be imposed upon women expected to fulfil the role of conveyors of culture, often respond more positively to the role of mother in general. Passing stories and language from mother to daughter is seen as potentially opening up sites of 'contest [and] revolutionary struggle'.[43] The idea that the domestic, as opposed to the public, sphere may constitute an important site of resistance is also recognized in studies of diasporic peoples or of those who have experienced cultural dislocation through colonization. In such cases, the home may become the only place where a subaltern culture may be transmitted.[44] Passing on an unofficial, 'native' language such as Welsh, at a time when parents were actively choosing *not* to pass on the language to their children, can be viewed as an explicit act of resistance

to cultural imperialism. This complicates a straightforwardly conservative understanding of Mallt Williams's plea.

The social status of nineteenth-century women is touched upon in
'Lady Gwen', although motherhood is not discussed. The insistence on
the ability of women to benefit the nation through politics is sustained
and the unhappy lot of women forced to exist within the narrow
constraints of nineteenth-century polite society with only a meagre
education is forcefully outlined. But the story is clearly more concerned
with national and imperial politics than with the details of how women
might negotiate public and private life. In fact, on this score the story
does not seem to be quite so radical as it might first appear, and we
discover that Gwen would be expected to retire from politics were she
ever to marry. 'Lady Gwen', then, while declaring radical feminist
credentials, is more concerned with expounding the more usual
concerns of Liberal nationalism. Before concluding with a discussion of
just how Gwen's construction as a national allegory might inflect her
status as a feminist figure in this text, it is worth briefly comparing her
with some other allegorical figures of Wales-as-woman.

Although a common trope in the nineteenth century, the figure of
woman-as-nation is complicated in a Welsh context by the construction
of the Welsh people as a feminine race, which would naturally benefit
from the masculine guidance and rule of a colonial power, in line with
wider imperial discourse employed in India and Greece, for example.[45]
Thus to construct Wales-as-woman is not only to make use of a
common motif, it is also to negotiate the complex array of gendered
roles associated with the figure of a woman with reference to wider
national and international power-relations. For example, a feminized
(weak and subordinate) Wales could be pictured as 'married' to a
masculine (strong and guiding) England. Alternatively, a similarly
feminine, alluring Wales might be pictured as a damsel in distress or as
an attractive and nubile woman (such as Lady Gwen) in order to
engender manly Welsh valour to save her (a common manifestation of
national allegories in female form). Again, nation-as-woman might be
fiercely maternal and protective of her 'children', or could sometimes
appear, as in cartoons by J. M. Staniforth of the *Western Mail*, as
'Dame Wales', a rather inconsequential matronly figure who might
be able to stick up for her charges on minor domestic issues but who
could be safely ignored on the subject of more worldly matters.
Needless to say, the female allegories of Wales could be a mix of all
these images.

The various relationships between nations which could be represented by allegorical national figures and the possibility of double-coded meanings embodied in such national allegories are explored in a different national/imperial context in a study, by Rodanthi Tzanelli, of the Anglo–Greek dialogue of the 1860s and 1870s.[46] Tzanelli examines the way Greek discourse both adopted and adapted (subverted) the imagery and language of the British overlords, which constructed the relationship between Britain and Greece in familial terms. In British discourse, a paternal Britain protected a childlike Greece. Greek discourse, on the other hand, while mimicking British imagery to some extent, engineered an important slippage in which Greece was represented as a mother who must protect her children – both those (such as the Ionian Islands) who were already in her care, and those (such as Macedonia) who remained within the Ottoman Empire. This mother figure, however, could mimic British discourse and undermine it, by simultaneously presenting an image of Greece as a mother searching for lost sons, while retaining the image of an impoverished female figure who remained subordinate to the British father/husband. Thus Greece produced a forked dialogue in which Greece played to a split audience of 'Britons and subjected Greeks'.

> When addressed to the British, the Greek discourse would present the mother figure as a weak degraded creature. When addressed to the non-native Greeks of the Ottoman Empire, the very same maternal image would become the patron, which all the unredeemed Greeks ought to love and respect.[47]

Tzanelli's descriptions of the two versions of Mother Greece, presented to two very different audiences, might perhaps offer a model for exploring the potential for Welsh allegories of nation to signify different things to different audiences.

Instances of the coexistence of irredentist and subordinate or loyalist agendas may be found embodied in single figures as well as in different incarnations of Wales-as-woman. 'Dame Wales', a common appellation for the embodiment of the nation in female form, has been scripted into various national pageants and, most famously, perhaps, the Welsh National Pageant of 1909. Hywel Teifi Edwards has described how this pageant, with a cast of thousands, including many Welsh notables, was intended not only to secure the status of Cardiff as an important and enterprising Welsh/British city and of Wales as an important nation within the British Empire, but also to teach the people of Wales about their heroic past and thus engender self-respect. Thousands of schoolchildren from across Wales were brought to Cardiff to witness the spectacle, which was staged daily for nearly two weeks. The Dame Wales of this Pageant, played by Lady Bute, was a regal figure, nothing like the national-costumed peasant of Staniforth's well-known newspaper cartoon. Yet perhaps her role was not all that different. J. M. Staniforth's Dame Wales first appeared in 1900 and, while she would occasionally appear in the guise of an enraged and protective mother, she was most often depicted as a ridiculous matron of rather lowly origins, whose natural place in the social hierarchy emphasized Wales's subordinate position within the UK. Hywel Teifi Edwards has eloquently described Staniforth's 'caricature' of the nation as a

> dwmplen afrosgo o werinreg yn ei phais a'i betgwn a'i chlocs, yn rhadlongroesawgar wrth bawb, yn syml-fucheddol, o blaid 'trefn naturiol' pethau . . .[48]

> [plump, ungainly peasant woman, clad in her petticoat, Welsh dress and clogs, who would graciously extend her welcome to all and sundry, while simultaneously observing basic morals, and supporting the 'natural order' of things . . .][49]

Staniforth's Dame Wales was, as Hywel Teifi Edwards has suggested, an emblem of the Wales summed up in the phrase 'Cymru Lân, Cymru Lonydd' ('Pure and Peaceable Wales'); that is, she was fundamentally subservient to England, capable of sticking up for 'fair play' in London's treatment of the principality, but ultimately a loyal unionist.

Lady Bute's infinitely more commanding figure appeared in the Prologue and Finale of the National Pageant of Wales, which offered a discursive frame for the historical scenes depicted in the pageant proper. The pageant began with her entrance, along with thirteen women who represented the shires of Wales, and accompanied by other attendant fairies and heralds. Significantly, this prologue enacted Wales's own 'Empire-building', or, as it was represented in the pageant, the reclamation of rightful territory. Dame Wales calls her counties together by name (incidentally, calling 'Glamorgan, to the front'[50]) and then beckons to Monmouthshire, not at that time a part of the principality, to join the group:

And thou, dear Monmouth, stand beside thy kin;
For though great England claims thee for her own,
Cymric thou art, and Cymric thou shalt remain.[51]

Although this irredentist act and assertion of Welsh unity is immediately undermined by the comic bickering amongst the counties, over who might rightfully claim as their own each of the Welsh heroes to be celebrated in the pageant, the finale attempts some form of closure with the assertion of the territorial unity of the Welsh nation. After the final scene of the central historical drama, Dame Wales, surrounded by her shires, and a multitude of other women dressed as the *tylwyth teg* (fairies) form a map of Wales with their bodies, constituting a living, all-female emblem of the nation. Unfortunately I have been able to find no detailed description of how this impressive spectacle was arranged, nor any pictures of the tableau, but the images suggested by the description available in the pageant's *Book of Words* might be interpreted as offering an intriguing display of Welsh pride and unity, although not one which supports any anti-colonial or Home Rule reading.

As already mentioned, the National Pageant aimed to put Wales on the imperial map, but it was also intended to engender a new (or rather an old) Welsh self-respect and to impress upon the Welsh the full glory of their ancient history. The personification of Wales, the live allegory played by Lady Bute, was, as we have seen, a long way from the matronly figure who regularly graced the pages of the *Western Mail*. This mother figure was regal, irredentist, a force to marshal a nation, not a subservient dumpling. Is it possible that the pageant's dual function, of engendering nationalist self-esteem but also reinforcing a stake in the United Kingdom and its Empire, might have produced a forked image, similar to that described by Tzanelli above? While it is perhaps possible that the pageant's multiple functions might have thrown up some ambiguities, and it is quite possible that English and Welsh audiences (or various sections within these) may have read the performances very differently, it would be misleading to try to argue that the 1909 National Pageant constituted any significant challenge to English hegemony, either in intention or possible interpretations. Compared with a similar tableau of nation from a contemporaneous piece of theatre in the colonized Philippines, the Cardiff Pageant is characterized by predominantly conservative themes rather than any subversive undertones. A scene in a 1907 Filipino performance was highlighted in the Australian paper *The Theatre* (1907):

[The costumes are] so coloured and draped that at a given signal or cue the actors and actresses rush together, apparently without design, and stand swaying in the centre of the stage, close to the footlights, their combination forming a living, moving, stirring picture of the Filipino flag. Only an instant or so does the phantom last, but that one instant is enough to bring the entire house to its feet with yells and cries that are blood-curdling in their ferocious delight, while the less quick-witted Americans in the audience are wondering what the row is about.[52]

This performance is cited as a paradigmatic instance of imperial resistance through theatre by the authors of *Post-Colonial Drama: Theory, Practice and Politics*, Gilbert and Tompkins. The National Pageant of Wales can hardly claim to perform anything like this. Rather, such a comparison with an openly hostile piece of anti-colonial nationalism as that described above underlines the point that even displays of intense national pride could underwrite loyalist rather than separatist national feeling in Wales. The nation was concerned more with proving itself a worthy partner (a wife to England's royal consort, perhaps) in the British imperial enterprise than with attempting to extricate itself from any perceived status as a colonized nation within Britain.

For all the National Pageant's irredentist 'frame', and its patriotic procession of heroes, the final historical scene ended with an assertion of Welsh loyalty to the United Kingdom. Henry VIII announces, amid a 'general uproar' of joyous shouts and pealing bells, the Act of Union between England and Wales at Ludlow: 'My kin and faithful liegemen, I have harkened to your prayer and granted your petition. Here is the Act of Union between England and Wales for ever.'[53] Thus Wales's loyalty within the United Kingdom is reaffirmed in terms highly suggestive of a marriage ceremony: (Dame) Wales is unified – 'made one' – with England, embodied here not by any androgynous or feminized Britannia but by the hyper-masculine Henry. Of course, the marriage vows ironically, or perhaps rather appropriately here, include the woman's promise to 'love, honour and *obey*' the man. Thus a comedic closure to the pageant is achieved and, although Wales claims to have participated in British greatness (the penultimate scene, for example, shows the crowning of 'Harry Tudor' on Bosworth Field, and a note reinforces not only his Welsh ancestry but the fact that this Welshman is regarded by 'scholars . . . as the founder of the British Empire'), this participation is clearly in the role of a minor partner, aptly suggested in the figure of the weaker sex.[54]

If the female allegories discussed may be employed to suit a variety of different national(ist) agendas, their potential to act as feminist icons is a little more questionable. Marina Warner has argued that not only is there little sense of the individual in 'live' allegories of nation (for example, the female flagbearers of the French Revolution: the Mariannes who embodied the spirit of the Revolution), but that the sex and gender of these female forms are largely effaced. She argues that 'Justice', for example, was not represented by a woman 'because women were thought to be just, any more than they were considered capable of dispensing justice. Liberty is not represented as a woman, from the colossus in New York to the ubiquitous Marianne, figure of the French Republic, because women were or are free.'[55] Indeed, she suggests that 'the recognition of difference between the symbolic order, inhabited by ideal, allegorical figures, and the actual order, of judges, statesmen, soldiers, philosophers, inventors, depends on the unlikelihood of women practising the concepts they represent.'[56] That is, men are individuals who strive towards the virtues represented by female forms, who are able to function thus because of their actual distance; the appropriateness of the female form is its perception as a 'tabula rasa'. Nevertheless, there remains some room for female/feminist appropriation, however problematic. Warner rightly argues that allegories can offer a 'symbolized female presence [that] both gives and takes value and meaning in relation to actual women, and contains the potential for affirmation not only of women themselves but of the general good they might represent'.[57] Classical feminine allegories were indeed used by the various women's movements. Nike, the winged goddess of Victory, was used by Sylvia Pankhurst in the Women's Social and Political Union paper, *Votes for Women*. This suffragist angel, with her trumpet and a banner with the word 'Freedom', was depicted in the white, purple and green of the militant suffragette movement.[58] Nike/Victoria also appeared in feminist publications elsewhere with a more specific national agenda. *The Dawn: A Journal for Australian Women*, for example, sported this classical figure, again with a trumpet, flying above the sun rising over an Australian coastline.[59] It seems that women at the centre of the fight for women's rights in general, and the vote in particular, believed that such allegories of Victory could represent their causes as well as, they hoped, inspiring women themselves.

In discussing the use of allegories of nation in Ireland, Margaret Ward argues that images of nation-as-woman could be appropriated usefully by the women's movements of the time. Her argument might allow for Lady Gwen/Wales to be interpreted and appropriated as a feminist as well as a nationalist icon. Discussing women and the national liberation movement, Ward considers the figure of Cathleen ni Houlihan and the significance of 'Ireland-as-woman' for the turn-of-the-century women's movements. She acknowledges that Cathleen (and the other female personifications of the nation) were primarily constructed by male-orientated discourses that presented Ireland-as-woman as a victim needing to be rescued by a chivalric, valorous and thoroughly masculine Irish manhood. But, quoting Belinda Loftus, Ward also points out that Cathleen ni Houlihan symbolized 'individual as well as national freedom'.[60] She goes on to argue that:

> unlike their male comrades, the women were not undertaking some chivalric rescue but were fighting on their own behalf – they were Cathleen ni Houlihan just as much as Cathleen was the personification of the ideal. When Maud Gonne, founder of the nationalist-feminist organisation Inghinidhe na hErieann (Daughters of Ireland), played the title role in W. B. Yeats's play *Cathleen ni Houlihan*, she symbolised nationalist women's determination to break with the tradition which relegated them to a purely supportive role.[61]

Thus, although the figure of Lady Gwen seems to conform to a male-centred discourse and was, in all likelihood, the creation of a man, she might still be seen as appealing to Welsh feminists as well as being an alluring figure for male readers. The themes of temperance and dis-establishment prominent in 'Lady Gwen' were, for example, widely supported by various women's movements which, although not prim-arily established with a national(ist) agenda in view, nevertheless reinforced a sense of 'connection . . . between temperance, womanhood, the Welsh language and the sense of belonging to a Welsh nation'.[62] Gwen's uncompromising stance on the sale of alcohol (demonstrated by her refusal of a request to allow celebrating regiments access to alcohol and her diatribe on the social evils of drink), is just one of the ways in which we might see her as acting as a role-model for real Welsh women, engaged in real social and political campaigns during the late nineteenth century.

In this chapter, then, it has been possible to look at only a few examples of the interpenetration of what are often viewed as disparate discourses of feminism, nationalism (in anti-colonial or more loyalist forms) and imperialism. But even in this short discussion, if just one point emerges clearly, it is I hope that the readings which are available when all these strands of the texts are considered in relation to each other are far richer than if each strand were to be considered alone. Furthermore, such a study demonstrates the point that binary constructions which place anti-colonialism and imperialism at mutually exclusive ends of a political spectrum, or which assume a similarly conflictual relationship between nationalism and feminism, are, at best, highly reductive.

4

The Battle for the Hills: Politicized Landscapes and the Erasure of Place

There are places in Wales I don't go:
Reservoirs that are the subconscious
Of a people, troubled far down
With gravestones, chapels, villages even
R. S. Thomas, 'Reservoirs'[1]

Place (that is, 'space to which meaning has been ascribed'[2]) is one of the most important organizing concepts in postcolonial discourse, including postcolonial literature. The investment of a familiar landscape with enormous emotional and, often, political importance is also a clearly recognizable feature of Welsh culture, finding expression in a range of Welsh writing in both languages, as well as in other forms of artistic expression.[3] In a passage in *The Welsh Extremist*, Ned Thomas evokes the experience of affinity to a particular landscape and locality by suggesting that the very geography of an area embodies the qualities of a close human relation. In the process of espousing the strength which may be drawn from 'resist[ing] on his own territory the dehumanizing forces that are to be found everywhere', Thomas writes: 'One should not underestimate what it means to live in a country where fields and rivers and hills and villages conserve old and human feelings, and where the consciousness of these things is still widespread and can move one like the contours of a loved face.'[4] Here, the land itself conserves the essence of the human communities which have inhabited it. Jan Penrose has asserted that some sense of 'a mystical bond between people and place' is a fundamental part of the construction of nation, and of the representation of such nations as 'natural'.[5] What I want to suggest here is that this 'mystical bond' – or, more specifically, the destruction of this bond – is an important feature of the construction of Wales as a nation by a number of Welsh- and some English-language writers of the twentieth century; a nation, moreover, that has been repeatedly subjected to the imperialist actions of a London administration.

While more recent theorists of place have challenged portrayals of place that construct community, culture and place as coterminous, the links between land and culture, place and people have been highly politicized in Wales, a feature also commonly found in postcolonial writing. Pyrs Gruffudd's work on the Welsh and the land highlights issues such as the spiritual significance of the Welsh countryside, as well as the inter-war fashioning of rural, agricultural Wales as the cornerstone of the nation by Plaid Cymru, especially by Iorwerth Peate. During these early days of Plaid Cymru, Gruffudd convincingly argues, 'Welshness was understood in profoundly geographical terms', and indeed it is not unusual to find Welsh history and therefore culture explained in geographical terms, especially in the first half of the twentieth century.[6] The relationship between the Welsh geographical imagination and the nation as imagined community is indeed a complex and multifaceted one, and it is not possible to do more than explore just one aspect of what in fact constitutes a much wider discourse on land, community and nation. This chapter will focus on the role of the Forestry Commission in Wales, and specifically its construction as an alien, colonizing force by Welsh writers, who depict the afforestation of the hills as the erasure of place (as space which has been imbued with meaning through language, history and human occupation). Such erasure of place is, of course, associated with the postcolonial concept of exile which 'involves the idea of a separation and distancing from either a literal homeland or from a cultural and ethnic origin'.[7] Albeit in a localized framework, exile in this sense refers to an unbridgeable distance, since there is no possibility of return to a place which has effectively ceased to exist.

Symbols of the perceived disregard, or undervaluation, by the London government of the rural Welsh and their culture – the forests, reservoirs and military ranges – are numerous. They have become powerful and immediately evocative nationalist tools, as the enduring graffiti 'Cofia Dryweryn' ('Remember Tryweryn') testifies. But for all that Tryweryn is an immediately recognizable icon of the nationalist movement, a symbol of the disregard of Wales and particularly the Welsh language by London, the flooding of Capel Celyn was hardly the first such instance of the appropriation of land for the benefit of England or Britain at the expense of a Welsh-speaking community.[8] The first major symbol of nationalist resistance against the appropriation of Welsh territory by the London government came in 1936, when a bombing school, which had been established on a site of historical and cultural significance at Penyberth, on the Llŷn peninsula, was set on fire by Saunders Lewis, Lewis Valentine and D. J. Williams (whose writing is discussed below). In his compelling Caernarfon Court speech, Saunders Lewis defended this act of arson in what we might recognize as clear anti-colonial terms, highlighting what he saw as the plundering of Wales by England, and describing himself and his co-defendants as 'leaders of a struggle for the defence of a nation's culture against an alien and heedless state'.[9] Wales is represented as subordinated by a form of internal colonialism, and Lewis draws attention to the way the London government disregarded the widespread protest in Wales at the proposals for a bombing school.

The Ministry of Defence was also behind other controversial land-acquisitions in Wales. In 1940, at very short notice, Mynydd Epynt was compulsorily purchased and there is evidence to suggest that the community was deliberately left in the dark until the last minute about the Ministry's plans, which may have been in place long before the war.[10] Although the English-language press largely ignored the fate of the people of Epynt, there was some protest in the Welsh press, as well as a short-lived campaign orchestrated by Saunders Lewis and Gwynfor Evans, among others. In a satirical article in *Y Faner* (13 March 1940), Saunders Lewis wrote that 'Step by step the Government of England is devouring Wales', comparing the actions of the 'English' government to the aggressive empire-building of Germany in Europe. The Revd J. Dyfnallt Owen also wrote powerfully and dramatically about the implications of the loss of Epynt, not just for those directly affected but for the nation as a whole. He described the appropriation of Welsh land by the London government in terms of a violent policy of cultural annihilation:

> The despoliation means uprooting part of our nation which has been here for generations. They will be exiled from their own land and homes.
>
> It is obvious that behind this catalogue of the destruction of our patrimony there is one over-riding intent, and that is nothing less than an attempt to destroy our nationality. We are face to face with a power which, in the end, will strangle the personality, the soul and the religion of our nation.[11]

In addition to the permanent loss of Epynt (it remains a military training-range to this day), many other sites in Wales were requisitioned. A number of reservoirs were created (in Claerwen, Clywedog and Tryweryn valleys) with the aim of supplying water to those outside Wales. Such incursive developments brought little or no profit to Wales, but sometimes demanded enormous sacrifices. A much resisted nuclear power-station was opened at Trawsfynydd in 1963, an act which antagonized CND supporters and pacifists in general, and an overwhelmingly pacifist nationalist movement in particular. Not all such proposed acquisitions or 'development' of land were successful, however. An attempt in 1947 by a Labour government to turn part of the Preseli mountains into a military range was defeated, for example, and proposals to construct a reservoir in Cwm Gwendraeth Fach were also successfully resisted. In the meantime, the Forestry Commission was pursuing its task of acquiring land for its policy of afforestation. Although the Commission was given powers of compulsory purchase in 1945, the only attempt to use them – to acquire 20,000 acres in Carmarthenshire in the early 1950s – failed, after what was known as 'The Battle of the Towy'. Compulsory purchase was never attempted again in Wales, but in the event the Commission found there was no shortage of 'voluntary' sales.[12]

The use of Welsh land to meet the needs of a wider British public may not always have disturbed those communities who were either not directly affected, or who viewed Wales as a region of Britain and themselves as British first and foremost – and there were and are, of course, many Welsh people who would identify themselves as such. The attitude towards the Forestry Commission, even in rural Wales, for example, was ambivalent. On the one hand, its activities were perceived to be a threat to a way of life – epitomized by the almost biblical figure of the shepherd, who stood for struggling tenant farmers and other minor landowners; on the other hand, the Commission was often the only buyer to be found for agricultural land which was otherwise almost worthless, and farmers were thus able to sell all or part of their land at an inflated price. Nevertheless, the depth of feeling engendered by the perceived disregard of Welsh interests by the London government can be traced in Welsh-language writing, particularly of the 1950s, whilst English-language writing on these losses of land and community came a little later, from the 1960s onwards. While a sense of affinity to place is important across the whole of Wales where native locality forms an important signifier of identity,[13] it is predominantly rural, agricultural, Welsh-speaking places that are considered in this chapter.[14] Of course, those areas which could be most readily appropriated by the government in one form or another, indeed those areas most useful to

London, tended to be sparsely populated, economically disadvantaged and, crucially, Welsh-speaking rural areas.

In any discussion of the construction of place as more or less coterminous with culture and community – and by extension nation – a number of important questions must be asked. While the principal aim of this chapter is to illustrate one of the ways in which Welsh writers have self-consciously constructed Wales as a colonized nation (although not necessarily in such explicit terms), there must also be some consideration of exactly whose version of nation is supported in such imagining of the affinity between place and people. I do not wish to enter into the familiar – and ultimately unhelpful – argument in which mutually exclusive versions of rural and industrial Wales battle for superiority, but, rather, to complicate the primary subject of this discussion with a consideration of gendered interpretations of place, home and exile. Stasis and nostalgia, for example, have been highlighted as central features of the construction of place as the location of culture – key features of an escapist wish to return to some former more desirable era, and the sense of place as a source, or site, of authenticity.

What becomes immediately obvious when one surveys the Welsh writing that directly comments on afforestation and the erasure of place is its gender imbalance – all the authors discussed below are men. R. S. Thomas and Harri Webb have written poems in English, which draw on a much more extensive and earlier concern amongst Welsh-language writers, such as Gwenallt, Waldo Williams, Islwyn Ffowc Elis and Tryfan, who recognized the threat of the ambitions of the Forestry Commission and Ministry of Defence, not to mention the Water Board, to traditional Welsh life. Geographers, such as Annette Kolodny, Bronwen Walter and Doreen Massey, have emphasized that the experience of space and place is inflected by gender, in that the 'same' places may have very different meanings for the different sexes according to how gender roles are defined within these spaces/places, although Bronwen Walter also recognizes that '"race" and ethnicity [may] cut across these gendered meanings'.[15]

Thus, in examining how place is constructed by the writers discussed here, one must remain alert to the fact not only that these representations of place tend to be dominated by rather patriarchal understandings of the meaning of home and belonging, but also that they are inflected by a powerful sense of cultural threat. While perhaps working to romanticize (home) places as static, such discussions may also act as strategic interventions which aim to change the present, rather than simply articulating a longing for the past. Nevertheless, while we may note the use of threatened localities within a broader nationalist agenda, which seeks to highlight the difficulties Wales faces in the light of England's dominant position within Britain, we must also attempt to see beyond this strategic function to explore the language, imagery and other nuances of such constructions of place.

In its consideration of the project of afforestation in Wales, this chapter contrasts the discourse of the Forestry Commission and other government bodies with the work of Welsh writers who make direct reference to that afforestation. Both the government and the Welsh writers considered here were acutely aware of the crisis of depopulation in rural areas and of the struggle of rural communities to survive under an array of different pressures. There is, however, a clear gulf between them. The Commission lays emphasis on bringing work to those areas suffering from economic decline and depopulation, and thus sees the policy of afforestation in such areas as doubly beneficial, in helping to slow or reverse rural decline and in increasing the supply of British timber. The Welsh view, by contrast, presents the policy of afforestation as a danger to the Welsh nation: Welsh writers portray the areas appropriated by the Forestry Commission as the home of communities that are the 'last outposts', or, in less fatalistic language, the vibrant, if threatened, heartlands of Wales.[16] The contrast in these ways of viewing the same territory as very different 'places' may be discerned when one juxtaposes the rhetoric of the Forestry Commission with the work of Welsh-language writers, in both poetry and prose. Although these are very different media, the divergent values and world-views encapsulated in each are both fascinating and revealing: Welsh writers emphasize the cultural significance of the relationship between people and land, while the government tends to portray the land as empty, under- or unproductive, almost *unpeopled*. The function of this rhetoric is not dissimilar from the function of colonial constructions of the New World as 'empty space' rather than as places that were peopled (albeit sometimes sparsely), while (often at the same time) promoting the 'clearing' of these lands through acts of genocide.

AFFORESTATION: GREENING THE DESERT?

'. . . better a forest than a desert . . .'
The Land and the Nation: Rural Report of the Liberal Land Committee 1923–25

The government policy of afforestation in Wales, as administered by the Forestry Commission, has had a profound effect upon the landscape (both *tirlun* and *tirwedd*[17]) of the Welsh uplands and an equally significant impact upon the imagined geographies of the hills. The policies and practices of afforestation remain a bitterly contested issue, with the vested interests of the timber lobby, agriculturalists, environmentalists, the tourist industry and others often in direct conflict.[18] The true economic and social impact of Forestry Commission policies over the years is difficult to assess, not least since the rapid pace of technological change (both within the timber industry and beyond, for example, in associated industries such as mining) has rendered irrelevant and obsolete many of the forecasts of employment benefits to the afforested locality which were made earlier in the century (see pp. 88–91). For the purposes of this discussion, the actual achievements or failures of the afforestation policy are of little importance – since the focus is on the *perceived* (as distinct from the *stated*) role of the Forestry Commission, as one arm of a centralized, often arrogant and alien, London government. It is interesting, however, briefly to look at the rhetoric of this government department in relation to Wales. The self-image of the Commission, in its first fifty years, is of a body active in the regeneration of the countryside, providing employment and stability and reversing rural depopulation, as well as making a vital contribution to the security of Britain. This is a long way from its portrayal in some canonical Welsh literature, and even the members of the Commission itself were aware of a wider mistrust and hostility among the Welsh people. In his sensitive history of the first forty-five years of the Forestry Commission, the former deputy-general, George Ryle, acknowledged that in Wales the Commission was regarded 'almost as a disease spreading its slime of black fir trees over hill and dale'.[19]

The Forestry Commission was brought into being in 1919 as a direct result of the First World War, during which conflict existing concerns about the deplorable state of timber management and the lack of a coherent forestry policy in the United Kingdom before 1914 were transformed into an acute awareness of the vulnerability of Britain in this crucial area of defence. Thus, although the Forestry Commission would evolve and justify its continued existence in different ways over the following decades, as the nature of both industry and warfare changed, at its inception it was primarily concerned with the safety and defence of Britain: it was a military concern. As such, there was no initial commitment to commercial viability, although the generosity of the first budgets quickly fell victim to the government spending cuts of the early 1920s (appropriately known as Geddes' Axe). If the cost of afforestation was regarded as necessary public expenditure, the newly formed Forestry Commission was eager to justify its existence in terms broader than the mere production of a military and industrial commodity. From the outset, the subject and language of reports emphasized the benefits of afforestation to local communities as well as to 'the nation' as a whole.

This position was echoed by other post-First World War political documents, such as *The Land and the Nation: Rural Report of the Liberal Land Committee 1923–25*, which championed the cause of afforestation. In this report, the land upon which it is proposed trees should be planted is portrayed as a picture of neglect and is repeatedly referred to as 'lying waste'.[20] In a survey of forestry in Europe the report cites instances of the use of 'waste land' in Germany and Denmark and the planting of 3,000,000 acres of 'sandy waste' in France, thus instilling the idea that afforestation occurs on *empty* land.[21] The report suggests that there is plenty of such land in Britain: 'It may be as well to reiterate that not only has Great Britain a smaller proportion of forest area than other countries, but that she also has a larger proportionate area of *wholly unproductive land* than any comparable country.'[22] And again: 'It is beyond question that some land now lying waste in Great Britain would not carry trees. It is equally beyond question that an immense area of land which, in other countries would be carrying trees, is now lying waste.'[23] Since the section on timber is less than ten short pages, the repetition of the image of vast tracts of Britain lying waste is amplified, and there is even a lengthy quotation from Sir Daniel Hall's *A Pilgrimage of British Farming* (1913). First published in *The Times* (1910–12), under the subheading 'No Excuse', it paints a very sorry picture of the British countryside.

> From Stratford we struck across the edge of the Lias clay and limestones and the New Red Sandstone to Droitwich, through a poor country as badly farmed as though it were a thousand miles from a market. On the low limestone hills field after field was entirely derelict, given over to briers [*sic*] and rabbits, with the stones protruding through the thin scurf of vegetation as on a Bagshot common or the driest and thinnest scarps of the chalk. It may be true that it is a waste of money to try to farm on bad land and make a soil where nature has not supplied the foundation, but *for such entire neglect there can be no excuse in England*. . . . Some people have no great opinion of the future of forestry in England because it can never

support the proportion of men to acres which ought to prevail in our densely populated island. But better a forest than a desert . . .[24]

Although this passage refers to a place in England, and the following commentary laments the state of English agriculture, the discussion is clearly applicable to the whole of Britain: the use of 'England' and 'Britain' interchangeably was, of course, common practice at this time.

The need for timber in mining areas of Wales was great, and Wales is singled out in this report as particularly suitable for planting, with its 'unsurpassable' climate which would allow the country to become self-sufficient in timber. There is some acknowledgement, however, that there might be some contest over land use in Wales and that the half-a-million acres identified as 'forestable' are not 'deserts', or 'lying waste', although the report argues that the land is 'more suitable for forestry than for agriculture'.[25] The battle between afforestation and agriculture (or 'Y Bugail a'r Coedwigwr' (The Shepherd and the Forester), as Richard Phillips put it in 1963) was to be a crucial chapter in the history of the Forestry Commission, especially after the Second World War when government policy on food production at home lent the Department of Agriculture no small authority in the determination of land use in Britain. From the very beginning, however, the Commission was engaged in making a forceful case for the coexistence of farming and afforestation in Wales, while simultaneously putting forward figures to show that the latter would sustain more men per acre than farming. Again, the rhetoric of such forecasts is revealing. On the basis of R. D. Acland's Forestry Commission Report, *The Land and the Nation* suggests that 'if the Forestry Commission is allowed to carry out its original 10 years programme, it will in that time have settled 6,000 *families* in permanent employment who would otherwise not have been so settled',[26] while ultimately the afforestation will be able to maintain 17,770 men, having displaced 2000 men from sheep-farming. Thus, the Forestry Commission offers to settle new families while displacing (unattached, mobile?) men who will be easily absorbed back into this new industry; indeed the report argues that the 'right grounds' of an argument for afforestation are 'that afforestation helps to stabilise rural population by providing a certain amount of skilled employment, by making smallholdings economic, and by bringing into existence rural industries providing alternative employment for agricultural workers'.[27]

The Forestry Commission's actual record on its most widely advertised and philanthropic policy of promoting and providing rural jobs, and therefore strengthening local community is rather less positive than was predicted in those early reports, which painted pictures of wasteland turned into forests supporting thriving local communities. In 1957, John Saville could still write that:

> It is now accepted that a more active policy of afforestation would tend to increase the local populations in the districts where planting is undertaken. A recent Welsh survey noted that 'though the numbers employed in the early stages of afforestation are not large, even from the outset forestry employs from three to four times as many men, area for area, as agriculture . . .' The Minister for Welsh Affairs, commenting on these remarks, agreed the 'Forestry can do much' to arrest the drift from the countryside.[28]

Even while problems and difficulties with 'settlement policy' are acknowledged to exist, Saville asserts that 'there is no question that afforestation would exercise a beneficial effect upon all rural areas where it was undertaken, and not least in the hill and marginal land areas where the volume of migration has been greatest in the past'.[29] Yet Steve Tompkins's more recent survey of the timber industry in Britain, *Forestry in Crisis: The Battle for the Hills* (1989), suggests that the projected jobs never materialized and that the government simply created and subsidized an expensive, environmentally damaging, economically unsound, yet increasingly powerful and vocal industry. While it is notoriously difficult to measure the creation of employment opportunities by afforestation due to the long timescale involved (and while these same factors allow for the exaggeration of the number of jobs created), the 1972 Treasury Review concluded that:

> Given the very high implied costs per job in both resource and Exchequer terms, it would appear doubtful whether more effective forms of supporting employment cannot be found nor indeed whether this degree of support is equitable to other areas of long-term unemployment.[30]

Tompkins also compares the subsidies for afforestation with those for agriculture in the same areas and notes that grants for afforestation 'dwarf' the subsidies needed for sheep-farming. If this analysis is correct, then the benefit of hindsight lends another degree of poignancy to the protests of those writers who rejected the claims of the Forestry Commission to Welsh land.

In a later Forestry Commission publication, the pamphlet *Forestry in Wales* (1949), afforestation is again presented not only as a means of settling families on the land, but also as a solution to the depopulation of the hills. On the front cover, beneath a picture of the Lledr Valley that shows farmland on the valley floor and a variously wooded hill behind, is the inscription:

> The most urgent problems facing rural Wales are how to arrest depopulation of the countryside; how to attract and establish families on the land; and how best to utilise land in the interests of the nation.
> FORESTRY HELPS TO PROVIDE THE ANSWERS

There are a number of assumptions being made here that might be challenged, particularly from a nationalist perspective. While few would dispute the first statement about arresting depopulation, the attraction of new families to the land would probably need qualifying, in the light of the potential impact of attracting non-Welsh-speakers to Welsh-speaking communities. Although this was a concern which was to gain far greater prominence during the inward migration of the 1960s, it was already an issue in Wales, triggered by the influx of evacuees during the Second World War, for example. Exactly what the 'interests of the nation' are depends, of course, on which nation is referred to; although the pamphlet is about forestry in Wales, the nation in question is undoubtedly Britain. Inside, under the heading, 'Why Wales Needs Forests', the pamphlet details how 'Forest means a prosperous country-side', and describes the 'contribution to Britain's needs' made by Welsh afforestation. It gives details of the numbers employed and mentions that in '1948 the Commission paid its forest workers in Wales nearly £600,000 in wages'. Welsh involvement in the programme of afforest-ation is also emphasized, with remarks on the densely wooded history of Wales and pictures of the forests and of healthy young men at the training schools. The tone of the pamphlet chimes well with the aims of the new Welfare State being created by the Labour government after the Second World War, but it is also a continuation of the earlier idealistic ethos of the Commission's conception of its paternalistic role, which was greatly influenced by 'the father of the Forestry Commission', Lord Lovat.[31] This fostered the belief 'that the Forestry Commission was a fixed part of the nation's structure and that it was safe to build upon it in providing permanent employment for men whose families would be rooted to the soil in their holdings'.[32]

In response to increasing unemployment in heavy industry, the Forestry Commission also cooperated with the Ministry of Labour to provide work. 'Many unemployed colliery workers were in fact trained at these camps, but for obvious reasons it was considered wise not to open up camps too close to the Welsh or other coalfields.'[33] Despite the 'obvious reasons', whatever these might be, in the mid-1930s further joint projects were launched to aid those 'Special Areas' decimated by the Depression. Residential camps were set up in various new forests, including Brechfa, and although they were 'initially for the training of men for settlement overseas, . . . this element of the training soon gave way to rehabilitation works to refit men for tough work at home'.[34] At an experimental non-residential camp at Rheola, men 'brought in by omnibuses each day from Aberdare, Merthyr Tydfil and other unhappy towns would be provided with strenuous work under conditions of reasonable outdoor hardship and, perhaps more important, would start the day with a good hot snack and have a really nourishing hot midday meal'.[35]

The sincerity of the notion of public service and the idea of a wider national and social duty, which was established and maintained in the first decades of the Commission's existence, comes across very clearly in George Ryle's history of the first forty-five years of the Forestry Commission. It is a slightly nostalgic, if not wholly uncritical, document, which is particularly valuable for the fact that, since so much of Ryle's work was conducted in Wales, his history also contains a wealth of anecdotes about his dealings with the Welsh. These can be patronizing (reflecting differences of class), but there is no shortage of passages which reveal some sympathy and involvement with local rural life. Ryle was neither able, nor seemingly eager, to escape the generous hospitality of the local farmers. He describes how, having newly arrived in 'central Wales', he was, within an hour, invited to a neighbouring farm for tea. There he and the farmer

> talked and talked while his 'Barnado's boy' – now a wizened little man in his fifties – kept the open fire going with logs and brewed countless pots of stew-black tea. I heard the whole story, from the local farmers' angle, of the Battle of the Towy, as well as the life stories of all the neighbouring farmers, and the age-old legends of Twm Shon Catti whose cave was in the hillside across the river. I learned that 'the fforestry' was not in itself so evil but that its men and its ways had been bad. I managed to get away a little before midnight.[36]

As mentioned above, 'The Battle of the Towy' refers to the Forestry Commission's arrogant and misguided attempt to purchase 20,000 acres of land compulsorily. George Ryle comments that

The Commissioners, and ultimately the Minister of Agriculture, were persuaded that this was a wise, if drastic course to adopt in view of the long-term economics of the zone. Each of these men was perfectly correct in his opinion, but each appeared to have forgotten that he was viewing a little piece of Wales which belonged to individuals: Welsh farmers who had inherited from their fathers and their father's fathers, and who dwelt therein.[37]

The 'battle' was won by the farmers, the policy of compulsory purchases was abandoned and, according to Ryle, the problem of opposition to afforestation was resolved through making 'personal contact' and, ultimately, 'genuinely good friends' within the representative farming bodies.[38] In the case of the land in Carmarthenshire which the Forestry Commission had attempted to acquire by force, Ryle comments that, by 1965, 'the friendliness and understanding of the local foresters had already resulted in the voluntary purchase of 16,000 acres of potential forest, while private investors had bought up several thousands of acres more to plant alongside the State-owned land'.[39]

The Forestry Commission's desire to acquire land in the more conventional manner was not necessarily unwelcome among the agricultural landowners of Wales – indeed, the Commission's quest for land could be beneficial to farmers, who were able to sell off less profitable land for a good price, such as happened in the Berwyn Mountains, and could thus raise revenue to put back into their farms.[40] However, for tenant farmers the story is rather different, and even Richard Phillips, who argues that afforestation has benefited Wales without damaging sheep-farming as an industry, acknowledges that 'mae'n wir fod llawer tenant weid colli ei le drwy orfodaeth ar ôl i perchennog [sic] werthu'r tir i'r Comisiwn' (it is true that many a tenant has been forced out after the owner-landlord had sold their land to the Commission).[41] Ryle remarks that 'the big-stick attitude [has never] really been necessary. There has always been ample land available for purchase or for lease by free negotiation.'[42] His statement is somewhat undermined, however, by another description of his which suggests there was little room for 'free negotiation' on the part of farmers whose farms were heavily mortgaged. George Ryle's history suggests that, by the time the Forestry Commission arrived, the farmers were barely in possession of their own farms:

far and away the most interesting bargaining was with owner-occupier, hill farmers and Welsh to the backbone. With them there was always the opportunity to walk the boundaries which so often could not be identified from old title deeds, but knowledge of which was passed down from father to son. During this walk – or there might be the offer of a pony – no negotiating business was done, but there was invaluable talk about the neighbours or about more distant sheep folk who might have land to sell. Then, returned to the farmhouse, there would be a meal and further talk – anything to delay the business which was uppermost in the minds of both parties. In the end, of course, nothing would be settled because, though he would not admit it, the farmer could do nothing without consulting his bank manager, since most of these hill farms were heavily mortgaged. So there would be a parting amongst a swirl of sheepdogs, with strong advice to go and see Tom Bevan up the valley there, and William butcher the Hafod who wanted to sell, and with a hearty invitation to come back again soon. Maybe on the second or more likely the third or fourth visit, a final settlement and a handshake would seal a mutual friendship. But Savile Row never got over their disgust that a document named 'Form of Terms Agreed' bore no signature of the prospective seller. They could not understand the farmer's conviction that if his word was good enough throughout the county, it must be good enough in London.[43]

We might conclude then, that the Forestry Commission saw itself as a positive force in areas undergoing severe economic depression – either in the 'distressed' or 'special areas' of the industrial south or the strained agricultural uplands of Wales. The poignant description by Ryle above offers some insight into the reasons why the Commission was regarded with ambivalence in Wales, offering farmers a relatively good price for increasingly uneconomical farms yet also planting over the fields and boundaries of farms 'which [had been] passed down from father to son'.

AFFORESTATION: THE ERASURE OF PLACE

> *Coed lle y bu cymdogaeth,*
> *Fforest lle bu ffermydd,*
>
> [Trees where there was a community,
> Forest where there were farms,]
> 'Rhydcymerau', Gwenallt[44]

The postcolonial understanding of place is produced at the inter-sections of language, community and landscape. Displaced peoples struggle to develop a language that allows them to engage with new spaces so as to develop a sense of place. Equally, a fracture in the relationship between people and place may occur for the colonized in their homelands. The loss of place experienced by communities who have remained 'at home' (described by J. R. Jones as 'your country leaving you'[45]) through the appropriation of actual land or through the experience of cultural fracture, 'exile' or alienation from their own cultures, through which a sense of place was negotiated, is an important theme of postcolonial writing and is also found in Welsh writing.[46] The literal erasure of place (where place is understood as the named, imagined space described in the introduction) performed by the planting of impenetrable conifer forests, functioned as a potent symbol of the perceived destruction of a way of life often presented as synonymous with Welsh-language culture. All the texts under discussion here are concerned to some extent with making a political, implicitly anti-colonial, point. Forestry policy, directed from London, is viewed at best as further evidence of London's indifference to Welsh culture and community, and at worst as proof of outright hostility. In the poem 'Afforestation', by R. S. Thomas, Forestry Commission plantations are explicitly presented as yet another colonial instrument designed to usurp traditional Welsh life:

> It's a population of trees
> Colonising the old
> Haunts of men;[47]

In the writing explored in this chapter, physical and cultural landscapes are inseparable, and the threat of one concomitantly becomes a symbolic threat to the other. However successful, or however problematic, one considers such constructions of place to be, one point emerges clearly from these writings – that the threat to place, culture, language, community, even history, and by extension to the Welsh nation itself, is perceived as emanating from the imperialist dominance of England over Wales. A brief glance at the writing selected for discussion here – *Hen Dŷ Ffarm* (The Old Farmhouse) (1953), by D. J. Williams, 'Rhyd-cymerau' (1951), by Gwenallt, 'Preseli' (1946), by Waldo Williams, *Wythnos Yng Nghymru Fydd* (A Week in Future Wales) (1957), by Islwyn Ffowc Elis, 'Cwm Carnedd' (1957), by Tryfan, and poems by R. S. Thomas and Harri Webb – is enough to reveal that far from bolstering rural communities, as the Forestry Commission would have it, these writers perceive afforestation as contributing to the death of the nation by ousting the 'rightful owners' of the land and decimating the indigenous culture.

Tryfan's eisteddfod-winning *awdl* (a long poem in traditional metres), 'Cwm Carnedd', covers a plethora of economic and social failures which have led to the abandonment of the valley, drawing clear parallels between the twentieth-century depopulation of the hills and other historical betrayals and evictions of common people. The Highland Clearances are evoked in the line: '*Troi y crefftwyr o'u crofftydd*' (turning the craftsmen from their crofts),[48] an echo reinforced by the earlier reference to the valley 'smallholding' as a '*tyddyn*', which may be translated as 'croft'.[49] His reference to enclosing the free acres, '*Cau terfynau'r erwau rhydd*' (Placing lines/boundaries on free acres),[50] refers to another injustice inflicted by a government indifferent to the interests of commoners, the eighteenth-century Enclosure Acts. Tryfan makes especially powerful use of the image of a Forestry Commission plantation to emphasize the finality of the dissolution of an imagined Welsh-speaking community. The language and imagery of the eleven stanzas which focus on the erasure of place occasioned by afforestation are dramatic and compelling. The forest threateningly encircles the old village, an action reminiscent of military attack, but also recalling Waldo Williams's famous poem, 'Preseli', which, having described an intimate rural community backed by the strong wall of the Preseli mountains ('*Mur fy mebyd, Foel Drigarn, Carn Gyfrwy, Tal Mynydd*' (Wall around my boyhood, Foel Drigarn, Carn Gyfrwy, Tal Mynydd)[51]) concludes with the terrible lines: *Mae rhu, mae rhaib drwy'r fforest ddiffenestr. / Cadwn y mur rhag y bwystfil, cadwn y ffynnon rhag y baw* (There's a roar, there's a ravening through the windowless forests. / Keep the wall from the brute, keep the spring clear of filth). The image of pollution and death associated with the trees here is a familiar one and in 'Cwm Carnedd' this metaphor is sustained, with the trees described as some sort of invasive, perhaps fungal, disease:

> *Ymleda'r fforest, gan estyn – ei gwraidd*
> *Dros y grib i'r dyffryn*
> *Dirfawr ei gwanc diderfyn*
> *Am rynnau gweirgloddiau'r glyn.*[52]

> (The forest spreads out, reaching its roots
> Across the top and down to the valley
> Great is its unappeasable hunger
> For the ribbed meadows of the vale.)

Thus the forest saps the agricultural land of its fertility, an apposite allusion to the environmental as well as the human cost of spruce plantations. The profoundly alien nature of these poisonous all-consuming trees is repeatedly emphasized: they are '*gelltydd o dram-orwydd*' (groves of foreign trees/plantings); '*estrongoed*' (literally foreign-trees) and '*coed aliwn*' (alien woods).[53] Symbolically, the native trees which formed part of the intimate landscape and lives of the former inhabitants of Cwm Carnedd – lovingly described groves of oak and brushwood, interwoven with human paths, and boundary markers of ash, trees which themselves formed part of the meaning of the place – are swamped by an invading sea of fir trees, described in language which would not be out of place in the rhetoric of the xenophobic far right.

In *Hen Dŷ Ffarm* (1953), D. J. Williams chronicles life in a small part of Carmarthenshire during the lives of his parents and grandparents, and makes repeated attacks on the Forestry Commission. Using the image of the ultimate Welsh cultural event, the eisteddfod, Williams powerfully suggests the low worth accorded to Welsh culture by London through the policies and actions of the Forestry Commission. The image of the division of community (and, by implication, nation) is significant here, suggesting tactics of oppression from an imposed, rather than representative, London government:

> Rhydcymerau and Gwarnogau are some four miles apart across the hills, and the eisteddfod brought them together in a warm cultural alliance. To-day wooden walls miles thick separate them, the Brechfa Forestry, and many homesteads where song and verse flourished have fallen into decay, thanks to the London Government's care for Welsh rural life.[54]

The actions of the Commission were also criticized in a wider context, highlighting the (military) function of the trees, which was in direct conflict to the pacifist beliefs of some of the most important figures of Welsh nationalist and literary circles. In Gwenallt's 'Rhydcymerau', whose dramatic and chilling opening line reads '*Plannwyd egin coed y Trydydd Rhyfel*' (The seedlings/saplings of the Third War were planted here),[55] the poet signals not only his protest, like Williams above, at the substitution for verse and scripture of ranks of uniform trees, but also his pacifist objection to the appropriation of Welsh land in preparation for war. The poem also voices fear and anger at the perceived Anglicization of Wales, or, to express it differently, the homogenization of Britain, and the forests again provide a fertile metaphor with their dark, undifferentiated ranks of trees. In the depths of the forests where once a cultured Welsh-language community thrived, Gwenallt pictures an English Minotaur amid the crucified bones of poets; the Welsh of Pantycelyn usurped by 'the South's bastardized English' ('*Bratiaith Saeson y De lle bu barddoni a diwinydda*'[56]).

The death of the language is linked explicitly with the drowning of valleys and the afforestation of the hills in almost all the writing of place considered here. R. S. Thomas's poem 'Reservoirs', quoted at the beginning of this chapter, ends with a description of the English 'elbowing our language / Into the grave we have dug for it'.[57] In 'Cwm Carnedd' Tryfan attacks young people who prefer the town and '*Ei hiaith lithrig Seisnigaidd*' (its slippery English dialect) to the home valley and the Welsh language. The most memorable and chilling passage in Islwyn ffowc Elis's *Wythnos Yng Nghymru Fydd* (a novel which imagines two very different futures for Wales: one a vision of a successful, independent nation, embracing a vibrant, if patriarchal, culture, the other a nightmarish 'West England', dominated by military ranges and forestry land) describes the encounter with the last native speaker of Welsh in a militarized, afforested Wales. Perhaps predictably, this last vestige of Welsh culture is embodied by a woman, an elderly and frail figure who is coaxed into admitting she remembers Welsh only when the words of Psalm 23 ('*Ie, pe rhodiwn ar hyd Glyn Cysgod Angau . . .*' (Yea, though I walk through the valley of the shadow of death . . .)[58]) are, rather ominously, recited. The importance of the language in the construction and contestation of place is central, and the Welsh language has certainly been represented in certain discourses as intimately, even organically associated with place. Ned Thomas explains this in terms of J. R. Jones's notion of *cydymdreiddiad*:

> that subtle . . . interpenetration, which, he says, grows in time (in people's consciousness) between a territory and its people and their language creating a sense of belonging to a particular stretch of the earth's surface. From the point of view of an established and secure culture such as that of England, this may seem a rather vague and mystical notion. The secure culture takes it largely for granted and therefore leaves it undefined. But in various parts of the world, the absence or loss of this *cydymdreiddiad* focuses the mind powerfully upon the idea.[59]

One implication of this idea of *cydymdreiddiad* is the question that perhaps the English language does not offer an equivalent (or adequate?) means of interpreting the Welsh landscape. In other colonized territories, the inadequacy of English to describe a foreign landscape has resulted in a situation where the Anglophone inhabitants of such territory have suffered from a sense of distance and cultural dislocation from their environment, a gap which has been bridged by linguistic and imaginative innovation. This is not an experience which finds parallels in Wales, not least, perhaps, because similar landscapes are found in England and Wales, although this is not to suggest that the nuances and specificities of Welsh may be translated directly into English. Nevertheless, since most areas of Wales bear Welsh place-names, there is some sense in which monoglot English-speakers (whether native or incomers) are inevitably excluded from much of the cartography which is offered through them. This dislocation, which is the result of the fractured linguistic history of Wales, is explored in Christopher Meredith's *Shifts* (1988), where, although the marks of industry upon the landscape are easily read by the trained eye of the insider, who can discern the difference between natural hillocks and grassed-over slag-heaps, for example, the older, Welsh-speaking history of the area is obscured, even when it is inscribed in place-names such as 'Henfelin' ('Old Mill').[60] This feature of Meredith's novel is discussed further in chapter 5, but the importance of naming in the production of meaning and, crucially, ownership of landscape is a point worth pursuing here.

The role of cartography in the colonization of land is now well known, thanks to studies such as *The Road to Botany Bay* (1987) by Paul Carter, and compelling dramatizations of this imperial tool, such as Brian Friel's play *Translations* (1981), in which the translation or Anglicization of Irish place-names forms a central part of the re-mapping of Ireland as a colonized country. In the prose and poetry which symbolically engages with afforestation, naming is also recognized as fulfilling a crucial role in the inscription of meaning and belonging upon landscape, and the recitation of place names becomes a form of protest against the erasure of place. In contrast, and in opposition to the 'wilderness created by the London Government to bear the high sounding name of Brechfa Forest'[61] is the litany of place-names, the names of farms and fields intimately associated with those who live and work on them, that resonate throughout *Hen Dŷ Ffarm*. This not only emphasizes the long association of people and language with the land, it also reads like a roll-call of the dead, forcing an acknowledge-ment and re-membering of community and nation. Gwenallt too, in

'Rhydcymerau', uses the lyricism and the implied specificity of place-names to suggest the enormity of the loss of land, to contrast the human investment in land and place with the desert of over-planted land where 'place' (as a lived-in space invested with human meaning) has been destroyed by trees destined to become part of a larger human atrocity, perhaps even Armageddon:

> Plannwyd egin coed y Trydydd Rhyfel
> Ar dir Esgeir-ceir a meysydd Tir-bach
>   Ger Rhydcymerau[62]

> (They have planted the saplings to be trees of the Third War
> On the land of Esgeir-ceir and the fields of Tir-bach,
>   Near Rhydcymerau)

Tryfan, in 'Cwm Carnedd', also suggests peoples' sense of belonging and ownership of the land through naming. He describes the old people unwillingly (but ultimately with a certain servility) leaving their homesteads to the stranger, to the '*Comisiwn*':

> Gado Cae'r Ogof a'i chwyn a'i glofar,
> A Chae Rhiw Bychan lle llechai'r buchod,
> Cae Rhyd Olau a'r balc ar ei dalar'
> Gwrychoedd y Gelli a'u rhesi o rosod,
> Clos bach y Llain a eginai'n gynnar,
> A llyn yr Efail a llwyni'r Hafod.[63]

> (Leaving Cae'r Ogof with its weed and clover,
> And Cae Rhiw Bychan where cattle sheltered,
> Cae Rhyd Olau and the ridge of its furrow
> The hedges of the Gelli with its rows of roses
> The 'Clos bach y Llain' that budded early
> And the lake of Efail and the bushes of Hafod.)

In *Wythnos Yng Nghymru Fydd*, an afforested Wales is renamed 'West England' performing an elision comparable to that of Brechfa Forest, mentioned above.

It should be clear from the discussion thus far, then, that this writing of place and protest constitutes much more than an antagonism towards Forestry Commission plantations. In Harri Webb's poem, 'Cwmtaf Bridge', the appropriation of Welsh land for afforestation, as well as to supply water and for military training, becomes a metaphor for Welsh decline which embraces the problems of the industrial south as well as of the rural uplands. The poet describes standing in a flooded valley, surrounded by 'pinetrees marshalled' in 'mathematical ranks', looking down the valley to 'the tip above Aberfan' and the poem ends with the image of Wales dead under a shroud of trees, water and slag.[64]

How best to manage the complex and dramatic economic and social changes behind the 'depopulation of the hills' (not to mention the decline of heavy industry) is a difficult issue, and one which remains a pressing concern into the present. In the face of what often seem the impossible odds stacked against farmers, Welsh writers in both languages sometimes revert to an impractical, but no less poignant romantic idealism; this is all the more moving, and perhaps pathetic, because of the self-awareness of these writers, who seem simultaneously to sense a certain futility in their acts of protest, literary and practical, whilst using elegy and nostalgia strategically to engender and encourage protest in their readers. D. J. Williams describes his own attempt to resist the complicity of other farmers in the project of afforestation, those who have sold their land to the Forestry Commission. The author clings on to an ancestral farm, despite its being uneconomical:

> Between the cost of upkeep and the depreciation in the value of the place due to the increasing importance of convenient roads, you can obtain some idea of the right royal profit the landlord gets by to-day! Because of the Uncle Jâmsian [that is, obstinate] and sentimental stubbornness of its owner in refusing to the end to sell it to the Government, Penrhiw is a kind of peninsula to-day in the sea that has submerged the Lowland Hundred, the Brechfa Forest.[65]

The safeguarding of this place is an act of symbolic as well as a concrete gesture of resistance to the destruction of the Welsh-speaking, rural culture of these hills – of which the forests are a symptom, rather than a cause, a fact implicitly acknowledged by Williams in his nonetheless hostile description of the Commission as the 'imperialist vulture from London' – albeit that the author realizes the ultimate impracticality of the gesture.[66] R. S. Thomas's romantic and yet detached perspective on agricultural Welsh lifestyles is briefly discussed in chapter 2, but it might be epitomized here by the lines from 'Too Late', which are addressed to his archetypal Welsh farmer, Iago Prytherch: 'I would have seen you poor and in rags, / Rather than wealthy and not free.'[67] (Yet, as we would expect of Thomas, he addresses the problematic nature of this stance in other poems.) In 'Above Tegaron', Harri Webb is concerned to highlight the temptation to romanticize ways of life that are in decline. Surveying the 'high ground / Between Irfon and Camddwr', Webb is aware of a certain ambivalence of perspective:

> Look on it for the last time; in a few years
> The pinetrees will have hidden it in their darkness.
> Even now perhaps it is not quite right
> To take this road when there are easier routes.
> Flying from madness, maybe we bring it with us,
> Patronising romantics, envying the last survivors
> Of an old way of life, projecting our dreams
> On this conveniently empty scenery, deserted
> By its sons for the hard bright streets we come from.[68]

Perhaps it is not insignificant, too, that in this mixed portrayal of the countryside as a romantic retreat Webb ironically evacuates the uplands of people, so that the landscape becomes 'conveniently empty scenery'.

The aim of this chapter has been to consider the construction of Wales as a colonized or otherwise subjugated nation by Welsh writers in English and Welsh, through their utilization of Forestry Commission plantations (as well as reservoirs and military ranges) as potent symbols of the appropriation of Welsh land by the London government. The consequences of this policy for Welsh community and culture were perceived to be catastrophic, even fatal, and the actions of the London government could be seen as those of an imperialist overlord. Before concluding, then, it is worth pausing to consider more explicitly just what kind of place, *whose* place, the Wales produced by this discourse is. Writing, as these authors were, from a particular if protracted moment of crisis, a portrayal of the erasure of home-places in Wales is ideologically loaded, raising questions about their use of gendered tropes of authenticity, history and exile.

There is no space to enter into a protracted discussion of gendered home-places here, but with reference to the related issues of nostalgia, stasis and exile it is worth noting Bronwen Walter's assertion that: 'The fixed and bounded understanding of place, with its connections to a romantic view of place as "home", a haven of rest and retreat, is a masculine characterisation.'[69] Doreen Massey associates this static and therefore restrictive idea of home, which is coded female by male exiles, with an essentialist and ultimately reactionary construction of place, 'always constructed with reference to the past'.[70] Massey also suggests that the identities supported by nostalgic images of home, place and nation are primarily those of white western males. This grouping of white western males together, however, does not allow for a consideration of power differences within this group, such as may be discerned between England and Wales, for instance. In her study of Irish emigrants, however, Bronwen Walter qualifies this homogenization of whiteness to reflect the possibility of subordination and dominance within this ethnically diverse group. Drawing on the work of bell hooks, Walter acknowledges that:

> Whereas homes may signify control and imprisonment for women in dominant societies, they may represent places of safety for racialised groups whose physical and cultural integrity is threatened by the dominant group outside. They can also provide subversive sites where valued aspects of the culture, disallowed in the dominant culture, are maintained and passed on to children.[71]

In this understanding, the home as a site of cultural authenticity or refuge becomes a politically powerful one – Welsh after all is revealingly known as a 'language of the hearth' – which may find resonance in the experiences of those Welsh for whom a stable idea of a secure home-place (with its associations of language and other markers of ethnicity) is absent.

For all the problems with the 'nostalgic' construction of home-places, which are recognized just as they are evoked by most of the writers discussed here, the tendency towards nostalgia may equally be regarded as an effective and evocative tool in their work. The *hiraeth* (in the sense of a longing which it is impossible to assuage) which permeates this writing reflects perhaps an inevitable response to the very literal loss of place, a response to the condition of exile from these home-places to which there is no possibility of return, except in memory. Nevertheless, each writer – Tryfan, D. J. Williams, Gwenallt, Islwyn Ffowc Elis and, in different ways, Harri Webb and R. S. Thomas – is writing *against* the loss of a culture, against the loss of memory of a place; so, in (re)populating the places that have been both portrayed as empty and actually emptied by the policies of central government, these writers seek to re-member past and place and so to change the present and future of Wales. In *Yearning: Race, Gender and Cultural Politics*, bell hooks echoes Milan Kundera in emphasizing that for African-Americans (and other colonized or postcolonial peoples) 'our struggle is a struggle of memory against forgetting'[72] and this statement has deep resonance in the context of the projects of the Welsh writers discussed here. While hooks recognizes the pitfalls of nostalgia and stasis that often accompany a 'sense of place', she points out that what is important is 'a politicisation of memory that distinguishes nostalgia, that longing for something to be as once it was, a kind of useless act, from that remembering that serves to illuminate and transform the present'.[73] While this politicized act may drift close to sentimentality at times, the writing of place discussed here constitutes part of a wider, sustained, self-conscious and powerful effort of 're-membering' which attempts to 'illuminate and transform the present'.

5

'Devices of Otherness'?
Code-switching, Audience and the
Politics of Language

INTRODUCTION: NEW 'ENGLISHES'

Raja Rao once eloquently remarked that the problem which confronted him, as an Indian writer who had inherited the language of the colonizer, was to 'convey in a language that is not one's own the spirit that is one's own'.[1] This is a comment which might at first seem to have no small resonance in Wales, especially among those authors – R. S. Thomas and Emyr Humphreys, for example – who have felt a mixture of guilt and resentment over their use of English rather than Welsh in their work. However, since the early twentieth century, English has been the language of the majority in Wales, and for this majority any sense of Welsh cultural or national identity has been experienced through the English language. As Janet Davies explains in her informative book, *The Welsh Language* (1993):

> Until the twentieth century, it was possible to define the Welsh as a people who were predominantly Welsh-speaking. That definition was no longer viable [after 1911], and a new definition was needed. Welsh-speakers continued to use Cymro to mean Cambrophone and Sais to mean Anglophone, but when the words were translated as Welshman and Englishman they carried the suggestion that those lacking a knowledge of Welsh were not part of the Welsh nation, a suggestion fraught with controversy and bitterness.[2]

It might be argued that Welsh writers using the English language are particularly sensitive to such tensions since their language use is inevitably self-conscious, and those writers who consider themselves Welsh rather than British must be aware of the 'spectre' of Welsh-language literature, as well as the politics of language, which looms over their endeavours. The relationship between English-language writers and their Welsh-speaking contemporaries and forebears is complex but often sympathetic (see M. Wynn Thomas's *Internal Difference* and *Corresponding Cultures*, as well as chapter 4 of this book). The position of Welsh writers in English in relation to the canon of English literature or literature in English is uneasy and critics such as Ned Thomas have tentatively tried to align Welsh writing in English with postcolonial writing in English. In a book on Derek Walcott, Thomas writes that:

> Those in Wales who write in English, no less than Derek Walcott write a *new* literature. West Indians can say with R. S. Thomas: 'Despite our speech we are not English.' Because Derek Walcott has some small affinity with his situation we may identify with him beyond obscuring guilts and stereotypes.[3]

Showing just *how* Welsh writers in English may be regarded as using a *new* English, which is to some extent distinct from that of English-language writers from England, is an ambitious project which has yet to be tackled in any systematic way, although it has been argued, for instance, that Dylan Thomas's use of the language was influenced by a residual knowledge of Welsh as a literary and spoken language.[4] The defining characteristic of postcolonial writing in a European language is that the writer approaches the language from the outside, often as a second language, or even as a first language which does not quite reflect the history and culture of the speaker, and therefore is more able to innovate, to introduce productive slippages, create hybrid discourses, to write 'english', not English (see n. 69 on p. 164). To some extent this description might be seen to merge with certain features of the post-modern, although the attempt to register and incorporate alternative (non-English) englishes goes back at least as far as the late eighteenth century, as found in Sir Walter Scott's historical novels. It was also, of course, a feature of the early 'renaissance' in both Ireland and Scotland. In recent decades, however, it has surely been postcolonial writers, sometimes with a knowledge of languages other than English at their command, and certainly with a knowledge of cultures and landscapes

which may not be adequately described by English, who have not
infrequently made the most startling and exciting innovations within
'english' literature.

Such innovative use of European languages by postcolonial writers
has been described by Bill Ashcroft as acting metonymically to suggest
the cultural, and possibly linguistic difference of the author. The
'aphasic cultural gulf' may be referred to, constructed 'most strikingly
by uses of language which we could call the "devices of otherness", the
devices which appear specifically utilised to establish the difference and
uniqueness of the post-colonial text'.[5] These techniques include:

> direct glossing in the text, either by explanation or parenthetic insertions,
> . . . syntactic fusion, in which the english prose is structured according to
> the syntactic principles of a first language; neologisms, new lexical forms in
> English which are informed by the semantic and morphological exigencies
> of a mother tongue; the direct inclusion of untranslated lexical items in the
> text, ethnorhythmic prose which constructs an english discourse according
> to the rhythm and texture of a first language, and the transcription of
> dialect and language variants of many different kinds, whether they come
> from diglossic, poly-dialectical or monolingual speaking communities.[6]

One might think of a number of Welsh writers who make use of one or
more of these 'devices' and whose use of the English language might be
usefully explored more fully in terms of these postcolonial paradigms.
Caradoc Evans is an obvious and exciting example of a Welsh writer
approaching the English language from outside and making dramatic
alterations to great effect, although whether his writing fits neatly into
any of these categories is another matter. In Caradoc Evans's *My
People*, generally regarded as the first example of a distinctive Anglo-
Welsh literature, the syntax and choice of language are highly stylized
so as to render the English language unfamiliar, foreign even, to a
speaker of standard English. Evans does not simply impose a Welsh
syntax on his written English, and his use of 'untranslated lexical items
in the text' is limited. Evans's short stories are written in what we might,
following Ashcroft, describe as an 'ethnorhythmic prose', but this prose
is inflected in a variety of ways. The main body of the narrative is
written in a kind of claustrophobic biblical language which, while
lending a certain majesty, as John Harris comments, reinforces the
horror of the corruption of the characters. The dialogue, although
clearly deriving something from the Welsh language, is not simply a

'translation' of Welsh idiom but a far more artistic creation, playing on deliberate mistranslations to create 'a range of startling expressions purely of his own devising: they have no parallels in the Welsh language or in the English spoken in Wales'.[7] In his use of an 'english' which is clearly transformed by the influence of another pre-colonial language, Evans's writing can easily be located in the tradition of postcolonial literature. What may confuse a discussion of Evans's writing as offering an accomplished example of adapting the language of the colonizer to represent a culture lived through a different language, is the fact that Evans's representation of 'the Welsh peasantry' – still contentious nearly ninety years after the work was first published – does not seem to fit quite so neatly into an anti-colonial model. The furore and objections surrounding the publication of *My People* are well known and do not need to be rehearsed here. I raise the matter simply to point out that this problem of content, of Evans being 'off message' in postcolonial terms, illustrates both how far postcolonial literature is defined by its content and also the potentially reductive capacity of such a definition.

Other writers who use a non-standard english to create a sense of cultural specificity and difference include Mike Jenkins, who transcribes Merthyr english, and Niall Giffiths, who represents a variety of dialects and accents in his novels, although how successful these accented inscriptions are is debatable. Equally interesting are those authors who attempt to convey cultural difference through apparently standard English, as Emyr Humphreys does in *Outside the House of Baal* and other novels. Although much more difficult to pin down and define, even here there is what might best be described as a certain self-consciousness in the use of language, which contributes to an individual style that is often a little heavy or slow in its deliberateness. For the purposes of this chapter, however, only one method of suggesting cultural difference through the use of language as metonymy will be explored: the way Welsh writers in English make use of the Welsh language through code-switching in their work – a practice which is inevitably inflected by the intense and often bitter politics of language in Wales.

This study addresses two important essays on the subject: Bill Ashcroft's 'Is that the Congo? Language as Metonymy in the Post-Colonial Text', and Elizabeth Gordon and Mark Williams's 'Raids on the Articulate: Code-Switching, Style-Shifting, and Post-Colonial Writing'.[8] These essays are not without their problems. It becomes immediately clear, especially in Ashcroft's essay, that very large assumptions are being made about the nature of language and its relationship to culture, which must be more explicitly considered. Moreover, for our purpose, Ashcroft's thesis needs to be inflected, or modified, in such a way as to accommodate the specificities of the language–culture debate in Wales. Ashcroft looks at the way in which what he calls 'language variance' (that is, the use of 'foreign'[9] words in a text – code-switching – or the grammatical/syntactical disruption of one language by another) functions to represent cultural difference in postcolonial literature. He suggests that when postcolonial writers, using a European language of colonization, insert words or phrases in their 'native' language (usually but not always pre-colonial – think of Caribbean languages, for example) into the text, these words work as metonymic signifiers of the culture of the linguistic group from which they are drawn.[10] More specifically, Ashcroft suggests, this oxymoronically 'foreign' native word acts as a synecdoche of culture. A synecdoche is defined in the *OED* as 'a figure of speech in which a part is made to represent the whole or vice versa'. The suggestion that a single word of a language can be understood to *represent* the whole language should not cause any problems. However, to suggest that a word can signify an entire culture does raise some important questions – particularly in a country such as Wales, which has more than one language. Wales has often been represented as having two cultures: English-language culture most obviously associated with the industrial south, and Welsh-language culture, associated with the more rural west and north, thus producing a more or less essentialist version of Welsh culture(s) as defined by language. Essentialist claims that construct language as synonymous with, or at least the vehicle of, a particular culture are abundant in Wales and elsewhere, and can be persuasive, if ultimately reductive. Given the linguistic situation in Wales, these assumptions can also prove to be deeply and destructively divisive, and it seems more appropriate to consider Wales as a culturally composite nation where language plays a great, perhaps paramount, part in the variety of Welsh 'cultures', but where it is also recognized that linguistic groups are not culturally homogeneous, nor are different cultural groupings always divided along linguistic lines. Before attempting a study of individual texts and their authors' use of code-switching, however, it is necessary to consider some of the contentions of the language debate in Wales, with particular reference to more or less essentialist notions of the relationship between language and culture.

LANGUAGE POLITICS AND CONTESTED CULTURAL IDENTITIES IN WALES

An understanding of language as essential to culture is based on an understanding of the uniqueness of the reciprocal relationship between language and culture, where each shapes the other. Languages are shaped by the linguistic community and, in turn, 'Language constitutes reality in an obvious way. It provides some terms and not others with which to talk about the world.'[11] Kenyan writer Ngugi wa Thiong'o, describing the development of language in terms of production and labour, where language is the result of a historical social need for humans to cooperate and communicate to secure the materials necessary for life, draws attention to the profound cultural significance of language:

> over time, a particular system of verbal signposts comes to reflect a given people's historical consciousness of their twin struggles over nature and over the social product. Their language becomes the memory-bank of their collective struggles over a period of time. Language thus comes to embody both continuity and change in that historical consciousness. It is this aspect of language, as a collective memory-bank of a given people, which has made some people ascribe mystical independence to language. It is the same aspect which has made nations and peoples take up arms to prevent total annihilation or assimilation of their languages, because it is tantamount to annihilating that people's collective memory-bank of past achievements and failures which form the basis of their common identity. It is like uprooting a community from history.[12]

Linguistic difference is often regarded as the most important distinguishing factor between groups of people and the implication, then, is that just as a language is created by a community, a community is defined by its language. Marx expressed it thus: 'Language itself is just as much the product of a community, as in another respect it is the existence of community: it is, as it were, the communal being speaking for itself.'[13] In a comment such as this, however, we may begin to see some of the problems which assertions of language as the essence of culture and community can raise. Marx, in describing a 'communal being speaking for itself', evokes the image of a nation speaking with one voice – with one language? – and there seems to be no space for difference in this construction of community. Of course, much has changed since Marx wrote those words, and yet the idea that the ability to speak Welsh is a prerequisite of a Welsh cultural identity is still common in some circles, as is suggested by Janet Davies above p. 104. Saunders Lewis, driving home the centrality of the language to the nationalist movement, declared in his lecture, *Tynged yr Iaith* (The Fate of the Language), that 'Wales without the Welsh language will not be Wales'.[14] R. Tudur Jones is even more explicit in excluding non-Welsh speakers from claiming a Welsh identity: 'They call themselves Welsh-men and yet they lack the one distinctive qualification that gives the Welshman his cultural uniqueness, namely command of the Welsh language.'[15] This position, which regards the majority of the Welsh-born population as not 'qualified' to be Welsh, is, of course, vigorously challenged by others.

Dai Smith has argued that the English-speaking culture which has grown up around the valleys (around 'my Wales') is not only a vibrant and uniquely Welsh culture, but, given that this English-language Welsh culture has been the experience of the majority, it can be claimed to be the 'true' culture of modern Wales.[16] Strangely, perhaps, for a historian, this position implies a rather limited historical perspective, failing as it does to look beyond the late nineteenth century, when English did become the language of the majority. Dai Smith is not alone in ignoring the significance of such history, however, and Tim Williams asserts the precedence of an English-language Wales (specifically his version of a socialist, industrial south Wales), recalling an idealized culture of 'social cohesion and political cleverness, cosmopolitanism and an educated bolshiness, a delight in rhetoric and an informed love of our *real* mother tongue'.[17] Indeed, Williams goes further, to imply that what he describes as 'eisteddfodic Welshness – that phoney and pernicious cultural nationalism . . . committed in equal parts to the second rate and the second language, . . . has advanced in the ruins of a better Wales. My South Wales.'[18] This is a revealing passage, settled firmly in the limiting dichotomy which persistently constructs Wales as divided into two mutually hostile and exclusive groups – those of an English-speaking, socialist, industrial south Wales and a Welsh-speaking, nationalist, Nonconformist, rural west. It employs all the usual emotive imagery – a heroic past, a sad future, the extinction of one language by an unworthy usurper. If it were not for the depressing frequency with which this image of Wales is evoked, this absurdly simplistic and cripplingly reductive construction would be laughable.

Tim Williams's emphasis on the status of the Welsh language in Wales as a 'second language' not only suggests the minority status of the Welsh language, while taking a swipe at the fact that it is often an acquired second language; it also tries to turn the tables on an attitude among some Welsh-language advocates which has worked to devalue English-speaking Welsh people as second-class, as 'underqualified' (to borrow R. Tudur Jones's vocabulary), Welsh men and women. The label also makes an implicit reference to a book published nearly thirty years before Williams published *The Patriot Game*, Robyn Lewis's *Second Class Citizen*; this book described the position of Welsh speakers in a Wales which denied them the right to live through the medium of Welsh. In this 1969 volume, it is Welsh speakers who are 'second-class citizens in their own land' by virtue of the fact that they are unable to use their first language in all aspects of national life.[19] The battle to assert a dominant version of Welsh culture, which is part of the language–identity debate in Wales, inevitably constructs hierarchies of identity, just as it works to deny the possibility of cultural variations within Wales. Diversity is sacrificed for a limited ideal of a homogeneous, ideally monoglot Wales, and yet to imagine that diversity may exist without inequalities and potential conflict may also be naive, as critics of the rhetoric of multiculturalism, for instance, have argued. Indeed, it is increasingly acknowledged that tension, conflict and power struggles are fundamental to 'culture', that is, culture is always and inevitably in a 'conflicted' state of existence.[20]

Part of the language–identity debate in Wales focuses on *which* version of Welsh culture is associated with the Welsh language. For example, the political, economic and cultural-linguistic position of Wales within Britain has had some interesting effects on the way reactionary and revolutionary forces have been associated with the different languages of Wales. In addition to the pressures upon the Welsh language from massive in-migration, unsupportive educational policies and a lack of institutionalization, the late nineteenth and early twentieth centuries in Wales saw what might be described as the damaging 'ghettoization' of the role or sphere of the Welsh language in modern life. Ieuan Gwynedd Jones is one of many who have argued that the Welsh language increasingly became the protected domain of religion, while English was portrayed as 'the language of infidelity and atheism, of secularism, of higher criticism, of extreme liberality in theology'.[21] While the Welsh language had not always been allied with reactionary forces, by the end of the Victorian era the language had 'entered into alliance with the chapel on the terms of the chapel . . . and English became the language for what [Welsh] scorned or feared to express'.[22] Ieuan Gwynedd Jones goes on to argue that the result of this alliance was the rejection of the language, along with the ideology:

> To abandon Welsh became not only a valuational but also a symbolic gesture of rejection and affirmation – the rejection of the political philosophy and the sham combination of Lib-Labism and the affirmation of new solidarities and new idealisms based upon a secular and anti-religious philosophy. Fifty years earlier the new unions of the coalfield had issued their pamphlets, transacted their business and organised themselves politically in Welsh. *The Miners' Next Step* was written in English and never translated. What some thinkers had consistently feared had come about: the language and the religion which had grown together would decline together.[23]

On a more contemporary note, Janet Davies draws attention to a similar conflation of language and a specific version of Welsh culture in her postscript to *The Welsh Language*. Davies tries to distinguish between contemporary fears that the Welsh language is experiencing an irreversible decline (a position she rejects) and distress over the disappearance of particular traditions of Welsh life:

> A great deal of the panic and despair [over the supposed decline/death of the Welsh language] stems, not so much from the erosion of the language in many of its former strongholds as from the realization that the way of life associated with the language in those strongholds has passed away. I did not know that way of life, and so its passing leaves me unmoved. Indeed, it could be argued that the association of Welsh with a vanishing way of life was detrimental to the language, and that its continuance is dependent upon its ability to anchor itself in modernity, an ability which it has, to some extent, shown.[24]

Emphasizing a certain distance between the language and the culture(s) of Wales both past and present, Janet Davies challenges the *equation* (if not the interaction) of language with culture and, in doing so, she frees language from the burden of association with a *fixed* (and therefore reactionary) cultural moment. It is worth noting in passing, however, that if the association with 'a vanishing way of life' may be considered to be detrimental to the place of the Welsh language in the modern world, for some this perceived quality has been its main attraction.[25]

If national identity cannot be defined exclusively in linguistic terms, the linguistic history and contemporary situation of Wales are nevertheless profoundly important to Welsh identity. This is not, however, to suggest that one can divide the Welsh into English-speaking and Welsh-speaking groups, label the nation as somehow bilingual and leave it at that. Quite the reverse – irrespective of which linguistic group people consider themselves to belong, their Welsh identity will also be affected by the other linguistic group.[26] That is to say, it is impossible to ignore either of the languages of Wales – for some Welsh speakers English is a universal and well-used second language; for the monoglot English-speaker there is the experience of living in a country which has conducted the greater part of its long history in a 'foreign' language until the very recent past, and in which Welsh is becoming a resurgent force in public life. Indeed, the prominence and contentiousness of the language debate is surely, by now, an intrinsic *part* of the cultural landscape of Wales. Of course, the debate in which the two linguistic groups battle to claim authority as the 'true' culture of Wales is as futile as it is absurd, as revealing of the cultural tensions within Wales as it is symptomatic of them. Bearing in mind the sensitivity and complexity of the language debate in Wales, the language an author uses for his or her work not only has a direct bearing on the audience available, but also has a wider politico-cultural significance.

'CHOOSING' A LANGUAGE

In a book on Englishness, Jeremy Paxman describes the punitive laws against the Welsh and their language, and notes that: 'Despite these inhibitions, the Welsh continued to use their own language between themselves, so that it is estimated that as late as the 1880s, three out of four Welsh people still spoke it by *choice*.'[27] Paxman's statement suggests that one *chooses* a language much as one would choose an (in this case hopelessly unfashionable) outfit. We must hesitate, however, before using the word 'choice' so freely when referring to the use of language. Writers such as Chinua Achebe, R. S. Thomas and Christopher Meredith have all made the point that one does not choose one's first language, nor, usually, the language of one's education which may come to supersede the language of the home. Achebe defends his use of English thus: 'for me there is no other choice. I have been given this language and I intend to use it.'[28] This is echoed by Christopher

Meredith's assertion that: 'A language chooses its writer.'[29] However, where the author does have a choice – where he or she already possesses or learns more than one language – the decision to write in one language or another, or to code-switch in a single text, must result in the selection/construction of a particular audience, as Ngugi wa Thiong'o has pointed out: 'the choice of a language already pre-determines the answer to the most important question for producers of imaginative literature: For whom do I write? Who is my audience?'[30]

The famous argument between Ngugi and Achebe over the choice of language of an African writer has revealing and sometimes paradoxical implications for Wales. Achebe has advocated the use of the English language by African writers, for a number of reasons, not least because of its accessibility, its supposed ability to 'transcend' the many linguistic borders within Africa, not to mention its appeal to those beyond that continent, controversially positing lesser-used Nigerian languages as 'tributaries to feed the one central language enjoying nationwide currency. Today, for good or ill, that language is English.'[31] What is presented here as a practical solution is, of course, a rather naive representation of the power relationships between languages and the potential consequences for literatures in 'tributary' languages, a fate ironically hinted at in his essay 'The African Writer and the English Language', when Achebe states his 'hope . . . that there will always be men, like the late Chief Fagunwa, who will choose to write in their native tongue and ensure that our ethnic literature will flourish side-by-side with the national ones'.[32] The fact that Achebe choses to refer to a *late* writer of 'ethnic literature' seems highly suggestive of the ultimate fate of this 'tributary' literature, although the irony here seems to go unnoticed by him.

Ngugi, on the other hand, has argued that an African writer ought to use his or her own tongue, not only because it is more relevant to the experiences of the various peoples of Africa, but also because he believes it is the duty of an African writer to address the masses, the peasantry, in the language they understand, rather than in the language of the colonial or neocolonial elite.[33] Interestingly, if we translate this into the contemporary Welsh situation, then the argument would support the use of English rather than Welsh. If, however, we look at Ngugi's arguments in the context of (early) nineteenth-century Wales, there is no need for any modifications. While postcolonial studies have highlighted the dangers of denigration implied in the construction of Africa as an underdeveloped Europe, or, to phrase it differently, as Europe's prehistory, given the fact that Wales is in geographically closer contact with England than is Kenya and has been subject to English influence for much longer, it seems fair to consider Ngugi's discussion of twentieth-century Kenya as it reflects upon the linguistic situation at an earlier period of Welsh history.

Aside from the class- or nation-based politics of language usage, as Ngugi has pointed out, an author's 'choice' of language has profound implications for the readership he or she might reach. For Ngugi, the decision to write in Gikuyu is to curtail the possible size of his audience radically, not only in linguistic terms, but also because of the poor rate of literacy and purchasing power of the majority of Gikuyu-speaking Africans. In 'Writing on the Edge of Catastrophe', the acclaimed Welsh-language author and playwright Wiliam Owen Roberts strips down the situation in Wales to a bleak set of numbers: 'The population of Wales is about 2,500,000. Out of this, about 400,000 to 500,000 speak Welsh. This includes everyone and as a writer that's my entire audience. The percentage of people who actually read literature in Welsh must be anyone's guess.'[34] At least as important as this initial choice of language, however, is the issue of the access to an audience gained through a publisher. The location of a publisher outside the writer's own nation can result in a conflict between the author's imagined or intended audience, that is, the audience implicitly addressed by the text, and the publisher's intended market. The lack of English-language publishers in Wales until the 1960s and 1970s forced Welsh authors writing in English to publish in England and therefore fulfil the requirements of an English audience, or to turn to more accessible Irish periodicals, again with their own agendas. The lack of a home press may result in failure to find a publisher at all for certain texts and will necessarily affect the very text itself (according to the popular Welsh writer Siân James, locating a novel in Wales remains unpopular with English editors/ audiences and she meets with some resistance every time she chooses a Welsh setting for her novels).[35]

Addressing a particular audience may inflect the very fabric of a text, perhaps enriching it, perhaps necessitating unhelpful compromises. For whom does a Welsh writer using the English language write? An English audience? A monoglot English-speaking Welsh audience? Or a bilingual Welsh audience? How do these different readers approach an English-language Welsh text? Even for an author who uses standard English, there will be decisions to be made about how far one wishes to 'explain' or 'gloss' details of Welsh culture, history or geography for the benefit of readers outside Wales. Some of these issues have been considered in relation to the regional novel. K. D. M. Snell's definition, in *The Regional Novel in Britain and Ireland, 1800–1990*, emphasizes that one necessary quality of the regional novel is a sense of the distinctiveness of place, but the question of the location of the audience is implicit in any such discussion of region. Snell refers, for example, to Margaret Drabble's *Oxford Companion to English Literature* where the following definition of the regional novel is provided: 'a novel set in a real and well-defined locality, *which is in some way strange to the reader*'.[36] It is a profound irony, and one that is the result of English cultural and educational hegemony in Britain, that a novel set in 'a real and well-defined' part of Wales may remain 'in some way strange' to a local Welsh reader. The nature of the media and education in Wales, until fairly recently largely controlled from London, means that even those living within Wales may be fairly familiar with English history and signifiers of culture and fairly ignorant of the Wales beyond their immediate experience. Thus the Welsh writer in English is in the anomalous position of having to explain elements of Welsh culture, history or geography to the Welsh themselves.

Having thus far contextualized the cultural political climate in which Welsh writers must take the political and artistic decisions over linguistic and stylistic issues, as well as deciding how far to 'explain' the content of their work to audiences within and outside of Wales, we are now able to consider in more detail one way in which Welsh writers may signal their difference from English-language writers outside Wales: code-switching. As the discussion above suggests, for authors who choose to use Welsh words in the text, or a non-standard form of English (either for dialogue or for the entire text), issues of readership groups within their possible audience are complex and politically fraught. Tensions between advocates of the Welsh language and those within Wales who bitterly resent and are hostile towards Welsh cannot be ignored, and the polarity of the language debate and the strength of feeling attached to it do not allow the author to withdraw from the arena of the debate. Intrinsic to the language issue, as we have seen, is an examination of definitions of Welshness. Is language the essence of Welsh culture, or at least the primary marker of difference? Can Welsh identity exist in and be expressed (solely) through the medium of English? In the discussion which follows, the problems of the audience and the language–identity debate described above must be a continual consideration.

LANGUAGE AS SYNECDOCHE: CODE-SWITCHING IN
WELSH WRITING IN ENGLISH

In 'Raids on the Articulate', Gordon and Williams divide the use of code-switching in literature into three categories. The first of these is 'extrinsic' code-switching, defined as the use of italicized 'foreign' words or phrases merely to provide local colour, as in the French exclamations of '*Mon Dieu!*' and '*Parbleu!*' uttered by Agatha Christie's Poirot, words which are untranslated but are likely to be understood by most readers.[37] Indeed, since the exact meaning is irrelevant it does not matter whether the reader understands them or not, as it is clear that these words are excited exclamations. The use of the word '*bach*', for example, in Welsh texts could be seen as falling into this category of providing local colour. Gordon and Williams, however, go on to note that Agatha Christie's use of French is socio-linguistically inauthentic and that code-switching of this kind 'is only ever used by people whose second language ability is extremely weak'. This analysis does not necessarily hold true in the Welsh instance, where *bach* is a term of endearment commonly used in English exchanges. It might, perhaps, be considered a 'borrowing' – a word incorporated into the English language (or into Welsh English, at least).

A second type of code-switching, termed 'organic' by Gordon and Williams, might also be seen as providing local colour, yet it has a far greater significance in expressing cultural difference. The 'foreign' words are usually italicized (drawing attention to their difference from the rest of the text) and are often used where no equivalent translation is available (for example, *eisteddfod*). Nevertheless, an explanation within the text, or a glossary, is provided so as to allow the reader access to the culture represented by these 'foreign' words. Glyn Jones's use of the italicized words *gymanfa ganu* and *seiat*, for example, in the volume of short stories *Welsh Heirs* (1977), comes under this category of 'organic' code-switching. As the title implies, the stories describe Welsh life, and the Welsh words used generally refer to cultural events and practices specific to Wales, and are explained in the text. For instance, in the story 'Robert Jeffreys', where the narrator is addressing a 'Mr Herbert' throughout the narrative, the meaning of *gymanfa ganu* is clarified thus: 'I know you have learnt, Mr Herbert, that the chapels in this valley hold at Easter an united religious festival, a *gymanfa ganu*.'[38]

The third category of code-switching described by Gordon and Williams is termed 'political'. Unlike 'organic' code-switching, 'where the introduced material is translated or explained in the new context so as not to alienate the reader', the object of political code-switching 'is often to discomfort the reader by confronting him or her with an apparently uncrossable cultural boundary'.[39] This description of code-switching is very interesting with regard to Welsh writing in English, although I would question the usefulness of Gordon and Williams's terms 'extrinsic', 'organic' and 'political'. 'Extrinsic' may be a helpful and suggestive description, but 'organic' (especially when differentiated from or juxtaposed to the term 'political') seems to lend a misleading degree of authority or normalcy to the language into which the 'foreign' word is translated. While the term 'organic' can be understood as refer-ring to the linguistic cohesion of the text, surely if the decision not to gloss is a political one, then the contrary decision to provide transla-tions and glossaries must also have profound political implications, which are ignored by the overly neutral term 'organic', with its holistic overtones.

In Bill Ashcroft's essay, 'Is that the Congo? Language and Metonymy in the Post-Colonial Text', the author refers to the techniques of disrupting and adapting standard English, or the use of 'foreign' words in the text, as constituting 'an "overlap" of language'.[40] Describing such writing as 'cross-cultural', his essay constructs these texts as some sort of palimpsest, where we glimpse a different and 'original' language and culture through the overlay of a colonial, European language.[41] Significantly, both the implied audience of Ashcroft's essay and the readers of such 'cross-cultural texts' are always native speakers of the European language; that is, the readers are always outsiders to the 'other' culture, which intrudes into the (ex-)colonial European language. So this writing is presented in terms of offering European readers the possibility of learning about exotic cultures; that is, the perspective is thoroughly Eurocentric. If we were to apply the paradigms of Ash-croft's essay directly to Welsh writing in English, then, we would end up with an equivalently Anglocentric view of the way Welsh words may be used in an English-language Welsh text to signify the cultural otherness of Wales. While this perspective might be apt in a discussion of texts which are aimed at a non-Welsh audience, such as Emlyn Williams's *The Corn is Green* (1938; which generally played to audiences in England when it was first written, and in which the overtly colonial Welsh setting and the difference of the Welsh are emphasized through the use of many untranslated Welsh sentences), it does not seem an appropriate perspective from which to view Welsh writing in English as it is published or read in Wales. This divergence not only highlights the complexities and apparent paradoxes of the cultural situation in Wales which may be illuminated by postcolonial paradigms, it also reveals some of the problems which may attend the attempt simply to *apply* postcolonial theories in a Welsh context. Significantly, however, another outcome of reading Ashcroft's essay in a Welsh context is that attention is drawn to the flaws of this and other postcolonial theory that tends to address itself exclusively to those outside the culture under discussion. The complexity of the linguistic and cultural situation in Wales means that if we carry over such perspectives to Wales, all too often significant elements of the Welsh population end up being pushed into the position of the 'outsider' who is the reader constructed by the discourse of some postcolonial critics. Are English-speaking Welsh people to be produced as outsiders in their own country, where the Welsh language constitutes an other, exotic culture?

Providing a direct translation, through a glossary or note in the text, obviously assumes a readership that will not understand the word, and the author helpfully and authoritatively supplies the meaning. This does not necessarily diminish the power of the word as a synecdochic signifier of cultural difference, but in the choice to use a 'foreign' word and then to render it transparent for the reader, the otherwise uncom-prehending reader is privileged, since 'glossing gives the translated word, and thus the "receptor" culture, the higher status'.[42] So, when Margiad Evans, in *Country Dance* (1932), writes the line, 'Then you shall dance with me, fy cariad anwyl (my dear love), until the day breaks',[43] her translation is not a neutral act. The translation implies a monoglot English audience, which is hardly surprising, perhaps, given that the book was published in London. Within the confines of the text itself, however, the provision of a translation is also loaded. *Country Dance* purports to be the transcription of 'Ann Goodman's book', a journal which Ann keeps at the request of her jealous fiancé, so that he may monitor her behaviour while they are apart.[44] Ann's fiancé, Gabriel Ford, is an Englishman, and so the translations of the unwanted attentions of the Welshman, Evan ap Evans, as quoted above, take on a new significance. The politics of translation in this text are further complicated when we remember the first line of the author's 'Introduction' to Ann's story: 'The struggle for supremacy in her mixed blood is the unconscious theme of Ann Goodman's book.'[45]

Ann's relationship with the Welsh language is shown to be rather ambivalent; although she understands the language she avoids using it, and resents the way Evan ap Evans speaks to her in Welsh. Indeed, she tries to deny her Welsh identity completely: 'I am English. I was with English folk in Wales and I hate the Welsh and all their shifty ways of dealing. "Taffy was a Welshman, Taffy was a thief." '[46] This outburst comes after Ann's accusation that Gabriel has rejected her in part because of Evans's inappropriate remarks to her in front of her fiancé, under the cover of the Welsh language, the meaning of which Gabriel has nevertheless caught the gist. Yet *Country Dance* (and its heroine, Ann) is more sympathetic to the Welsh language than the above quotations might suggest and it is interesting that the Welsh words in the text are *not* italicized and thus normalized in the context of the printed page. It is also worth considering the complexities of another act of translation when Ann provides her father with a Welsh phrase to speak to his dying wife, who seems unable to understand – or even hear – English in her last moments:

> 'What is she saying? What does she want?'
> 'She is asking for you, Father.'
> 'Myfanwy, Myfanwy, I am here. Speak to her, Ann! Can't you? Speak her own tongue!'
> 'Father is here,' I tells her.
> She grabs my wrists.
> 'Oh be quick, Ann dear, be quick, I am dying.'
> 'He is here,' I cry over and over.
> At last I tells my father to say:
> 'Rwaf yma wrtheich ymyl' (I am here beside thee).
> He tries, word for word, after me, and she smiles as best she can.[47]

This is a curious passage. Much of its drama comes from the shortness of time, the urgency of communicating before death, and the present tense works to suggest a sense of immediacy and intimacy between the reader and the family group. Yet, as Ann apparently speaks, ' "Father is here," I tells her', it becomes clear that we are not witnessing the scene as it occurs; Ann does not actually say 'Father is here', since she is speaking Welsh and is more likely to be saying something like '*Mae nhad yma*'. To have provided the Welsh for the whole exchange, even if this were within the capabilities of the author, would have reduced the dramatic tension. While the immediacy of the writing is perhaps undermined by the knowledge that we are reading a 'simultaneous translation', for our purposes the portrayal of the language within a story is of less concern than the way in which the 'foreign' words are handled

within the text. Interestingly, it is here in the Welsh words themselves
that Margiad Evans's writing is most revealing. Although a monoglot
English reader is implicitly privileged by the provision of translations of
Welsh in parentheses, a Welsh-speaking reader may ultimately access a
more illuminating reading of this novella. As Clare Morgan has pointed
out in her essay 'Exile and Kingdom: Margiad Evans and the Mythic
Landscape of Wales', Margiad Evans used the Welsh language very
deliberately as a signifier of cultural difference, but she also used these
signifiers ignorantly, or carelessly, making mistakes in her use of the
Welsh language. '*Rwaf yma wrtheich ymyl*', for example, is incorrect in
the use of the formal '*eich*' instead of the familiar '*dy*', '*rwaf*' ought to
be '*rwyf*', and '*wrth*' and '*eich*' are two separate words. Elsewhere, '*fy
cariad*' ought to be '*fy nghariad*' and Clare Morgan draws attention to
the line '*Mae arnafeisian gweld John*', which should read '*Mae arnaf
eisiau gweld John*', and to Evans's 'transposing [of] names from North
Wales'[48] to the border country where she sets her story. Thus I would
suggest that while *Country Dance* seems to conform to 'organic' code-
switching, where (glossed) Welsh words and phrases are used to indicate
a different language being spoken and to emphasize the coexistence of
two (rival) linguistic and cultural groups in the story, the code-switching
is ultimately 'extrinsic'. Here, then, the use of the Welsh language seems
to be an attempt to stress Welsh difference for a metropolitan audience,
even while Margiad Evans's story engages with issues of border
identities.

   Thus far, then, I have suggested that to provide a gloss on a 'foreign'
word, specifically a Welsh word in an English-language text, is to
privilege the English language (and a monolingual English-speaking
audience). This is all the more significant given the relative strengths of
the two languages; as Gayatri Chakravorty Spivak notes, '[t]he status of
a language in the world is what one must consider when teasing out the
politics of translation'.[49] The refusal to translate is a political act which
asserts the validity of the untranslated language and signifies both
difference and absence; difference in the sense that the untranslated
word acts as a synecdoche for the cultural differences of the linguistic
group to which it belongs, and absence in that the word and therefore
the culture is opaque and unknowable to the reader. Ashcroft writes
that 'language variance is a synecdochic index of cultural difference
which affirms the distance of cultures at the very same moment in
which it proposes to bring them together', and he goes on to suggest
that one of the most distinctive acts of such texts is the way they

inscribe '*difference* and *absence* as a corollary of that identity'.[50] The untranslated word acts as a timely reminder to the arrogant Euro- or Anglocentric reader of the limits of his or her knowledge but also, crucially, in an English-language Welsh text the use of untranslated Welsh asserts the cultural difference of 'English'-language Welsh writing. Monica Heller describes code-switching as 'a boundary-levelling or a boundary maintaining strategy', and the refusal to provide a translation draws attention to boundaries and differences between linguistic groups.[51] Gordon and Williams observe that 'deliberate code-switching may serve as a conscious technique for undermining the confidence of readers who belong exclusively to a dominant linguistic group, reminding them that they are thereby excluded from other groups, and are in fact outsiders'.[52] Indeed, in the face of resentment from monoglot readers, Spivak defends the leaving of words and passages untranslated, in both literature and criticism, making a strong case not only for the right of any writer to do this, but also for the effectiveness of this approach in communicating otherness and the 'non-transcendability' of linguistic difference. In an interview with the editors of the *Spivak Reader*, Spivak says:

> I had in 'Echo' a footnote which was just two lines of Bengali poetry. Now this footnote will be incomprehensible to non-Bengali readers. Now, in order for me to explain this footnote, I would in fact reduce the power of the footnote to a zilcho . . . To an extent that is also my way of pointing at what the arrogance of multiculturalism quite often forgets, that there are very strict limits to multiculturalist benevolence.[53]

In this view then, the refusal to translate is a very articulate statement to the 'uncomprehending' reader.

Furthermore, while the refusal to translate is a technique which can provoke frustration and indignation in the monoglot reader, even appearing to be a threatening exercise of cultural power, to insist upon translation is equally to engage in a struggle for power, which can have an impact on constructions of identity. In an essay entitled 'Looking through Non-Western Eyes: Immigrant Women's Autobiographical Narratives in Italian', Graziella Parati discusses the use of code-switching by Maria Viarengo, who is the child of an Italian father and an Ethiopian mother. Viarengo grew up in Ethiopia, but was sent to university in Italy, and while she remained in that country she retained a profound awareness of her hybrid status and resisted total assimilation into Italy. Parati describes

how a journal, *Linea d'ombra*, translated into Italian the title of an autobiographical article by Viarengo which the author had written in her
maternal language, Oromo. '*Scirscir n'demna*', the original title, became
'*Andiamo a spasso*' ('Let's Go for a Walk'), which Parati says is 'the
"exact" translation, but not the same'.[54] Parati explains:

> In Viarengo's autobiographical act, her self is publicized in a superimposed
> translation that separates her from her mother and strengthens the link with
> her Italian father and, in the end, defeats Viarengo's initial act of resistance
> in which she had portrayed herself as that hybrid child that can never be
> totally 'assimilated'. This arbitrary use of the translation, therefore, colonizes
> Viarengo's voice in order to turn it into a 'more' understandable text for
> Italian readers and modifies the core of Viarengo's agenda.[55]

Thus to insist on a translation, or to impose one, can be a culturally
violent act.

If we return to the Welsh situation, however, we find that some of
these positions, particularly Spivak's statement about the limitations of
the benevolence of multiculturalism, have further complex resonances,
since the ability to speak Welsh is often closely linked to essentialist
constructions of Welsh authenticity. When only a minority of Welsh
people speak, let alone read, Welsh, how is a Welsh reader to react to
the untranslated Welsh word or passage in an English-language text?
What can this assertion of difference, through the use of language as
synecdoche, mean to a non-Welsh-speaking Welsh person? On the other
hand, almost without exception, Welsh speakers in Wales speak and
read English well, and may be just as likely to read an English-language
Welsh text. How will such readers respond to their unusually privileged
position in understanding parts of that text from which others are
excluded? The use of the Welsh language as a metonymic signifier for a
wider Welsh cultural difference *might* arguably be seen as reinforcing the
reductive idea that the Welsh language is more or less synonymous with
an authentic Welsh identity (national or cultural). But this understanding, which, in forging an essentialist link between Welsh language
and nationality/ethnicity, excludes the English-speaking majority of
Wales from claiming a Welsh identity, is not in fact inevitable. Is there
not the possibility of the Welsh language being regarded as an important aspect of Welsh culture and nationality even by those who do not
speak it? This is certainly an attitude which finds some resonance in the
generation of non-Welsh speakers who are ensuring that their children,

at least, (re)possess the language, or by those monoglots who support
the equal status of Welsh and English in Wales.

These questions may, in part, be answered by a consideration of some
texts which employ 'political' code-switching. A number of twentieth-
century Welsh writers in English use untranslated Welsh words in their
work; see, for example, such as Emlyn Williams's fairly extensive use of
Welsh in his plays *The Corn is Green* and *The Druid's Rest* (1944). The
fact that these are plays originally performed in but mostly beyond
Wales raises a further layer of issues about audience, performers and
political intention. There is insufficient space to discuss Williams here,
but it is worth pausing to consider the subtle use of code-switching in a
novel written in the closing decades of the twentieth century,
Christopher Meredith's *Shifts*, in more detail. This novel is set in
the late 1970s in an English-speaking area of south-east Wales, where
the imminent closure of a steelworks casts a shadow of futility over the
valley. Keith is a keen amateur local historian, trying to make sense of
his present through the past. In his attempts to reconstruct in his
imagination the Gwedog valley on the brink of industrialization in
1800, when the first iron was smelted there, Keith runs up against the
barrier of language. The sense of historical dislocation in this novel is
profound; not only does the declining steel industry signal the end of
the industrial era in the valley, but the pre- and early industrial history
of the area, which still manifests itself in old Welsh place-names and
tombstone inscriptions, is inaccessible to the non-Welsh-speaking
inhabitants of the district. In one scene, Keith stands looking out across
the valley, mentally erasing buildings and slag-heaps, according to their
age, in order to create a picture of what the valley would have looked
like before the arrival of the furnaces. He regards an old, detached
house: 'Old. Farm perhaps. He could see its name on the gate at the side
of the Lion. Henfelin.'[56] Not understanding Welsh, Keith does not
realize that the original function of the building is described in its name:
Henfelin, old mill. However, this irony will also go unnoticed by any
reader who does not understand Welsh, as the non-italicized name is
not translated in the text. Now this is hardly an essential aspect of the
plot; however, a point about the historical fracture brought about by the
loss of the Welsh language is being forcefully made here and is only
available to Welsh speakers, although this same point is made forcefully
and dramatically later in the novel in a manner available to all readers.
Thus Welsh speakers are privileged by the text while non-Welsh
speakers are excluded from the irony of this scene.

The example of 'Henfelin' is perhaps not the most radical instance of political code-switching available in Welsh literature, but it is a fascinating one, not least because it has far more complex resonances than the simple assertion of the existence of a cultural/linguistic group beyond the reaches of the monoglot English reader.[57] The name of the old building, 'Henfelin', is a residue from the Welsh-speaking history of the valley. In this sense, the use of the Welsh name in the text is not strictly an example of code-switching, but a naturalistic representation of the nomenclature of Wales. Although many towns and streets in south Wales have English names, such as Edwardsville or Quakers Yard, Welsh place-names are abundant. Indeed, Christopher Meredith has described how Welsh place-names – some understood but most not – formed an integral part of his sense of place, of home, of Wales.[58] In using this place-name, untranslated in the text, Meredith reveals the way that a form of code-switching occurs every time an English speaker discusses Welsh places. The decision not to translate 'Henfelin' can also be justified by the form of the novel, in which the story is narrated from the varying perspectives of the four main characters: Keith, his wife Judith, his friend Jack and 'O'. There is no space for authorial intervention, for the translation of a name Keith does not understand. Rather, we are asked to identify with the perspective of a man struggling to understand a history from which he has been severed, due to the linguistic transformation of the area. Meredith acknowledges that a Welsh reader will be in a privileged position, but states that this is simply a fact of linguistic superiority (with no moral overtones intended); yet he also suggests that a Welsh speaker may gain an insight into the position of non-Welsh speakers in Wales.[59]

Keith is not content to remain in ignorance of Welsh, which is poignantly described in a much-quoted scene as 'a language that was his own, but that he could not understand'.[60] By the end of the novel, Keith has equipped himself with a dictionary, and a book of place-names, and it seems that he will soon be making significant steps towards acquiring a sound knowledge of the language. Perhaps this is what the reader is also encouraged to do. In Gordon and Williams's study of code-switching in the work of Patricia Grace, the authors note that, despite the political aggressiveness of her use of code-switching, which serves as a boundary-maintaining technique, 'paradoxically it might be argued that by obliging readers unfamiliar with the Maori language to extend their knowledge in order to appreciate the text's full meaning, she also encourages the *inclusion* of such readers' (my italics), but on *her* cultural terms. It is not difficult to see how Meredith's novel functions in this manner; not only do we have Keith's own example, but the author's, too – like Patricia Grace, Meredith learned his 'native' tongue as an adult.

Another Welsh poet and novelist who learned Welsh as an adult is Emyr Humphreys. He too employs political code-switching in his work, perhaps most notably in his *Collected Poems*. In this volume, Welsh-language poems are printed along with English-language poems, the latter making up the majority. There are also poems which use both languages, and the theme of language is itself foregrounded in the collection. The issue of language choice is referred to directly by the poet in the 'Author's Note'. Significantly, although Humphreys uses English to introduce the collection, he raises the questions '*pa iaith, pa hunaniaeth, pa wrogaeth?*' (what language, what identity, what allegiance?) in Welsh.[61] No translation is provided, and implicit in this decision is the idea that these questions are quandaries faced by the Welsh speaker alone. As is common with such untranslated passages in otherwise English texts, there is a certain intimacy in Humphreys's address to a 'known' audience. One of the effects of this volume, particularly as Humphreys explicitly states that the collection is 'as close as I would ever venture to . . . [an] autobiography', is to offer some reflection of the way the two languages are present in the poet's life and in Wales.[62] To decide not to translate is certainly to exclude part of his audience, yet, since each poem is a complete whole and English-speaking readers can access the majority, I would suggest that the impact of this example of political code-switching is less significant than if it occurred within the text of a novel. It is in the poem 'Inscribing Stones', where both languages are used, as well as in the 'Author's Note' mentioned above, that the denial of access is most acutely felt.

Thus far, then, I have looked at a variety of uses of code-switching, paying particular attention to the way code-switching can be used as 'a means of contesting the cultural and linguistic dominance encoded in language'.[63] Untranslated Welsh words or phrases used in Welsh writing in English serve as synecdochic signifiers of difference and – potentially – of absence, while they may also work to undermine the balance of power between dominant and more or less subaltern languages. I would suggest, however, that there is another use of code-switching in this literature, where no translation is provided and yet the ultimate effect cannot easily be described as political, in the above sense. Peter Finch's poem 'Partisan', in the 1997 collection *Useful*, is a very good example of the way both the languages of Wales can be used in the same piece of writing without fitting into the categories of code-switching defined by Gordon and Williams. The poem weaves Welsh and English together to create a clever 'bilingual' poem which plays one language off against the other, transforming both English and Welsh words.

The first stanza 'conjugates' the verb 'to be', from the Welsh 'rydw i', with the balancing but explosive 'blydi I am', through to a disconcerting chant of 'I am I am I am'.[64] Finch's poem employs a variety of the techniques described by Ashcroft (see above p. 106), in his playful transformation of Welsh and English words and phrases to create at least an illusion of an 'ethnorhythmic' fusion of the two languages, including the transcription of a south Walian dialect; he also uses Welsh spelling to suggest this dialect, as in 'nasty blydi books we're a video neishyn', or 'rîl traditional blydi welshman'. His diglossic satire on Welsh icons of national identity erupts with energy in the use of Welsh and English idiom in the same phrase: 'rudin wedi dysgu hen ddigon ol' moldering / Welsh Saunders Mabinignog crap'.[65]

Behind much of the discussion in this chapter has been the unspoken assumption that complete accessibility of texts is what audiences, on the whole, desire and expect, and it is in the frustration of this expectation that the power of political code-switching lies. That art and literature should be inclusive and accessible is a fairly recent idea, and one that is not without its detractors, including those who would argue that elitism or inaccessibility are inevitable at the limits of the imagination or language. In a postcolonial context, where the interests of the subaltern are supposed to be paramount, the refusal to translate forms part of an anti-imperial resistance, which again justifies what it would be misleading to call 'elitism'. The Welsh writers discussed here who self-consciously choose not to translate, to some degree share an agenda of cultural resistance which insists upon the presence and importance of the Welsh language although, crucially, without necessarily supporting any idea of Welsh identity as coterminous with the Welsh language. In Finch's poetry there is a sense of liberation in his creative embrace of Welsh diglossia, but of course it is not only the language of Finch's poem which forms part of an internal discourse about Welsh cultural and linguistic identity. Readers will need to be not only at least partly bilingual, but also familiar with some of the cultural icons of Wales, be these 'Pantycelyn Rhydcymerau Pwllheli', or 'alcoalcohol' or 'imperialist long-nosed pinky cottagers'.

This said, however, and Finch's linguistic genius notwithstanding, the lack of any gloss on this poem is clearly an impediment to those with no grasp of the Welsh language, and it is noteworthy that while the poet provides two pages of explanatory notes in *Useful* there are none on 'Partisan'. While all the authors discussed here could be argued to be using the Welsh language in a way that reflects a variety of different linguistic realities in Wales, in their exercise of authorial control, in their decision to provide or exclude explanatory notes or translations, they inevitably construct an audience (or perhaps, more accurately, respond to an anticipated audience). For writers in colonial or post-colonial countries, or anywhere where multiple languages coexist and compete for dominance, language use is bound up with the politics of power, and the building or levelling of linguistic boundaries (as discussed here) seems to be an inevitable as well as intentional outcome of their handling of 'foreign' words in their work. In the fraught cultural climate of Wales, questions of translation and exclusion remain complex, but potentially enriching literary issues.

6

Hybridity and Authenticity

Hybridity is a versatile and apparently endlessly fertile metaphor and cultural descriptor, most often used to refer to a process of transculturation which occurs in colonial contact zones, but also extended to refer to a variety of cultural 'exchanges'. One of the most notable examples of the use of this multifaceted and sometimes problematic term is to describe the ambivalent, in-between (linguistic) space which Homi Bhabha suggests is the location of cultural production. In addition to Bhabha's thesis of slippage and the impossibility of mimesis, the figure of the hybrid (individual, text, cultural expression) is associated with ideas of exile (including a metaphorical exile from one's native culture brought about by alienation from language, landscape or the like) and the concomitant experience of self-division, dislocation or alienation experienced by the colonized.

While hybridity seems to offer a space which privileges cultural *différance* (in the Derridean sense), the etymology of the term (originating as it does from the biological sciences) suggests a certain tension between postcolonial usage of the word to represent a release from ideas of cultural authenticity and the implied fixity of the two (or more) 'parent' cultures 'in-between' which the interstitial, hybrid space is formed. Robert Young points out that the term 'hybridity' is inescapably linked to racial ideologies of purity and miscegenation; so, in evoking ideas of mixture and interchange, we must be wary of inscribing the 'originary' cultures as static or somehow authentic (as implied in nativist constructions of authenticity, which look back to the precolonial past in order to salvage what is conceived to be the essential, pure culture that existed prior to the moment of colonization). While

this problematizes, it does not necessarily undermine the cultural significance of (re)invention of traditions as a revivifying cultural force.
Such a remembering of history and tradition is, of course, more about
the present than the past. As Neil ten Kortenaar points out:

> neither authenticity nor creolization has ontological validity, but both are
> valid as metaphors that permit collective self-fashioning . . . Authenticity
> and creolization are best regarded as valuable rhetorical tools that can be
> made to serve liberation. It may also be liberating to remember that these
> constructions are effectively rhetorical.[1]

The term 'synergy' provides a more positive alternative to the problematic 'hybrid', as it emphasizes the productive qualities of complex and
multiple forces (rather than the two essential strands which are implied
through the biological reproductive elements of hybridity), which contribute to something new that is not reducible to any of its constitutive
elements.[2] This idea of synergetic cultural production might be
especially helpful in the Welsh context, since one of the most limiting
discourses of Welsh cultural identities has been that which is confined
to binary constructions of Welshness as being reciprocally linked to
degrees of difference from, or similarity to, Englishness.

Rhetorically useful – and perhaps irresistible – as the use of binary
constructions of hybridity and authenticity might be, the postcolonial
concept of hybridity is far more complex and productive than the biological origins of the term might suggest. This discussion seeks to
illustrate, through the close reading of a few texts, how authors from
different ends of the twentieth century have engaged with the rhetoric of
ethnic hybridity, authenticity and the cultural flux defined in the terms
'assimilation' and 'acculturation'. Postcolonial descriptions of the impact of acculturation on the colonized inform a reading of 'The Way He
Went', a 1912 novella by Bertha Thomas, as involving self-division,
alienation and partial assimilation. These descriptions also facilitate a
wider consideration of the role of education in the process of acculturation. Then, in the second part of this chapter, we explore a text
which (re)writes the colonization of south-east Wales by the (Anglo-)
Normans, emphasizing the shifting, hybrid nature of Welsh ethnicity,
while simultaneously inscribing such hybridity with a sense of
authenticity.

Cultural assimilation (the process of absorption of a foreign element
into a 'wider society or culture', *OED*) or acculturation ('the adoption

and assimilation of an alien culture', *OED*) are crucial issues in Welsh history and culture and, in the earlier part of the twentieth century, tend to be imagined in terms of a fairly fixed, binary model of culture, such as is later found in the theoretical writings of Memmi and Fanon. For many, assimilation into England or Britain has been a desirable route to social and economic success, and it must be remembered that the Welsh, after 1536, were not barred from such assimilation in the same way that other colonized peoples have been. The 'option' of acculturation which was available to the Welsh ought not, however, to obscure the some-times enormous psychological and emotional, not to mention cumulative cultural, cost of such a process which, for some, finds parallels in Fanon's descriptions of the psyche of the colonized. While many have acknowledged the appeal of exploring 'wider' cultures, it is important to be explicit about the dynamics of power at work in the relationship between assimilating and 'assimilatee' cultures. The nature of cultural exchange in 'contact zones', be these created by brief encounters or sustained and complex relationships, colonial or other-wise, is intimately linked to the relative economic, political and/or military status of those involved. Before going any further, it is as well to clarify my use of the words 'cultural exchange', since the word 'exchange' has caused some unease amongst postcolonialists, who have rightly pointed out that it may erroneously be taken to imply an equal or free interchange between different cultures in contact zones. Of course, processes of assimilation and acculturation are not always about conquest and domination, but they are about the encounters between peoples, and factors of cultural dominance or hegemony need to be taken into account. The dynamics of power between any two cultures that come into contact are unlikely to be entirely balanced and in colonial situations they were often grossly mismatched. Indeed, just as Spivak has drawn attention to the need to be fully aware of the dynamics of power which lie behind acts of translation, it is necessary to be sensitive, in the circumstances of cultural exchange, to the relative status of the cultures involved.

Prys Morgan's history of eighteenth-century Wales, for instance, describes the profound effect upon Welsh culture of English appropri-ation of Welsh stories and traditions. English dominance meant that their assimilation of these aspects of Welsh culture resulted in them being *lost* to Wales; assimilation in this instance was a form of cultural robbery:

> Over the centuries the British-Welsh hero, Arthur, had been filched by the English, and transformed into an English hero, now the Tudor dynasty turned Welsh princely tradition and prophesy to their own ends; and, lastly, the Anglican church in the Reformation period cleverly took over the Welsh tradition of the Early British Church, founded by Joseph of Arimathea, and used it for its own purposes . . . The consequence was that the Welsh no longer appeared to have a distinct history, but only traditions which were either discredited or merely contributory to English traditions. This had a debilitating effect on the self-confidence of the Welsh.[3]

This cultural phenomenon is not confined to Wales, although Welsh experience certainly affords one of the older examples. In other colonial/postcolonial societies where significant inequalities between different ethnic groups persist, the issue of 'cultural theft' remains highly contentious. In 'Stop Stealing Native Stories', Lenore Keeshing-Tobias argues uncompromisingly that the depiction of Native Canadian (hi)stories by non-Native writers and film-makers amounts to a disempowering 'culture theft, the theft of voice'.[4] Thus assimilation is not necessarily a neutral act, nor is the effect on the 'assimilatee' culture negligible. Acculturation to an imperial hegemony, however, could be an even more uncomfortable imperative.

Welsh culture, raided for its 'valuable' artefacts, its useful stories, whilst being derided for less 'desirable' attributes, was seen as inferior to English culture. An obvious way to avoid the inferiority attached to Welshness was to become English – a solution denied to most of the subjects of the British Empire. Yet the possibility of 'full' acculturation, while offering certain privileges, is not without serious problems of its own. For all the difficulties of learning a new language and adopting new manners, changing oneself is surely much easier than challenging the hegemony. How many would not, to put it in personal terms, rather change something in themselves to fit the values of the status quo than attempt to battle against entrenched social and institutional prejudice, often having first to overcome some internal resistance? To return to the issue of skin colour – despite all the movements to assert the worth and beauty of dark-skinned people, there are still those who would rather submit to plastic surgery, skin bleaches and hair straighteners to conform to dominant cultural aesthetics. That the Welsh could 'become' English and were afforded the opportunity to erase or hide significant cultural or linguistic difference may actually be regarded as a severe disadvantage in terms of cultural and linguistic survival. A Welsh person is so labelled by virtue of her or his culture alone, and is therefore easily assimilated invisibly into another white country. Thus, for example, in the years following the penal laws passed during the rebellion of Owain Glyndŵr, when the Welsh were relegated to the status of what Gwyn A. Williams calls 'unpersons', some of the Welsh *literally* became English to escape these laws: 'Successful Welshmen escaped the penal laws by buying letters of denizenship which declared them to be English.'[5]

If the lack of a colour bar in the case of subordinate white ethnicities, like the Welsh or the Irish, inflected the experience of cultural and racial inferiority in different ways to that of non-white subordinates, the methods of achieving acculturation had many points of similarity right across cultures during the nineteenth century. In Wales, as in India, education was seen as a primary tool for establishing and maintaining cultural dominance and control. Postcolonial critics, such as G. Viswanathan, have described the way that English literature was taught as a subject in India, where it was intended to impart the values and tastes of the colonizer so as to create, according to Babington Macaulay's infamous 1835 'Minute on Indian Education', a class of people 'Indian in blood and colour' but 'English in taste, in opinions, in morals and in intellect'.[6] Not only was it supposed that this class would then readily comply with the colonial project; the very process of teaching an imperial literature, which was in great demand from the Indians themselves, would emphasize the inferiority of the Indians compared with the colonizer, who had a 'natural' access to this literary culture.[7] Education policy in Wales during the nineteenth century reflected a similar imperialist project, as expressed in the 1847 Report into the State of Education in Wales. Indeed, until recently, state education policy has been largely directed from without, and Glyn Jones's description of his schooldays in the early years of the twentieth century, at Cyfarthfa Grammar School, Merthyr Tydfil, might perhaps hold true even for present-day pupils:

> The establishment might have been in the middle of the Broads or up in the Pennines for all the contact it had with the rich life of the community surrounding it. We had no school *eisteddfod*, we heard nothing of the turbulent industrial history of the town itself, nothing of its Welsh literary associations, nothing of its religious history.[8]

This invisibility of Welsh history and culture in Welsh schools would surely lead to a problematic sense of dislocation – the result of identifying with the perspective of the Anglocentric hegemony – for the Wales portrayed within the classroom or pages of a book might actually be shown in such a way that its depiction encouraged a sense of the otherness and inferiority of the Welsh.

While an Anglocentric formal education might, in a Welsh context, become an important feature of the process of coming to see oneself as other, the message that a colonized group is of little worth – its achievements negligible and its subjection justified – is reinforced outside the walls of the classroom through a variety of media, including literature. It is worth pausing to examine one such example of a text which, aimed at children in the early decades of the twentieth century, might force Welsh children to read themselves as other, or to detach themselves from the Welsh people constructed as other in the text. *On the Welsh Marches* was published by Blackie and Son in February 1906 as part of a successful series of Reward Books. These books were designed to be given as Sunday school prizes or to be distributed to poor children, and they were largely selected on the basis of appropriate moral content. Although by the early twentieth century these books had become more enjoyable and less overtly pious, it seems such Reward Books were still intended to contribute 'to the process of socialisation' of children.[9] *On the Welsh Marches* is in fact an abridged extract from Sir Walter Scott's 1825 novel, *The Betrothed*, which complicates any interpretation of the content and style of the text. Nevertheless, as a Reward Book which sold over eleven thousand copies between publication in 1906 and going out of print in 1920,[10] it is relevant to a consideration of the position of young readers of the early twentieth century who were awarded it as a prize. Since Scott's text portrays the Welsh as a deservedly defeated people, it is perhaps puzzling that the book was given to Welsh children. It would be fascinating to know whether it was especially popular in Wales, chosen for its local colour, perhaps, despite its ultimately demeaning portrayal of the Welsh. For, of the three copies I have managed to trace, all were found in Wales, and two have Sunday school inscriptions supporting the thesis that it was given as a Reward Book to Welsh children.[11]

On the Welsh Marches tells the story of an attack on an Anglo-Norman castle by a Welsh prince, Gwenwyn, who is angry that his offer of marriage to the daughter of the Norman castellan, Raymond Berenger, has been spurned. The sympathy of the narrator – and therefore the reader – lies with the inhabitants of the castle, who display all the appropriately gendered ideal 'English' virtues. The Flemish are

industrious and inventive, while the Normans are brave and honourable
– the Norman lord, having made a playful, drunken challenge to the
Welsh lord, will not betray his word, even though it will cost him his life.

> When I promised to meet him in yonder field, I meant . . . to give the
> Welshman the full advantage of the ground. I so meant it – he so
> understood it; and what avails keeping my word in the letter, if I break it in
> the sense?[12]

Accordingly, Berenger dies a heroic death, hopelessly outnumbered on
the battlefield. Back at the castle the practical, if materialistic, Flemish
men are extremely clever and resourceful in their defence and susten-
ance of the fort. The lady of the castle is, of course, beautiful, graceful
and thoroughly religious, but, like her priest, not averse to joining in the
defence of the castle; and she is admirably adept at rallying the morale
of her flagging troops. The Welsh, on the other hand, are full of Celtic
vices: the empty pride of the Welsh prince leads him to believe, to the
amusement of the Normans, that his ancient genealogy will make him
an irresistible match for the lady of the castle, and the refusal of his
request provokes him to an instant and terrible rage. The Welsh display
underhanded deviousness in the attempt to get the Flemish captain to
betray the castle and, indeed, a Welsh speaker reading this story will
spot the significance of the prince's name, Gwenwyn, which *Geiriadur
Prifysgol Cymru* gives as 'poison; killer; slayer; venom; fig. baneful
influence or ideas; baneful element from without', this last being a
nicely accurate summary of the prince's role in the story, thus
highlighting the cultural perspective from which the narrative is
written.[13] In a story that lays so much store by skill and bravery in
battle, the Welsh are shown to be weak, undisciplined, badly equipped
and unskilled, and they display a crippling stupidity in supplying the
besieged castle, close to starvation, with a herd of cattle in an attempt to
bribe a possible traitor. Although the Welsh are portrayed as a warrior-
like people, they are also presented as unpredictable bundles of emotion
and as likely to fight amongst themselves as against a common enemy.
Most of the story is set behind the walls of the besieged castle, so the
one glimpse we have of the Welsh in their own halls is revealing:

> The mien and appearance of the company assembled was wild, and even in
> their social hours almost terrific. Their prince himself had the gigantic port
> and fiery eye fitted to sway an unruly people, whose delight was in the field

of battle; and the long moustaches which he and most of his champions wore added to the formidable dignity of his presence . . . Notwithstanding the military disposition of the guests and the danger arising from the feuds into which they were divided, few of the feasters wore any defensive armour, except the light goatskin buckler which hung behind each man's seat. On the other hand they were well provided with offensive weapons; for the broad, sharp, two-edged sword was another legacy of the Romans. Most added a wood-knife or poniard; and there were stores of javelins, darts, bows and arrows, pikes, halberds, Danish axes, and Welsh hooks and bills; so in the case of ill-blood arising during the banquet, there was no lack of weapons to work mischief.[14]

Thus, in a description which bears comparison with Scott's depiction of the Highlanders in *Waverley* (1814), the Welsh are portrayed as worthy enemies, descendants of Roman Britons, with a fearsome array of weapons and a willingness to use them. However, they are also seen as the inevitable inferiors of the disciplined and noble Normans. In the event, the Welsh fail to capture the besieged and poorly defended castle, and their camp is surprised by reinforcements because they have set no watch, the ultimate military folly. They are slaughtered like vermin, not like warriors; scattering in disorganized panic before the Norman knights:

Many threw themselves into the river . . . many dispersed, or in small bands fled in reckless despair towards the castle . . . while others roamed wildly over the plain, seeking only escape from immediate and instant danger, without knowing whither they ran.
   The Normans, meanwhile, divided into small parties, followed and slaughtered them at pleasure . . . [pursuing] the chase with shouts of exultation and of vengeance ringing around the battlements, which resounded with the cries 'Ha, Saint Edward! Ha, Saint Dennis! Strike – slay – no quarter to the Welsh wolves – think on Raymond Berenger!'[15]

Thus the Norman lord is avenged and the story ended (although this passage occurs less than a third of the way through Scott's original novel).

What was a young Welsh Sunday School pupil (or any other Welsh reader) to make of all this? With whom does she or he identify, if not with the castle dwellers against the heathen and savage Welsh? Charlotte Williams has discussed the troubling experience of being constructed as 'alienated, oppositional other' by texts from her mother country, Wales, and the uncomfortable position of being forced to 'read "white" ' '.[16] As we have seen, the text of the Reward Book discussed above offers just one example of the schizophrenic position of a Welsh reader or pupil who is forced to read 'English'. Thus, whether or not the child is conscious of this process, the effect of such a reader position is to illustrate something of what both Frantz Fanon and Ned Thomas have described in terms of alienation, dislocation and self-division (see chapter 1).

These themes of dislocation and self-division, and the role of formal education in the process of the assimilation of Welsh people into the dominant Anglocentric culture of the island of Britain at the turn of the century, are sensitively explored in a novella by Bertha Thomas published in *Picture Tales from Welsh Hills* (1912). In 'The Way He Went' Thomas explores the internal and inter-familial tensions and schisms created by the necessarily partial assimilation of Elwyn Rosser, a Welsh boy who receives an Anglocentric education in Wales before winning a scholarship to Oxford.[17] The details of Elwyn's education reveal his alienation from his native culture in terms of class, language, history and myth, and his untimely death at the end of the story seems to suggest that the dislocation occasioned by his educational experiences is profound. Hybridity is not a tenable position in this story and Elwyn is eventually crushed between two, perhaps oppositional, fixed identities. Yet, although Elwyn's fate seems inextricably linked with his (partial) acculturation, Thomas's story does not perpetuate simple dichotomies, and this fascinating story is worth studying in some detail.

Elwyn's only-ever-partial assimilation into the British hegemony through his Anglocentric education equips him with the desire, but not the means, to become part of the English establishment with its rigid class barriers and old-boy networks. While the impediment is primarily one of class, it is made clear at several points during the story that Elwyn's class is inseparable from his Welsh nationality. The story opens with an assertion of his humble, one might say 'authentic', Welsh origins: 'the home of his fathers' is a small tenant-farm which is presented as typical of Wales, and Elwyn's status as a rural *gwerinwr* is established: 'No gentleman-farmers, the Rossers. They might even have resented the term as being opprobrious.'[18] Another character is made to comment on the difficulty of defining Elwyn's place in the English class system. 'I can't quite make out where to put them [Elwyn's people] in

the social order; they seem simple but not common folk. I should think
hobereau would be the French for his late father, a genus that may thrive
down in Wales, but almost unknown among us here.'[19] Elwyn's class,
then, is based on Welsh social categories not easily transcribable into
the English class-system: yet his education is that of an English
gentleman. He wins a scholarship to 'an old-established college, on
English public school lines', despite his mother's fears that Elwyn might
be 'looked down upon' by the 'Gentlemen's sons [who] go there'.[20] He
quickly 'demonstrate[s] the superiority of the national intellect by out-
stripping the English boys'[21] at the college, but this happy educational
adventure begins to sour once he realizes that, although he has excelled
at Oxford, he is unable to follow his fellow students, who will leave
university to pursue careers within the spheres their class and their
familial connections have prepared for them. The equivalent arrange-
ments made for Elwyn's future, that he should take orders, are not to
Elwyn's taste, although they are represented as the only option for a
highly educated Welshman. The narrative repeatedly hints that Elwyn's
educational experiences have created in him a profound ambivalence
towards his native country and, in finally articulating his misgivings
about his future, he realizes that he is

> the dupe of a huge educational mistake. The true account now rendered of
> his scholarship was that it had unfitted him past redemption for the life
> that lay before him. Never could he again be understanded [*sic*] of his own
> people, never be at home in his real home again.[22]

The slow process of Elwyn's dislocation from Welsh culture is subtly
suggested in this narrative by anecdotes about his childhood education.
Although his fate as a cultural hybrid is ultimately tragic, through these
glimpses of his education we are offered a tangible idea of Elwyn's
excitement and sense of release from a sometimes suffocating traditional life in rural Carmarthenshire. As a child he revels in the classics
rather than in his own Welsh myths and legends; and he swaps his
laborious duties around the farm with a farmhand, David, who relishes
Elwyn's tales of Ulysses and Hercules, Perseus and Jason. Interestingly,
these apparently alien stories are given an explicitly Welsh and local
context in this story, bringing to mind for David

> that strange Roman temple whose remains underlie the ancient parish church
> of Llanffelix; the gold mines higher up in the valley, worked by the Latin

adventurers, and recently reopened after a fifteen hundred years' rest; the noble lord and lady owners of the coins and medals, gold necklaces, and other buried treasures, brought to light hereabouts now and again by the lucky.[23]

Thus the history of this part of Wales as an important centre of a Roman colony is vividly brought to the attention of the reader, just as the more recent Norman and Flemish colonization of Pembrokeshire and Wales's own transatlantic colonial enterprises will be highlighted later in the story.

Moving on from his childhood fascination with classical heroes, Elwyn begins to mock Welsh traditions openly: 'More than once he had cut [his mother] to the heart by poking fun at some immemorial national usage, reckoned sacred and beyond criticism.'[24] Although such actions are partly attributed to Elwyn's love of 'boyish pranks' (and the reader is perhaps encouraged to laugh at the 'pompous, fancy "bardic" names' Elwyn parodies during one attack on Welsh culture[25]) his mother blames his antagonism to Welsh traditions on his 'English' schooling: ' "If your English friends at Llanwastad College", spoke Mrs Rosser severely, "teach you to jeer at our old customs, I shall repent that I ever sent you there", silencing him for a moment.'[26] Soon, though, Elwyn is back from school, full of a fight between a Welsh boy and his English schoolmate which has been caused by national frictions. This serves the purpose of showing that Elwyn has not only rejected one of the most resonant organizing stories of the Welsh experience of the Saxon invasion and colonization, but he has done so on the authority of his admired teacher (who is, incidentally not English but Scottish). The cause of the fight is the story of the Treason of the Long Knives,[27] described as a myth by 'Old Foxy', the schoolmaster and gifted classicist 'who knows everything'.[28] The two boys come to blows over the taunt of the English boy 'that only a Welshman would make a grievance of a fourteen hundred years old old-wives' fable', while the Welsh boy shouts that the event 'cast an eternal disgrace on every Englishman, dead, living or yet to be born'.[29] As a microcosm of Welsh–English relations, this episode is a risible parody of the importance of Saxon invasions in Welsh memory and the anti-Englishness of much Welsh nationalism, while simultaneously suggesting that the English underestimate the grievances of the Welsh. Most importantly, however, it establishes Elwyn, the onlooker, as the product of his education; he describes the Welsh boy as 'a born fool'[30] and, in response to his mother's distress at the implication that he sided against his countryman, Elwyn asks 'would you have me so savage about a bit of ancient history, or ancient fiction, as Old Foxy . . . says it is, like that?'[31]

The doubtful influence of MacPherson ('Old Foxy') over Elwyn's education is questioned elsewhere with reference to Elwyn's competency in the Welsh language. In an important and lengthy debate between Mrs Rosser and MacPherson, MacPherson expounds the value of a classical Oxford education, which he defines as providing students with 'general culture'.[32] Mrs Rosser laments the fact that Elwyn is spending so much time on the study of the dead languages of 'nations which have vanished off the face of the earth'[33] and challenges MacPherson's assertion that a knowledge of these languages is necessary for 'the proper exercise of the clerical profession' with the assertion, ' "For Elwyn, a knowledge of Welsh is a first necessity. He has been tempted to neglect the study of his own language, with which he is very imperfectly acquainted." "Tempted by you" was implied, though unspoken.'[34] In this exchange we again see evidence of Thomas's ability to highlight important cultural conflict – the tension between an Anglocentric classical education and loyalty to Welsh linguistic and cultural difference – but also her simultaneous refusal to resort to simple binary opposites by making Elwyn a fluent, first-language Welsh speaker. Mrs Rosser's own background, for all that she is described as an 'austere patriot',[35] makes her in fact something of a hybrid herself and she is regarded as an outsider by her community. Albeit reluctantly, Mrs Rosser diligently attends the Anglican church, rather than the more popular 'Tabernacle of the Congregationalists', out of an old family loyalty to 'her late husband's uncle' who was a vicar in Worcestershire.[36] She speaks Welsh only as a second language – 'it was her misfortune, and not her fault to have belonged, by birth and bringing up, to recreant Radnor, that English speaking shire'[37] – although she is initially glad that her good knowledge of English helps her to bestow upon her son a significant educational advantage.

At Oxford (or Rhydychen, as it is known to the Rossers), Elwyn's educational and social success is presented as a feature of his outgoing and broad-minded personality. The experiences of other Welshmen at Oxford, however, are acknowledged to be rather more difficult, and the unhappy state of Welsh students there who fail to be assimilated is perceptively and convincingly portrayed. In a paragraph reminiscent of earlier novels where she portrays 'outsider figures',[38] Thomas describes the ambivalence of these Welshmen towards both Oxford society and their own national and cultural identities:

Many of his [Elwyn's] countrymen failed to make friends outside their clan, fearful of ridicule, always on the look-out for real or fancied slights. Not a few such hankered sorely after a wider social expansion, but found themselves not at home in the modes of expression habitual among the more cultivated, hence ill at ease; and preferred to hang together and criticise, nursing a sense of wrong; some burying themselves in theological or other deep dry study; but more than would own it, perhaps, echoing in their secret hearts the bitter cry of one of their number, bemoaning the restricted opportunities of a Welshman: –

'I sometimes wish the Welsh language had died before my mother had dropped its charm into my heart in hymn and verse! Will there be a chance for a Welshman in the next world, with no restriction of language – worse than restriction of sect?'[39]

This frustrated outburst, presented as the innermost thoughts of an unnamed and therefore representative Welsh student, highlights the potentially profound internal stresses for such students of being educated within one of the most important institutions of the Anglo-centric hegemony of Britain. Indeed, in this passage – which constitutes a sympathetic 'aside' and has no direct bearing on the experiences of the central character – Thomas goes to some length to convey to her readers the consequences of a naturally deep emotional attachment to the Welsh mother-tongue, and she draws attention here, as elsewhere in this collection of stories, to the singularly expressive, emotionally resonant and therefore valuable nature of the Welsh language.[40]

Having explored over the course of Elwyn's educational career various divisions and cultural tensions, which are foregrounded for the reader but of which the central character has remained oblivious, the narrative reaches the crisis of Elwyn's graduation. He is now expected to return home, if not to the family farm, then to be ordained and to minister in Llanffelix, or somewhere nearby. Irrevocably alienated from his home, Elwyn feels a desire to establish himself in middle-class England and to escape his claustrophobic home, and this is explored through the use of different women who 'compete' for his attention. Thomas's stories are generally peopled by a variety of strong, resourceful and quietly independent women, and 'The Way He Went' is no exception.[41] Although Trearavon is described as 'the home of his fathers', the farm is admirably managed by the widowed Mrs Rosser and her two daughters, Gwladys and Gwen, who 'of their own freewill, [were] walking the wise old Welsh ways'.[42] Elwyn's path takes him further and further from this traditional space of his mother and sisters.

He finally rejects Trearavon, never to return, by marrying Aline, the daughter of an English vicar and a woman of independent means. Aline is regarded by Mrs Rosser as a woman 'of an alien nation and class' and her very name is an anagram of 'Alien'. The match between the graceful and dignified woman and Elwyn is valorized by the obvious love upon which it is founded, but it is also significant that the narrative includes an account of the futile attempts of two Welsh girls, Katie Evans and Mary Hughes (trainee teachers, a career Elwyn's own mother sometimes regrets not having pursued), to seduce him before he leaves for Oxford. One of the unrequited lovers, understanding her position at last, remarks to her equally frustrated friend that 'The boy is not for you, nor for me neither . . . I don't know where he belongs, but he's as far, far above, as far away from us as man on earth can be.'[43]

The marriage between Aline and Elwyn is finally roundly condemned by Elwyn's mother, who is symbolically enthroned upon 'the old family chair – an Eisteddfod prize and heirloom that might itself be imbued with the spirit of vanished generations – looking more like an avenging deity than a fond mother awaiting the return of her only and well-beloved son'.[44] Mrs Rosser's emphatic displeasure is consonant with her mistrust of outsiders, which shows itself throughout the story, but is tempered by the more accepting comments of the younger generation, as embodied by her daughters. That the demands Mrs Rosser makes of her son in the name of national and familial loyalty are excessive and oppressive is suggested by the description of Elwyn's love for his country (and by extension for his mother and perhaps his mother tongue – although, as we have seen, this last point is somewhat complicated). Elwyn, we are told, 'loved his country – in Cordelia's way – according to his bond, nor more nor less'.[45] Mrs Rosser's struggle to keep Elwyn at home finally ends in a bitter and hollow victory, when she insists that she bury him at Llanffelix: 'You have taken his soul – his immortal soul – from me and mine. These, at least – these mortal remains – let me keep!'[46] Yet Mrs Rosser is also forced to acknowledge privately that her judgements of Aline have been wrong and the story ends with the mother's plaintive admission: 'To you he is not lost, not utterly!'[47]

As should be apparent from the discussion of this text so far, the characters sketched here are no mere allegorical or symbolic figures, employed only to help dramatize the central theme of Elwyn's dislocation. The multi-layered portrayal of 'the way Elwyn went' is never allowed to become a piece of reductive polemic, and this is due not least to the ability of the author to add depth and interest to the most minor of characters with a resonant sentence or two. Aline, then, is not the monstrous stranger that Mrs Rosser first believes her to be, but neither is she able to help Elwyn overcome the ultimately fatal outcome of his divided self. She is herself keen to visit Elwyn's home in Wales, but her husband becomes increasingly unwilling to acknowledge his origins, even though he is unable to settle anywhere else, an ambivalence for which the narrator accounts in terms of the (essentialized) tensions between his original and adopted cultures:

> His baffling reserve on the subject of his native land and circle Aline longed, but had utterly failed, to break through. It seemed perverse, almost unnatural, and was, in fact, a thing inexplicable to any rational English-woman. Probably he could not have clearly accounted for it himself . . .
>
> True, he had been drawn out of his native medium, charmed into a vaster nationality and a still vaster world, a world where there are glories of many sorts and of all scales, and he had become in it and of it too, till the glory of a small, however peculiar nationality, was to him a thing ridiculously unsufficing. But a remnant of him was there, and its clutch on the secret places of his heart he could not altogether escape. He had never thought much about Welsh patriotism, and would never have any thought to give it now. Still, that ancient, traditional virtue of a cherished, indestructible nationality, of which none outside the fold, whether scoffer or admirer, can appreciate the peculiar sanctity and importance to insiders, its indirect or cross-working on Elwyn showed itself thus; prohibiting the shaping or thinking out of his own sentiments to himself. How then should he word them to another? His intercourse with kith and kin remained strictly amicable, but limited to trivial passing matters. No communion nor desire for it, on either side, regarding the things filling their minds – the things next their hearts. It was silence. The door was shut.[48]

Elwyn Rosser's assimilation into English culture, through the prepara-tory education system in Wales and the colleges of Oxford, and his marriage to Aline, is presented not only as irreversible, but as disab-lingly incomplete, his Welshness still producing mysterious 'cross-workings' in Elwyn and retaining 'its clutch on the secret places of his heart'. He must remain a hybrid and the strain of attempting to assimilate fully – to deny his past, his origins – appears to be a fatal rejection of an essential part of his being.

The location of Elwyn's death is interesting and ironic in its colonial credentials – he dies whilst on holiday in a place named only as 'Little

England beyond Wales', but which is obviously somewhere in south Pembrokeshire. Just as Elwyn's own Anglicization is problematized in the story, so the complex colonial history of Wales is again highlighted by Thomas; of the area, Aline observes that 'on the face of it, it didn't seem very Welsh. The language was seldom heard; the names, types, manners and address of these fisher-farmers and others in and about Port Alba were too like Wessex.'[49] Elwyn, feeling as if he has failed to satisfy her curiosity about his homeland, thinks 'It wasn't his fault. He really couldn't help it if some little foreign settlement as to whose exact origin opinions still differ had, like this, refused to be utterly absorbed by the Cambrians.'[50] Yet, although Wales is seen in the above quotation as the victim of invasion by a people and culture it has been unable to assimilate, this corner of Wales is also made to testify to Wales's own role as colonizer:

> though Newfoundland Farm, their present habitation, sounded colonial, the present fisher-farmer occupier[s] . . . were as thoroughgoing, fine old-fashioned specimens of the Welsh breed as she could wish to come across. Pam the father and Pat the son. No connections with English statesman or Irish saint; Pat being short for Patagonia, site of that successful Welsh colony which is not the least of the national glories . . .[51]

Thus Thomas, in her characteristic fashion, complicates any reductive reading of Wales and the Welsh as a colonized nation, just as elsewhere she avoids the use of markers of Cymric authenticity.

If the symbolism of Elwyn's coming death has not already been adequately presaged in the internal tensions of his identity and the difficulties of his hybrid state, then an explicit prophecy of Elwyn's doom is retold shortly before his death. During a happy cliff-top walk with his wife, Elwyn relates how, as a child, he was forced to submit to 'a medical examination by a local celebrity, whom some called a quack'.[52] This man predicts, as the title of the story suggests ('The Way He Went'), that Elwyn's fate will depend on the path he chooses in life:

> It's early to pronounce, madam. If he goes on the farm, he may be there still, hale and hearty at eighty. If it's a professional gentleman's life he's to lead, buried in books and afraid of soiling his fingers, well – he must just take his chance with the rest.[53]

In response, Aline twice asks Elwyn if he repents his having chosen to abandon farming. In reply to her second query, he swears 'Though he slay me – no!'. Having dared the gods to contradict him, Elwyn is swiftly answered by 'Neptune or Nature' who sends up a wave that splashes at their feet where they are relaxing on the 'precipitous sea-cliff' that on this day 'overhangs an ocean smooth and motionless . . . as a mirror'.[54] Startled, Elwyn challenges the sea-god to repeat his trick, and is duly rewarded as the couple watch a 'vast sheet of water surge up the wall of rock, and break in a fountain almost over their heads'.[55] Elwyn explains that such freak waves are caused by 'the meeting of two undercurrents'[56] and the following day, Elwyn will wrestle for his life in these very 'cross-currents'[57] which form a textual echo to the strange 'cross-working'[58] of his 'bi-culturality'. Thus Elwyn's near drowning and eventual death a short time later are prefigured in this scene and linked to his rejection of his home and nation in favour of Oxford and Aline. That Elwyn's sickness and death are caused by his alienation from his cultural roots is further emphasized by the fact that his final illness is in fact a repetition of a mysterious illness which gripped him during his honeymoon in Italy. Towards the end of a lengthy tour of the cities and countryside of Italy, honoured by lengthy lyrical descriptions, Elwyn feels a sudden urge to return home (although here home seems to be Britain rather than Wales). The first words of a new subsection of the story announce the urgency of Elwyn's sudden desire, '*We must go back!*'[59] and his emotions are explained thus: 'The moment of reaction that waits upon the most enchanting pleasure-travel had come, with its warning home-ward tug. You feel your roots are being tampered with'.[60] Lingering in southern Italy for a few more days, Elwyn becomes dangerously ill. A retired English army doctor orders that he be taken home immediately, and indeed his health improves as he moves homeward.

Although there is great variation between the historical and cultural circumstances of Thomas's hero and other colonial subjects who have experienced a similarly dis-located education, parallels might be drawn between his case and what Benedict Anderson, echoing the biological language of colonial discourses of race, described as the imperial policy of 'mental miscegenation'.[61] That is, the underlying premise of the colonial education policy which instilled English tastes and values in the native population was, as Ania Loomba explains, 'that Indians [or other colonial subjects are able to] mimic but never exactly reproduce English values, and that their recognition of the perpetual gap between them-selves and the "real thing" will ensure their subjection'.[62] Thomas's dramatization of dislocation, destructive self-division and alienation from one's native history and traditions finds articulation forty years later in Frantz Fanon's important discussion, in *Black Skin, White Masks*, of the psychological effects of internalizing the perspectives of the colonizer, which result in 'self-division' for the black Antillean. 'Alienation' is described by Fanon explicitly in terms of an 'inferiority complex . . . created by the death and burial of local and cultural originality'[63] of the colonized and it is a description which, as we have seen, finds echoes and even literary precedents in Wales. Significantly, with reference to the interpretation of Thomas's focus on the educational destiny of Elwyn, Fanon also points out that the sense of dislocation and separation brought about by the forces of colonization (and specifically by the use of a different language) becomes stronger, the greater the level of education. That is, the internal conflict described by Fanon is greatest in the educated: 'the Negroes' inferiority complex is particularly intensified among the most educated, who must struggle with it unceasingly.'[64] While Elwyn, unlike the other Welshmen in the novella, is never presented as consciously feeling a sense of inferiority in his Welshness (indeed, Bertha Thomas goes to great lengths to emphasize the excitement and enjoyment with which he explores the worlds offered to him through his formal and informal educational experiences, as already mentioned), his sense of alienation from home is nonetheless profound, and his disastrous fate is clearly a symbolic expression of his self-division.

Thus far, then, we have considered some of the themes of acculturation as these are linked with education at the beginning of the twentieth century. The discussion of Bertha Thomas's novella illustrates the potential personal costs of the experience of partial assimilation or hybridity for the individual, although Thomas's refusal to resort to the use of narrow markers of cultural authenticity simultaneously asserts the complex palimpsest which constitutes the cultural heritage of the Welsh. Moving forward in time, to the end of the twentieth century, I want to look at another text which self-consciously places hybridity at the centre of Welsh experience and thus, while acknowledging the violence (cultural, territorial, physical) which is a feature of Welsh history, actively constructs an authenticity based on synergy.

Christopher Meredith's novel *Griffri* (1991) is set in an area of twelfth-century Wales experiencing the early colonialist incursions of the Anglo-Normans, or French, as they are referred to in the novel, in line with contemporary Welsh references to these invaders and colonizers. The depiction of a Welsh-speaking Gwent as a violent contact zone, in which the native inhabitants must contend with the pressures of territorial, political and cultural transformations, locates Wales, both past and present, within historico-cultural paradigms of colonial subjugation. The overt connections between this fictionalized historical contact zone and contemporary Wales, which echo through Meredith's novel, suggest that Wales remains a fraught arena of cultural and linguistic dispute, and Dafydd Johnston has suggested that the novel itself acts as an intervention into the discourse of authenticity which is often implicit in such cultural debate. Johnston argues that the novel works to authenticate the claims of the author's native Gwent to a Welsh identity: '*Griffri* can be regarded as an attempt to repossess Gwent's past and to reclaim it as an integral part of Wales.'[65] It is an authentication which is based upon relocating this Welsh borderland at the metaphorical centre of Welsh experience, thereby locating instability, change and hybridity at the centre of Welsh culture. Crucially, Gwynllwg itself exists on the border between the Welshries (where Welsh legal and economic systerms were allowed to persist in the less desirable uplands) and the more established Norman territories in the lowlands. The characters depicted in *Griffri* are perched on this border, falling to the 'Welsh' side, but aware of the existence of the strip-farming feudal estates and the money economy nearby.

If *Griffri* may be read as an intriguing exploration of the way historico-cultural forces have shaped and continue to affect Wales (and this aspect of the novel will be the primary focus of this discussion), then it is also a novel which questions the concept of reliable narratives, and particularly the construction of stories of the self, community and nation, whether by artists or historians.[66] Unsurprisingly, then, this is not an historical novel in any traditional sense. Meredith's avoidance of dates, as well as his decision not to include any maps, discourages a literal, historical reading of the narrative, thus allowing a greater fluidity of meaning through which we may read the text as engaging with issues central to contemporary Welsh cultural discourse. A pervasive sense of crisis which often seems to be an integral part of any cultural debate in Wales, informs Meredith's exploration of issues of language, Anglicization, the imperial dominance and cultural hegemony of (Norman) England, tradition and the significance of geography and place. The novel, which is narrated by Griffri, *pencerdd* (head poet) of Gwynllwg, tells the story of the apprenticeship and career of the poet against the background of increasing Anglo-Norman domination in Gwent. From a society which has a strong sense of itself and its history, where the *uchelwyr* (noblemen) of the *cenedl* (kin-group, or clan) can

declare 'my great-grandfather was a king',[67] we witness the fragmentation of power and identity to the point where Griffri, whose function
in society is to be the 'keeper of memory', 'the cauldron to contain a
people', the re-memberer, no longer knows who is 'us' any more.[68]
Meanwhile, all around him the fight for power draws his masters closer
and closer in behaviour (and perhaps in values) to the Anglo-Normans,
their enemies. Gwyn A. Williams describes the outcome of the Norman
occupation of Wales: 'The Normans made the Welsh a European
people.'[69] The Normans altered the centre of gravity away from the Irish
Sea and towards Latin Europe, and Williams describes how – in
response to the feudalism and money economy of the Normans, their
large-scale farming and towns, the European Church and so on – 'the
Welsh exploded into self expression and self assertion'.[70] Williams notes
the positive outcomes of the hybrid cultural production which
emanated from this contact zone (including the transformation of
Welsh 'oral culture into a scintillating literature, retaining its Celtic core
but glossing and enriching it from the new world'), as well as the
enduring 'scars' of the Norman occupation.[71] Meredith, on the other
hand, working through a first-person narrative, offers an imaginative
engagement which foregrounds the trauma of the contact zone and
represents cultural adaptation and adoption in a more disturbing light.
Cultural 'exchange' in the contact zone of Gwynllwg is portrayed as an
often violent process, in which the beleaguered Welsh are either impoverished, through the Norman assimilation of Welsh stories, or
complicit in the 'erosion' of their own cultural identity, through the
adoption of what appear to be the more effective military and legal
methods of their overlords.

The term cultural 'exchange', as already noted, has been eschewed by
some as obscuring the inequality of the dynamics of cultural
interchange in contact zones, which is dependent on the usually vastly
unequal dynamics of power between the two cultures. Indeed, in
Meredith's novel, acculturation is presented as largely a one-way
process, as Griffri's remarks when he and a number of other Welsh
dignitaries visit a Norman fortress at Abergafenni testify. The Welsh
have been led to expect a feast, and one of the party asks where the
tablecloths are (one of the signifiers of cultural difference between the
Welsh and the Normans). 'It was odd that the boards had no cloths.
"'Perhaps the spirit of compromise is going further than we thought", I
said. "They've started copying us." '[72] There are no cloths because there
is no feast; instead, they are slaughtered. The political inferiority of the

Welsh, which is implied in Griffri's recognition that the Welsh adopt
Norman culture but not vice versa, is lent dramatic impact by the
atrocity which follows these words. The term 'exchange' has been
retained here, however, to emphasize that there is, in fact, a two-way
process of cultural exchange, although this is far from being a benign
and equal phenomenon. The potential violence of cultural assimilation
for the 'assimilatee' culture is vividly portrayed in *Griffri*. Gwyn A.
Williams celebrates the fact that 'the initial form of what became one of
[Europe's] more brilliant and abundant literary-historical traditions'
was disseminated from Wales to Europe 'through the Norman March
or Borderland',[73] but Meredith's fiction tends rather to show this
process in terms of 'cultural theft', like that outlined by Prys Morgan
(quoted above, p. 132). In *Griffri* the appropriation of Welsh myths is
linked to the loss of Welsh territory and power when the main court of
Gwynllwg at Caerllion is captured by the Normans as a hunting lodge
on the whim of the king, who wants to possess what he believes to be
the court of Arthur. Significantly, it is complicit Welsh storytellers who
have fostered this belief: 'The French think that Arthur lived here',
Gwrgant tells Griffri on his first visit to Caerllion. 'Let them think', he
goes on, 'It's a pretty enough story', and since the overlords like this
version of the story, Rhys, a morally dubious storyteller, says also he is
'thinking of moving Arthur to Caerllion in future in his stories'.[74] Much
later in the novel Griffri relates how Norman soldiers turn the Welsh
out of their court:

> You could see it was more than a whim. The storytellers in Erging as well as
> Rhys Ddu and old Bledri had made Caerllion Arthur's main court for years
> by then, which is plausible enough, if wrong. I felt I could read the king's
> mind when he looked up. A man afraid of his own gut seeing himself as the
> great king, the mechteyrn [overlord], and seeing a pleasant reserve for the
> hunt, if only the inconvenience of the people could be shifted. Snatching a
> scrap of destiny and a little sport at the same time.[75]

Thus, cultural theft in this instance has dire material and political
consequences.

In fact, the Welsh are portrayed as eager to adopt Norman habits and
dress in their quest for power over their Welsh neighbours and Norman
overlords alike, and Meredith subtly shows the gradual, almost
imperceptible accretion of Norman ways among the Welsh of these
border territories: he reveals the apparent advantages of Welsh appro-

priation of the Norman practice of blinding hostages, for example, whilst
also instilling in the reader a revulsion at this practice, through his
dramatic and appalling descriptions. Blinding is first mentioned in the
novel as a Norman punishment for hunting on royal land. Later, in the
court of a neighbouring Welsh lord, Ifor Fychan, who seems to have made
some alliances with the Normans, we are treated to a vivid and profoundly
disturbing account of the blinding of a French prisoner by Ifor as part of
his wranglings with a Norman adversary. It is a scene which is made all the
more uncomfortable by the obvious unease the Welsh soldiers feel at the
blinding and their haste in leaving the unpleasant scene, although Ifor
himself performs the task 'with a kind of bored expertise'.[76] Later, blinding is used by Hywel and Iorwerth, Lords of Gwynllwg, to great effect
against the enemy during the siege of Caerllion – the Normans quickly
surrender rather than allow more of their number to meet such a fate.

While it might be argued that thus far the Welsh have merely fought
the Normans on their own terms, using their own weapons against
them, the third and most terrible blinding described in the novel reveals
the extent of the internalization of this foreign habit. Not only is the
blinding (and castration) of Owain Pencarn the first instance of this
torture being inflicted upon one Welshman by another, but the reader is
no longer surprised to witness this once alien practice being used by a
Welsh lord. Significantly, by the time he blinds Pencarn, Hywel is
described by Griffri as 'wearing one of those padded shirts the French
wear under their mail, though he hadn't at that time taken to wearing
stockings and shoes'.[77] The adoption of Norman dress is elsewhere used
to signify not only cultural erosion, but a concomitant moral degrad-
ation, linked as it is to the fratricidal Hywel. Commenting on Hywel's
adoption of Norman armour, Meilyr, a wiseman/seer/madman, notices
that the helmet 'has set a mark on him',[78] a comment which alludes both
to the effects of foreign influences on Welsh identity and to the idea of a
sinner bearing the mark of the devil. Meilyr goes on: 'Iorwerth and
Hywel can stride into their enlarged and Frenchified birthright [their
recaptured fort] wearing mail shirts and helmets. Won't that be glorious?
. . . Now we know ourselves.'[79] Cultural change, on the Welsh side, then,
tends to be portrayed as the result of fairly desperate reaction to the
pressures of the Norman colonization. In that the Welsh are complicit
within a framework of unequal power, *Griffri* offers a dramatization of
the early stages of the establishment of an imperial hegemony.

The pervasive effects of colonization, as portrayed by Meredith, go
beyond warfare, influencing, as we might expect, areas such as religion,

but also going beyond these 'public' spheres and into the more private
world of sexual relationships. The stone cathedrals of the Normans are
a powerful symbol of both the invaders' might and the alien status of
the European Church. The impact of the rise of this Norman-brought
religion on Welsh culture is expressed in Griffri's realization that the
Norman attempt to enforce celibacy on the Welsh Church will eliminate
future Angharads – a woman portrayed as beautiful, fertile and bare-
footed, this last a sign of Welsh authenticity, although she is later
discovered to be something of a Welsh Lady Macbeth. The native
religion is linked with sex, pleasure and innocence in the novel. Griffri
describes his adolescent sexual experimentation in religious terms, and
the body of his lover, Cristin (the name is also suggestive), in terms of
ecclesiastical architecture. In one scene, the lovers lie next to a 'dense
plait of tree roots' (at which Griffri peers through 'a thicket of [Cristin's]
hair'[80]). These 'living lines woven to the glory of God' are compared
with a Celtic cross.[81] Thus innocence, nature and sex are linked to a pre-
Norman Celtic Christianity which contrasts favourably with the wolf's
mouth, as Griffri perceives it, of the stone church being built by the
French. But the influence of the religion of the colonizers extends
further than the architecture of their religious buildings and seems to
permeate intimate relationships, as symbolized by the succubus, who
appears twice in the novel. While we might interpret the succubus as
expressing a fear of female sexuality (the transformation into a demon
seems to occur at and to echo orgasm), her appearances are also clearly
linked to the violence of the Norman colonizers. Meilyr's encounter
with the succubus is associated with the incursions of the French: 'It's a
bad sign when they come . . . Usually it's war . . . After she came some of
our neighbours were attacked by the French and the chief man was
killed and the sons were taken as soldiers and the daughters as slaves.'[82]
Griffri's own encounter occurs after he has escaped, physically
unharmed but psychologically violated, after witnessing the slaughter of
all his companions by the French, in a scene which recalls the Treason
of the Long Knives.

Meredith's novel, as Dafydd Johnston has described, goes to great
lengths to place Gwent at the heart of Wales: 'Gwynllwg is . . . [where]
the national crisis is taking place.'[83] This is a national crisis which is
shown to have profound resonances for contemporary Wales. By exploring the dynamics of cultural exchange, the constant flux and hybridity
of cultural production, Meredith produces a metaphorical as well as

geographical borderland as authentically Welsh. Yet, if Meredith could be said to conform to Neil ten Kortenaar's dictum of the strategic or rhetorical use of the ideas of authenticity and creolization, it is worth exploring further how his interstitial and fluid borderland is perhaps authenticated through images familiar from more traditional, even essentialist, constructions of national identity. In *Griffri*, I would suggest, the idea of hybridity and (ex)change offers a space, a 'cauldron', in which to make and remake a people through re-memory and storytelling. The role of memory and the instability of stories are questioned repeatedly in *Griffri*, with the effect of questioning notions of fixed cultural authenticity. The emphasis is on *re*-making and *re*-telling histories and identities, a position which sits comfortably with postmodern and especially postcolonial ideas of identity. Charlotte Williams has made a very strong case for understanding communities not only as 'imagined' but as perpetually reimagined, where cultural and personal identities are in a constant state of flux.

> [The] idea of moving away and moving back as continual processes of border crossing allows for a recognition of multiple points of identification . . . This positioning also acts as a counter-discourse to depictions of home and belonging that posit rootedness in specific locations and places and times. So the art of negotiating self lies in managing this dynamic where there is a constant mixing of heritage and traditions and a constant movement towards their identification and reformulation.[84]

Nevertheless, in addition to Meredith's rhetoric of flux and imagery of fluidity, we may find some traces of older, traditional signifiers of a more stable, essential identity, rooted in the land.

It is important to make the distinction here between land and place. Place (as discussed in chapter 4) is land or space to which meaning has been ascribed. As we might expect, in *Griffri*, different stories and meanings may be inscribed upon the same landscape. Thus, place in this novel, far from being 'purely' Welsh, is shaped by various cultures and peoples and their residual presence also shapes the various peoples who later move through the coded landscapes. Through one fascinating image, for example, Meredith creates a spatial metaphor of the cultural palimpsest which constitutes modern synergistic Wales:

> Gwrgant had shown me the remains of the old city from the age of giants. He said it was older even than the time when Macsen and Cynan from the

north had marched on Rome. I saw walls of rock and great cracked slabs. There were modern houses built among the stones and some of Morgan's soldiers had tents pitched in sheltered places along the southern fringes. The edges of the town were regularly patrolled and Iorwerth and Morgan themselves often did the rounds.[85]

At Caerllion the old Roman town determines the boundaries of the current one; it has been imbued with the myths of the contemporary occupants (soon to be overlaid with the Welsh-Norman stories of Arthur's court), while its structure determines the very paths of Welsh patrols. Though separated by centuries these various historical strands of Wales are brought together in space, space which postcolonial theory has 'privilege[d] . . . over time as the most important ordering concept of reality'.[86] Space in Meredith's fiction might certainly be understood as offering an important ordering concept of reality. Space as it is inscribed and reinscribed becomes a metaphor for containment of different stories, or, as Dafydd Johnston puts it, landscape may represent 'a rare element of continuity in a region which has suffered a fracture in its history as a result of Anglicisation'.[87] While I would question the assumptions of this statement, which conflates linguistic discontinuity with historical fracture, it accurately highlights one of the functions of landscape in Meredith's writing, which is even more pronounced when the parallel themes of *Griffri* and his earlier novel *Shifts* are examined in tandem. In *Shifts*, Keith is intent on 'reading' the landscape for clues of the pre-industrial history of the valley. In addition to Keith's self-conscious attempts to decipher the palimpsest of his surroundings, even the more cynical and nihilistic Jack unthinkingly 'reads' the coded landscape with the privileged perspective of a local as he distinguishes between natural hills and grassed-over slag-heaps.[88]

If the landscape may offer a continuity which extends across other historical or linguistic fractures, it may also be carved up literally, with dykes and ditches or more symbolically through cartography. These borders are a recurring motif in Welsh writing, in both languages. Gwyn A. Williams uses the image of a dividing line in his evocative description of the impact of the Norman conquest of Wales: 'The Normans . . . drew a frontier across the bony face of Wales. That frontier, in different form and circumstance, has appeared and reappeared as a shadow line across its human landscape. It exists today, more visible than ever.'[89]

The plurality and internal division suggested here are expressed elsewhere in Welsh writing in more personal or psychological terms,

which are yet intimately associated with a wider national identity. Bryan
Martin Davies's line, '*Ynom mae y clawdd*' [Offa's Dyke (that is, the
border) is within us],[90] and Waldo Williams's '*Ynof mae Cymru'n un*'
[within me Wales is one/whole][91] are thus simultaneously relevant in
expressing both the fractured nature of Welsh identity and the way this
sense of plurality, of hybridity, is coming to represent an 'authentically'
Welsh experience.

   The fractured self, and the related image of the individual within
whom (or space within which) a national or cultural divide is sur-
mounted, is a common feature of postcolonial writing. Charlotte
Williams borrows an image from Pauline Melville's short stories, in
which a character dreams she is suspended – perpetually in-between –
on a high-wire above the Atlantic, which is stretched between Big Ben in
London and St George's Cathedral, Demerara.[92] Homi Bhabha uses the
metaphor of a stairwell to describe his liminal space,[93] while the
departure lounge of an international airport has become a conveniently
liminal space which suggests travel, the to-ing and fro-ing from multiple
places of identification. Charlotte Williams makes use of just this kind
of space in her biotext, *Sugar and Slate* (2002), in which she uses an
airport lounge as a 'present' from which to articulate the criss-crossing
interconnections between Wales, Guyana and Africa.

   What has all this to do with Christopher Meredith, and the suggestion that he seems to foreground cultural fluidity and yet employ
essentialist and static markers of identity in his work? In *Griffri* the
metaphors of cultural borders and boundaries intersect with images of
a partitioned and fragmented country, where the hybridity and fluidity
of borderlands foregrounded in the novel are complicated by the
dramatic tensions, conflicts and deceptions which revolve around
territorial boundaries in the text.

   On an immediate narrative level, then, places of conflict, horror, danger,
betrayal and falsehood are central to the plot, but the fractured landscape
described by Gwyn A. Williams and Bryan Martin Davies (above) also
haunts the novel. The final 'vision' of the novel which has the quality of an
epiphany, comes after Griffri's most explicit acknowledgement of the
betrayals and deceptions which have been perpetrated throughout the
novel – each one linked to the dangerous borderland between Gwynllwg
and its neighbours, or bound up in fratricidal rivalry. Having survived a
terrible sickness, the narrator walks out on to 'an immense high moor of
heathclad peat', where he can look 'down from a high place' on the
mountains before him.[94] He tells us that 'As I walked in the spring sun I

had the sensation that this place was without boundaries'.[95] I have chosen to read the words 'this place' as anchoring the expression to a Welsh context, without, of course, excluding or invalidating other readings, but this scene, which is also a poetic representation of Griffri's return to life, seems to offer a powerful fantasy of transcending the conflicted internal borders of Wales, as well as, perhaps, suggesting a wider supranational vision, reminiscent of Alun Lewis's story, 'The Orange Grove', with its universalist fantasy of a transcendent world community without borders.[96] There is also the echo here of a fantasy scene of cultural equality from Meredith's earlier novel, *Shifts*, in which Keith imagines the occupants of two mountain-top graves, one English the other Welsh, 'meeting on the mountain . . . Talking each in their own language.'[97]

That this vision occurs on top of a mountain is not insignificant. The geography of Wales has been imbued with powerful historical, cultural and even moral significance. The historian E. G. Bowen and others have explained Welsh history in terms of that geography where the lack of natural defences in the south-east (what Bowen calls 'Outer Wales'), for example, are more 'open' to influences from the east, while the counties of the north and west ('Inner Wales') have the cultural high ground. Geography, in Bowen's historical narrative, becomes a powerful and culturally loaded signifier of authentic identity: 'the culture in the Inner Zone depends to a very large extent on the ability of the mountains to defend the culture of the valleys facing the west and north'.[98] Mountain-tops, as a space for meditation on the self or the world, or as a place to commune with 'the Big Man', abound in Anglophone Welsh literature, from Caradoc Evans through to industrial novels and short stories and beyond, but it is difficult to dissociate these places, as literary expressions, from the historical and cultural nuances outlined above, and the hills take on a sense of purity and morality which is directly associated with nationality and culture. Some of the most famous and suggestive images of the Welsh uplands emanate from the poetry of R. S. Thomas, for example, who consistently represents the (true) Welsh as a hill-dwelling people; the lowland is associated with the 'English plains';[99] 'down' is where the sinful, wanton, townspeople dwell;[100] freedom and dignity become, in metaphor, 'the high pastures of the heart'.[101] Meredith's poignant assertion of the wholeness of Wales, in this epiphany at the end of *Griffri*, is made using the traditional, essentialist imagery of authenticity.

Meredith certainly makes use of conventional emblems of cultural authenticity, such as the transcendent borderless uplands, but it would be a reductive reading of this novel that asserted *Griffri* is about *erasing* internal borders and differences. Heavily imbued with a sense of transcendence-as-closure though the final moving chapter is, the most powerful motif in the novel is the cauldron. This metaphor is a very fertile one, suggestive of re-membering a people whole, not in the sense of returning them to an earlier state, but in (re)making them *anew*. Even in the *Mabinogion* the cauldron does not return to life unchanged the slain soldiers put into it. Although it revivifies, the cauldron might also be figured as a liminal space of transculturation, of hybridity and cultural production. At the risk of simplification, or overstatement, it could be argued that Meredith's narrative to some extent works, as does the central character, as a 'cauldron of a people', by 'containing', or rather, making a space for, diversity and difference; strategically valorizing hybridity, ironically but no less successfully, as a form of cultural authenticity. The 'containment' offered by this cauldron – indeed, the interstitial space of cultural production opened up by the theory of hybridity – is not that of an impermeable or exclusive site, but rather one of continual flux, of making and re-making, re-membering, re-telling.

In Wales, the discourse of hybridity (if such a thing can be said to exist) can construct acculturation in terms of a cultural dilution or pollution. Alternatively, this discourse can be employed to offer an inclusive, participative and ultimately 'voluntary' or self-consciously constructed kind of Welsh identity. This notion of hybridity attempts to 'transcend' (admittedly a problematic term) the narrower, exclusive and often bitterly entrenched essentialist definitions of Welshness held by some, as well as the sometimes aggressively anti-Welsh attitudes of the 'British Welsh'. Such a positive understanding does not ignore the difficulties fundamental to hybridity. Bhabha's 'Third Space' does not *resolve* tensions but recognizes and valorizes them, as recognized in the critical approach of M. Wynn Thomas (*Internal Difference: Twentieth-Century Writing in Wales* (1992) and *Corresponding Cultures: The Two Literatures of Wales* (1999)). Thomas's is not a strategy which simply advocates tolerance and pluralism and thus sidesteps complex cultural tensions. For example, although his central concern of studying the way the two literatures of Wales may have 'developed in tandem'[102] might be described as an attempt to 'reconcile' the divide between linguistic groups by seeking to understand and explore the cultural interactions, the correspondences, it does not downplay the threat posed by the dominance of one language to the very existence of the other, recognizing 'the vexed problem of cultural confrontation' and 'in the case of the Welsh language, cultural survival'.[103] Rather, Thomas's approach contains such conflict within the notion of a complete whole that is the nation of Wales, so that difference – and *différance* – is perceived as central to Welsh culture itself; it thus allows a productive internal discourse – the correspondence between (competing) cultures.

To express this differently, a Wales constructed thus, as a not always coherent but culturally productive whole, unified in cultural hybridity or synergy, does not necessarily have to ignore the tensions of opposition or the senses of alienation and anger, neither does it elide or undermine the impact of Anglocentric cultural hegemony. Yet nor does it reduce Welsh culture to one essentialist definition (strategic or otherwise) which effectively renders most of Wales as not really Welsh at all – and so not really *Wales* at all. Rather, the conflicts and contradictions inherent in a culturally hybrid Wales (and the experience of the cultural imperialism of England, as well as versions of Welsh cultural hegemony) are 'contained' within what becomes an enabling and productive, if ambivalent, internal discourse. Containment in this instance should not be seen as reductive, rather as the opposite. It opens up a space where the complex cultural debate may be productively entered into, without the risk of shattering the nation into meaningless fragments. Indeed, in Bhabha's terms, it is this space of 'translation and negotiation, the *in-between* space – that carries the burden of the meaning of culture'.[104]

Notes

1 Theoretical Contexts

[1] Homi Bhabha, *The Location of Culture* ([1994], London: Routledge, 1998), p. 171.

[2] I use post-colonial here to refer to a post-independence colony and the non-hyphenated postcolonial to refer to the academic field (see p. 3).

[3] R. Shome, 'Caught in the Term "Post-Colonial": Why the "Post-Colonial" Still Matters', cited in Ismail S. Talib, *The Language of Postcolonial Literatures: An Introduction* (London: Routledge, 2002), p. 19. See Anne McClintock, 'The Angel of Progress: Pitfalls of the Term "Postcolonialism"', in Francis Barker, Peter Hulme and Margaret Iversen (eds), *Colonial Discourse/Postcolonial Theory* (Manchester: Manchester University Press, 1994), for a discussion of the wider issue of the prolific use of 'post' in academia and beyond.

[4] See McClintock, 'The Angel of Progress'.

[5] The lands formerly known as Czechoslovakia have a history of subordination to Germanic rule. Czech and Slovak 'nationalism' also provides instances of internal cultural hegemony, where Slovaks were relegated to the status of second-class citizens, not to mention both Czech and Slovak subjugation of the Roma up to the present day. Thus the history of the lands formerly unified as Czechoslovakia would seem to make a very interesting 'postcolonial' case-study.

[6] Bill Ashcroft, Gareth Griffiths and Helen Tiffin, *The Empire Writes Back: Theory and Practice in Post-Colonial Literatures* (London: Routledge, 1994), p. 33.

[7] Ken Goodwin, 'Celtic Nationalism and Postcoloniality', in Stuart Murray and Alan Riach (guest eds), *SPAN: Journal of the South Pacific Association for Commonwealth Literature and Language Studies*, 41 (October 1995), 23.

[8] Ned Thomas, *The Welsh Extremist: Modern Welsh Politics, Literature and*

Society (Talybont: Y Lolfa, 1991), p. 36. The first edition of *The Welsh Extremist*, subtitled *A Culture in Crisis*, appeared in 1971. A later edition was published in 1991, with a new introduction and without the chapter on S4C. The 1991 edition was subtitled as above. Both editions are referred to in the course of this book.

9   See, for example, Jane Aaron, 'Slaughter and Salvation: Welsh Missionary Activity and British Imperialism' and Aled Jones, 'The Other Internationalism? Missionary Activity and Welsh Nonconformist Perceptions of the World in the Nineteenth and Twentieth Centuries', in Charlotte Williams, Neil Evans and Paul O'Leary (eds), *A Tolerant Nation?: Exploring Ethnic Diversity in Wales* (Cardiff: University of Wales Press, 2003).

10 Declan Kiberd has made similar claims for Ireland, arguing that by considering postcolonial theories in relation to a country which has a complex and convoluted history of colonization/neo-colonialism, the exponents of such theories are forced 'to complicate and qualify them in valuable ways – most notably in recognizing that the Irish were both imperial and counter imperial, sometimes seemingly in the same gesture' (*SPAN*, 41, p. 40).

11 Bill Ashcroft, Gareth Griffiths and Helen Tiffin, *Post-Colonial Studies: The Key Concepts* (London: Routledge, 2000), p. 153. For a discussion of the significance of nomenclature see also Norman Davies's excellent 'Introduction' to *The Isles: A History* (Basingstoke: Macmillan, 1999), pp. xxi–xlii.

12 Robert Young, *Colonial Desire: Hybridity in Theory, Culture and Race* (London: Routledge, 1995), p. 3.

13 Dewi Z. Phillips, *J. R. Jones*, Writers of Wales Series (Cardiff: University of Wales Press, 1995), p. 55.

14 Seamus Heaney, 'Open Letter', in Seamus Deane (ed.), *Ireland's Field Day* (London: Hutchinson, 1985).

15 Britain means different things to different groups on the island. 'British-Welsh' might be shorthand for the 'Anglicized' Welsh of Pembrokeshire and the Marches, described by Denis Balsom in 'The Three-Wales Model', in John Osmond (ed.), *The National Question Again: Welsh Political Identity in the 1980s* (Llandysul: Gomer, 1985). Yet, equally for the Welsh, 'Britain' is a multi-layered idea which refers back to the period long before modern revival of the word in 1654. If the Welsh, or rather the *Cymry*, are the remains of the 'ancient Britons', then the island of Britain is remembered through a series of conflations as a 'Welsh' territory which has been lost through the incursions of 'the Saxon'. Moreover, Welsh poetry and mythology remembers connections across Britain. Our oldest Welsh poetry comes not from Wales but from what is now lowland Scotland. The location of the great eulogized battle at Catraeth (now known as Catterick) is in Yorkshire, and Arthur's court is generally located in Cornwall. In the *Mabinogi* London, or Llundain, is the final resting place of Bendigeidfran's head, from where he would protect Britain from invasion. The trauma of the

loss of the greater part of the island to invaders is implied in the legend of a Welsh/British hero returning to free the island and return it to the Welsh/Britons, most famously perhaps in the image of Arthur asleep in a cave. This myth has extended its influence beyond legend and into reality in the various campaigns of Owain Lawgoch, Owain Glyndŵr and Henry Tudor, this last apparently fulfilling the prophecy when he took the throne of England. Prehistoric monuments also connect modern Wales with other parts of Britain. The Preseli hills, which have been such an important feature of life, both spiritual and material, in west Wales, are linked to the West Country through the construction of the circles known today as Stonehenge. Of course, it is inaccurate and misleading to describe the people who constructed the megaliths of western Britain as Welsh. The Welsh can be thought of as coming into being, according to Gwyn A Williams, in about the fourth century (see Gwyn A. Williams, *When Was Wales? A History of the Welsh* ([1985], London: Penguin, 1991)). Nevertheless, the Welsh historical consciousness, aided in part by the Welsh landscape, which carries continual reminders of the history of this territory which stretches further back than the formation of the nation we call *Cymru* or Wales, may look back to 'their' history as Britons and find a sense of affinity with a much larger territory than that which lies within the borders of modern Wales. Wales's complex relationship with 'Britain', then, is in part a result of this affinity with the island as a whole, which looks back to the ancient Britons, coupled with an acceptance by many of a more or less complicated dual identity as both Welsh and British, and a sometimes simultaneous awareness that the ideology of 'Britishness' operates to mask the project of the assimilation of Wales into England/Britain. It is a further irony that the label 'British' has also been used as a means of maintaining the sanctity of Englishness, or, similarly, providing a label for those who do not feel comfortable with adopting the title 'English', a way of containing immigrant groups by providing a sense of partial belonging – it is easier to adopt the title 'British' than 'English'. If the process of devolution proceeds further and Britain ceases to exist as a political entity, the question of what happens to those who identify themselves as British rather than English, Welsh or Scottish (Black British or British Asian, for example) is an interesting and potentially revealing one.

[16] See, for example, Bronwen Walter, *Outsiders Inside: Whiteness, Place and Irish Women* (London: Routledge, 2001).

[17] I am slightly uneasy about the connotations of the term 'transcultural'; however, I use it here in its technical, postcolonial sense, after Mary Louise Pratt, to refer to the cultural 'exchange' which occurs in a contact zone and the synergistic cultural production which results from the meeting between two or more cultures. See Mary Louise Pratt, *Imperial Eyes: Travel Writing and Transculturation* (London: Routledge, 1992).

[18] See Jeffrey Jerome Cohen, 'Hybrids, Monsters, Borderlands: The Bodies of Gerald of Wales', in Jeffrey Jerome Cohen (ed.), *The Postcolonial Middle-*

Ages (New York: St Martin's Press, 2000). In the context of a discussion of 'Anglo-Welsh' poetry as a product of three kinds of frontier, Tony Conran has seen the whole of Wales as a frontier territory: 'Nowadays anywhere in Wales is frontier country', *Frontiers in Anglo-Welsh Poetry* (Cardiff: University of Wales Press, 1997), p. vii.

[19] Marc Ferro, *Colonization: A Global History* (London: Routledge, 1997), p. 3. In terms of colonial imagery, we might also see the European Wild Man as the forerunner of colonial savages.

[20] See R. R. Davies, 'Colonial Wales', *Past and Present*, 65 (November 1974), 3–23; 'Race Relations in Post Conquest Wales: Confrontation and Compromise', *Transactions of the Honourable Society of Cymmrodorion* (1974–5) 32–56; *Domination and Conquest: the Experience of Ireland, Scotland and Wales, 1100–1300* (Cambridge: Cambridge University Press, 1990); *The First English Empire: Power and Identities in the British Isles 1093–1343* (Oxford: Oxford University Press, 2000).

[21] Neil Evans, 'Internal Colonialism? Colonization, Economic Development and Political Mobilization in Wales, Scotland and Ireland', in Graham Day and Gareth Rees (eds), *Regions, Nations and European Integration: Remaking the Celtic Periphery* (Cardiff: University of Wales Press, 1991), p. 240.

[22] Williams, *When Was Wales?*, p. 119.

[23] Young, *Colonial Desire*, p. 71.

[24] Gwyneth Tyson Roberts, *The Language of the Blue Books: The Perfect Instrument of Empire* (Cardiff: University of Wales Press, 1998). See also Prys Morgan, 'From Long Knives to Blue Books', in R. R. Davies, Ralph A. Griffiths, Ieuan Gwynedd Jones and Kenneth O. Morgan (eds), *Welsh Society and Nationhood: Historical Essays Presented to Glanmor Williams* (Cardiff: University of Wales Press, 1984); Sian Rhiannon Williams, 'The True "Cymraes": Images of Women in Women's Nineteenth-Century Welsh Periodicals', in Angela V. John (ed.), *Our Mothers' Land: Chapters in Welsh Women's History: 1830–1939* (Cardiff: University of Wales Press, 1991); Jane Aaron, 'Finding a Voice in Two Tongues: Gender and Colonization', in Jane Aaron, Teresa Rees, Sandra Betts and Moira Vincentelli (eds), *Our Sisters' Land: The Changing Identities of Women in Wales* (Cardiff, University of Wales Press, 1994); and, most recently, Harri Roberts, 'Embodying Identity: Class, Nation and Corporeality in the 1847 Blue Books Report', *North American Journal of Welsh Studies*, 3, 1 (Winter 2003) 1–22.

[25] Interpellation is used after Althusser. See also pp. 20–2 and for a fuller, accessible definition of interpellation and subjectivity as they relate to postcolonialism see Bill Ashcroft, Gareth Griffiths and Helen Tiffin, *Post-Colonial Studies: The Key Concepts*, pp. 219–22.

[26] Bhabha, *The Location of Culture*, p. 171. For a fuller quotation see the beginning of this chapter.

[27] Lewis Jones, *Cwmardy: The Story of a Welsh Mining Village* ([1937], London: Lawrence & Wishart, 1978), p. 1.

[28] Ibid., pp. 94–5.

[29] Ibid., p. 97.
[30] Williams, *When Was Wales?*, p. 118.
[31] Ibid.
[32] See, for example, Charles R. Larson, *The Ordeal of the African Writer* (London: Zed Books, 2001); Greg Hill, 'Sisyphus Goes to School', *Planet: The Welsh Internationalist*, 161 (October/November 2003), 82–5; M. Wynn Thomas, 'Review of Sam Adams's Writers of Wales: *Roland Mathias*', *Planet*, 117 (June/July 1996), 105–6.
[33] See Albert Memmi, *The Colonizer and the Colonized*, tr. Howard Greenfeld, original intro. by Jean-Paul Sartre (1965), new intro. by Liam O'Dowd (London: Earthscan Publications, 1990).
[34] Raymond Williams, 'Welsh Culture', in Daniel Williams (ed.), *Who Speaks for Wales: Raymond Williams on Nation and Identity* (Cardiff: University of Wales Press, 2003), p. 9.
[35] See Ngugi wa Thiong'o, *Decolonising the Mind: The Politics of Language in African Literature* (London: James Currey, 1986).
[36] Williams, 'Welsh Culture'. See Daniel Williams's introduction to *Who Speaks for Wales* for a more detailed discussion of Raymond Williams's understanding of Wales's colonial status (especially pp. xxx–xxxii).
[37] Robert Crawford, *Devolving English Literature* (Oxford: Oxford University Press, 1992), p. 5.
[38] Leela Gandhi, *Postcolonial Theory: A Critical Introduction* (Edinburgh: Edinburgh University Press, 1998), p. 4.
[39] Bhabha, *The Location of Culture*, p. 63.
[40] See Prys Morgan, *The Eighteenth-Century Renaissance* (Llandybïe: Christopher Davies, 1981); 'From a Death to a View: The Hunt for the Welsh Past in the Romantic Period', in Eric Hobsbawm and Terence Ranger (eds), *The Invention of Tradition* (Cambridge: Cambridge University Press, 1983); 'Keeping the Legends Alive', in Tony Curtis (ed.), *Wales: The Imagined Nation* (Bridgend: Poetry Wales Press, 1986).
[41] Cited in Ania Loomba, *Colonialism/Postcolonialism* (London: Routledge, 1998), p. 17.
[42] R. S. Thomas, 'Welsh History', *Collected Poems: 1945–1990* (London: Dent, 1993), p. 36. 'Welsh History' was published in Thomas, *An Acre of Land* (London: Rupert Hart-Davis, 1952).
[43] See, for example, Patricia Daniel and Môn/Arfon Central America Group, *We Share the Same Struggle: Women in Wales, Women in Nicaragua* (Bethesda(?): Môn/Arfon Central America Group, 1996/1998), or the South Wales/South Africa Festivals of 1988 and 1990 which 'aimed to highlight the cultural, economic and political links between South Wales and South Africa'. See the introduction to 'South Wales/South Africa Exhibition' brochure, 1989, in Jerry Rothwell (ed.) *Creating Meaning: A Book about Culture and Democracy* (Blaengarw: Valley and Vale, 1992), p. 40. The brochure draws parallels between Steve Biko's description of colonialism and what it describes as the cultural domination which was espoused by Matthew Arnold. Biko's words are also printed alongside comparable

remarks by Gwyn Williams, and the tradition of using music and song in protest and resistance in south Wales and South Africa is highlighted.

44 Griffiths, *SPAN*, 41, 28.

45 Memmi, *The Colonizer and the Colonized*, p. 7.

46 See O'Dowd's introduction to Memmi, *The Colonizer and the Colonized*. Such identification in the Welsh context may be seen in the sympathy of Welsh nationalists with Gandhi (his pacifism could be particularly appealing); on a more contemporary note, the artist Iwan Bala has repeatedly expressed an affinity with the work of a variety of post-colonial artists, which he articulates within his model of 'custodial aesthetics'. See Iwan Bala (ed.), *Certain Welsh Artists: Custodial Aesthetics in Contemporary Welsh Art* (Bridgend: Seren, 1999).

47 Marie-Claire Boons-Grafé, cited in Ashcroft, Griffiths and Tiffin, *Post-Colonial Studies*, p. 170.

48 Ashcroft, Griffiths and Tiffin, *Post-Colonial Studies*, pp. 170–1.

49 Ashcroft, Griffiths and Tiffin, *The Empire Writes Back*, p. 8.

50 Ashcroft, Griffiths and Tiffin, *Post-Colonial Studies*, p. 221.

51 Roberts, *The Language of the Blue Books*, p. 24.

52 Williams, *When Was Wales?*, pp. 246–7.

53 Memmi, *The Colonizer and the Colonized*, p. 172. It is not difficult to find a variety of descriptions from Memmi's book which find resonances with the Welsh situation. For instance, Welsh-language activists of the 1960s might identify with the following comment: 'If only the mother tongue was allowed some influence on current social life, or was used across the counters of government offices, or directed the postal service; but this is not the case. The entire bureaucracy, the entire court system, all industry hears and uses the colonizer's language. Likewise, highway markings, railroad station signs, street signs and receipts make the colonized feel like a foreigner in his own country' (ibid., pp. 173–4).

54 Alun Rees, 'Anglo-Taffy', cited in Roberts, *The Language of the Blue Books*, p. vi.

55 Owen Sheers, *The Blue Book* (Bridgend: Seren, 2000), p. 20.

56 See, for example, Craig Cairns, *The Modern Scottish Novel: Narrative and the National Imagination* (Edinburgh: Edinburgh University Press, 1999), and Crawford, *Devolving English Literature*.

57 Memmi, *The Colonizer and the Colonized*, pp. 153–4.

58 Frantz Fanon, *Black Skin, White Masks*, translated from the French by Charles Lam Markham ([1967], London: Pluto Press, 1986), p. 12.

59 Ibid., p. 18. My emphasis.

60 Ibid., p. 192.

61 Ibid., p. 18.

62 Ned Thomas, *The Welsh Extremist: A Culture in Crisis*, (London: Gollancz, 1971), p. 58.

63 Raymond Williams, 'Welsh Culture', p. 9.

64 M. Wynn Thomas (ed.), *A Guide to Welsh Literature, VII: Welsh Writing in English* (Cardiff: University of Wales Press, 2003).

[65] Charlotte Williams, ' "I going away, I going home": Mixed-"Race", Movement, and Identity', in Lynne Pearce (ed.), *Devolving Identities: Feminist Readings in Home and Belonging* (Aldershot: Ashgate, 2000), p. 194.

[66] Neil ten Kortenaar, 'Beyond Authenticity and Creolization: Reading Achebe Writing Culture', *PMLA*, 110, 1 (January 1995), 30–42 (30).

[67] See M. Wynn Thomas and Tony Brown, 'Colonial Wales and Fractured Language', and Kirsti Bohata, 'Beyond Authenticity? Hybridity and Assimilation in Welsh Writing in English', in Tony Brown and Russell Stephens (eds), *Nations and Relations: Writing Across the British Isles* (Cardiff: New Welsh Review, 2000); John Pikoulis, 'Alun Lewis and the Politics of Empire', and Tony Brown and M. Wynn Thomas, 'Alun Lewis and the Politics of Empire: Two Replies', in the 'Forum' section of *Welsh Writing in English: A Yearbook of Critical Essays*, 8 (2003), 157–75 and 175–9, respectively.

[68] Williams, ' "I going away, I going home" ', p. 180.

[69] The un-capitalized word 'english' is used by postcolonial writers and critics to distance the language from England (or Received Pronounciation (RP) English) and thereby to assert their own claims to 'possess' the language and to reflect the way they have made it their own in other ways through creolization, syntactic adaptation, and so on.

2 Stereotypes of Alterity

[1] See, for example, H. L. Malchow, *Gothic Images of Race in Nineteenth Century Britain* (Stanford, CA: Stanford University Press, 1996), and Gayatri Chakravorty Spivak, 'Three Women's Texts and a Critique of Imperialism', in Bill Ashcroft, Gareth Griffiths and Helen Tiffin (eds), *The Post-Colonial Studies Reader*, (London: Routledge, 1995).

[2] Sander L. Gilman, *Difference and Pathology: Stereotypes of Sexuality of Sexuality, Race, and Madness* (London: Cornell University Press, 1985).

[3] See Malchow, *Gothic Images of Race*.

[4] Mark Valentine, *Arthur Machen* (Bridgend: Seren, 1995), p. 41.

[5] Originally part of *The Three Impostors*, this tale has often been anthologized as a short story, which is how it will be read here.

[6] Although, ironically, the English narrator of the story mistakenly describes the place as 'a country house in the west of England, not far from Caermaen [Caerleon]'; Arthur Machen, 'The Novel of the Black Seal', *Tales of Horror and the Supernatural*, intro. by Philip Van Doren Stern (London: The Richards Press, 1949), p. 12.

[7] Machen, 'The Novel of the Black Seal', p. 3.

[8] Ibid., p. 9.

[9] Ibid., pp. 33–4.

[10] Ibid., p. 32.

[11] See Jane M. Ussher, *Women's Madness: Misogyny or Mental Illness?* (London: Harvester Wheatsheaf, 1991), p. 74.

12 Thomas Jefferson, 'Laws', in *Notes on the State of Virginia*, cited in Emmanuel Chukwudi Eze (ed.), *Race and the Enlightenment: A Reader* (Oxford: Blackwell, 1997), p. 103. My italics.

13 Machen, 'The Novel of the Black Seal', p. 33. My italics.

14 See Charlotte Williams, ' "I going away, I going home" '.

15 Machen, 'The Novel of the Black Seal', p. 22.

16 Ibid.

17 Ibid., p. 34.

18 Ibid., p. 24.

19 Wirt Sikes, *British Goblins: Welsh Folk-Lore, Fairy Mythology, Legends and Traditions*, illustrations by T. H. Thomas (London: Sampson Low, 1880), p. 129.

20 Ibid.

21 Ibid.

22 Jonathan Ceredig Davies, *Folk-lore of West and Mid Wales* ([1911]; Lampeter: Llanerch, 1992), p. 89.

23 Ibid.

24 Bertha Thomas, *Picture Tales of Welsh Hills* (London: T. Fisher Unwin, 1912), p. 34.

25 Ibid., p. 35.

26 Ibid., p. 37.

27 See Kirsti Bohata, 'Apes and Cannibals in Cambria: Images of the Racial and Gendered Other in Gothic Writing in Wales', in *Welsh Writing in English: A Yearbook of Critical Essays*, 6 (2000), 119–43, for discussion of Bertha Thomas's 'The Madness of Winifred Owen'.

28 Arthur O. Lovejoy traces the history of the idea of the 'Great chain of being' back to Greece; however, he notes that 'It was in the eighteenth century that the conception of the universe as a Chain of Being, and the principles which underlay this conception – plenitude, continuity, gradation – attained their widest diffusion and acceptance'; *The Great Chain of Being: A Study of the History of an Idea* (Cambridge, MA: Harvard University Press, 1957), p. 183. The influence of Darwin's theories of evolution, were undoubtedly profound. However, despite his emphasis on the randomness of evolution, the revolutionary thesis of his work was often ignored or overlooked, while the language was adopted and adapted to support and perpetuate existing racial stereotypes. In *The Idea of Race in Science: Great Britain 1800–1960* (London: Macmillan, with St Anthony's College, Oxford, 1982), Nancy Stepan notes: 'By as early as the late 1860s, scientists embracing evolution found that, despite the novelty of Darwin's anti-creationism, evolutionary thought was compatible with the idea of the fixity, antiquity, and hierarchy of human races. Far from dislodging old racial ideas, evolution strengthened them, and provided them with a new scientific vocabulary of struggle and survival' (pp. 48–9).

29 The *OED* lists the earliest known use of the word 'lesbian' in the context of lesbian love as occurring in 1890, in *Billings Medical Dictionary*, II, 47/1.

This passage is translated from German (presumably by Sander Gilman, since no other is credited).

[30] Sander L. Gilman, *Difference and Pathology*, p. 89.

[31] Lisa Moore, 'Teledildonics: Virtual Lesbians in the Fiction of Jeanette Winterson', in Elizabeth Grosz and Elspeth Probyn (eds), *Sexy Bodies: The Strange Carnalities of Feminism* (London & New York: Routledge, 1995), p. 121.

[32] Lisa Moore, ' "Something More Tender Still than Friendship": Romantic Friendship in Early-Nineteenth-Century England', *Feminist Studies*, 18, 3 (Fall 1992), 499–520 (514).

[33] Ibid., 516.

[34] Margiad Evans. 'A Modest Adornment', in *A View Across the Valley*, ed. Jane Aaron (Dinas Powys: Honno, 1999), p. 235.

[35] Ibid.

[36] Ibid., p. 238.

[37] Ibid.

[38] Ibid., p. 239. Bad odour is also another example of the conjunction of many discourses concerned with others. H. L. Malchow suggests that in the nineteenth century body odour was the focus of an obsession which otherwise failed to find a place in polite discourse and so emerges in Gothic fiction associated with a variety of others: 'If one also considers the strong body odour associated in racist discourse with the animalistic African or with the unpleasant odours associated with the Jew . . . as well as that ascribed to prostitutes (owing, it was thought, to the retention of semen) and to menstruating women, it is clear that scent played a role in drawing together or bridging a surprising number of nineteenth-century middle-class prejudices. The discourses of racism, homophobia, misogyny, class hatred, and religious bigotry were all corroborated by this most penetrating of the physical senses' (*Gothic Images of Race*, p. 141).

[39] Evans, 'A Modest Adornment', p. 236.

[40] Ibid., p. 237.

[41] Ibid., p. 248.

[42] Ibid., p. 245.

[43] See Elizabeth Grosz, 'Animal Sex: Libido as Desire and Death', in Elizabeth Grosz and Elspeth Probyn, *Sexy Bodies: The Strange Carnalities of Feminism* (London & New York: Routledge, 1995), for a discussion of how attributes from the insect world have been projected on to female sexualities, especially p. 281; see also Bram Dijkstra, *Evil Sisters: The Threat of Female Sexuality and the Cult of Manhood* (New York: Alfred A. Knopf, 1996).

[44] Evans, 'A Modest Adornment', p. 235.

[45] Ibid., p. 259.

[46] Rhys Davies, *The Black Venus* (London: Heinemann, 1944), p. 1. The trial, conducted by the chapel, of the custom of courting in bed in general and Olwen's conduct in particular is described as a 'dark business' (p. 1), while the man who directly asks Olwen if she has had sex with any of her suitors is

addressed by Olwen as the 'dark gentleman' (p. 25). Much later, Olwen's sexual attraction to Rhisiart Hughes is intimated thus: 'yet somewhere dark and faraway in her she felt an urge to turn back' (p. 165).

47 T. Denean Sharpley-Whiting, *Black Venus: Sexualized Savages, Primal Fears and Primitive Narratives in French* (Durham, NC: Duke University Press, 1999).

48 Davies, *The Black Venus*, p. 1.

49 Ibid., p. 40.

50 Eric Smith, *A Dictionary of Classical Reference in English Poetry* (Cambridge: Brewer, 1984), p. 252.

51 Davies, *The Black Venus*, p. 177. My italics.

52 Ibid., p. 137.

53 Ibid., p. 24.

54 Ibid., p. 111.

55 Ibid., p. 110.

56 Ibid., p. 49.

57 Sharpley-Whiting, *Black Venus*, p. 168, n. 7.

58 Ibid., p. 34.

59 Ibid., p. 65. See Sharpley-Whiting for a discussion of Alain Corbin's *Women for Hire: Prostitution and Sexuality in France after 1850*, tr. Alan Sheridan (Cambridge, MA: Harvard University Press, 1990).

60 Ibid., pp. 107–8, original italics.

61 Ibid., p. 58.

62 Ibid., p. 52.

63 Ibid., p. 192.

64 Ibid., p. 3.

65 Ibid.

66 Ibid., p. 192.

67 Ibid., pp. 51–2.

68 Ibid., p. 45.

69 Ibid., p. 37.

70 Lizzie has a similar relationship with her statue; although she lovingly polishes the figure, she tells Olwen: 'See the black pearls in her hair? Pretty she is. But when I'm in a temper very handy she is to spit on' (ibid., p. 111).

71 Davies, *The Black Venus*, p. 111. This attention to the black Venus's 'backside' is significant in terms of the extra-textual Black Venus narrative discussed on pp. 36–7 and 42–3, for it was Saartje Baartman's buttocks that were the focus of the erotic gaze. However, it is also interesting that in another novel, *Ram with Red Horns*, in which Rhys Davies portrays female homosexuality, it is the buttocks of the woman which are eroticized. 'Rhonwen stared from the bed, eyes less milkily blue, a pin-point of fire within them. Eireen's apricot buttocks, a sepia birthmark on one, hypnotised her. She half-rose in the bed, and sank back, a wild impulse resisted' (Bridgend: Seren, 1996, pp. 98–9).

72 Davies, *The Black Venus*, pp. 111–12.

[73] Ibid., p. 139.

[74] Ibid., p. 142.

[75] More information about Rhys Davies's sources and his own views on race, for example, would be helpful here. It would be interesting to know not only whether he ever encountered any of the cartoons of the Hottentot Venus or perhaps visited the Musée de l'Homme in Paris, where Baartman's body-cast and preserved brain and genitals were on display until 1974, but also to what degree Davies may have been influenced by the anthropological studies of H. J. Fleure et al. A wider examination, which considered Rhys Davies's work in the light of his modernist contemporaries, would also be enlightening, particularly with reference to D. H. Lawrence who, notably, also used a black (African) statue of a naked female figure to facilitate a discussion of sexuality linked to the primitive, in *Women in Love* ([1920]; London: Wordsworth Classics, 1992). There are 'several negro statues, wood carvings from West Africa' in the flat of Rupert Birkin's Bohemian friends. One in particular, representing a woman giving birth, is singled out for discussion and Birkin, the Lawrence figure in the novel, describes the artistic culture behind the carving as 'pure culture in sensation, culture in the physical consciousness, really ultimate *physical* consciousness, mindless, utterly sensual' (p. 81, original italics). It is interesting that this description seems to be echoed by Olwen's perception of Lizzie's black Venus quoted on p. 42: 'it was clear from her aimless face that she had no brains to trouble her. Flesh she was, flesh's dark beauty, and no more' (Davies, *The Black Venus*, p. 111). It would also be interesting to examine the author's use of racial characterization and notions of heredity across his own fiction. Daniel Williams's essay, 'Withered Roots: Ideas of Race in the Writings of Rhys Davies and D. H. Lawrence', in Meic Stephens (ed.), *Rhys Davies: Decoding the Hare* (Cardiff: University of Wales Press, 2001), makes an excellent start on these projects. A comparison of the treatment of race and sexuality in *The Black Venus* and some of Davies's other works, such as 'Glimpses of the Moon' and 'Fear', would also be useful. 'Glimpses of the Moon' is a story about an ex-soldier who, once married to a black woman in Africa, goes after his errant common-law wife with a cattle cart and a 'cattle-net', to bring her home, pacified with alcohol, from the barracks-town where she has been enjoying herself. 'Fear' is a particularly fascinating story, and M. Wynn Thomas has already highlighted links between the sexual undertones of the story and the racial otherness of the stranger in the railway carriage in his essay, '"Never Seek to Tell Thy Love": Rhys Davies's Fiction', in Stephens (ed.), *Rhys Davies: Decoding the Hare.*

[76] Young, *Colonial Desire*, p. 17.

[77] John Beddoe comments, in *The Races of Britain: A Contribution to the Anthropology of Western Europe* (Bristol: J. W. Arrowsmith, 1885), on the subject of those persons belonging to the 'elevated districts of the West Riding': 'I can see nothing British or Iberian about them; they are the bold, rude, obstinate race so well depicted by Charlotte Brontë, who lived among

them' (p. 251). This use of literature to inform or support an observation suggests not only the rather unscientific nature of the observations themselves, but also the power of stereotypical images gleaned from popular cultural representations. While, in a similar evaluation of the Welsh, Beddoe quotes Giraldus Cambrensis' descriptions of the Welsh character, claiming the account 'may still, after 700 years, be read with instruction' and that although 'it presses very hardly on the worst points of the Welsh character; but some of the vices which he alleges are those with which their enemies still charge them' (pp. 261–2).

78 Beddoe, *The Races of Britain*, p. 246.
79 See, for example, Daniel Pick, *Faces of Degeneration: A European Disorder, c.1848–c.1914* (Cambridge: Cambridge University Press, 1989).
80 Tarnowsky, cited in Gilman, *Difference and Pathology*, p. 96.
81 Gilman, *Difference and Pathology*, p. 95.
82 Ibid.
83 Anthony S. Wohl, Professor of History, Vassar College, NY, notes, at his website on 'Racism and Anti-Irish Prejudice in Victorian England', that 'John Beddoe . . . wrote in his *Races of Britain* (1862) that all men of genius were orthognathous (less-prominent jaw bones) while the Irish and Welsh were prognathous and that the Celt was closely related to Cromagnon man, who, in turn, was linked, according to Beddoe, to the "Africanoid".' (*http://www.victorianweb.org/history/race/Racism.html* (28.10.03)).
84 Davies, *The Black Venus*, p. 1.
85 Ibid., p. 28.
86 Ibid., p. 5.
87 Ibid., p. 43.
88 Ibid., p. 107.
89 See Beddoe, *The Races of Britain*, for a description of how Celts, Saxons, Angles etc., could supposedly be distinctly identified in the population of Norman descent in Victorian Britain.
90 See Stepan, *The Idea of Race in Science*, where she describes how the eugenicist programmes of twentieth-century Europe continued apace until disrupted by the enormity of the Holocaust. Craniology was used to 'prove' the racial inferiority of Jews under the Nazi regime, which was, of course, at its height when *The Black Venus* was published in 1944.
91 Davies, *The Black Venus*, p. 131.
92 Ibid., p. 65.
93 Ibid., pp. 130–1.
94 Rhys Davies, 'The Chosen One', *The Chosen One and Other Stories* (London: Heinemann, 1967), p. 8.
95 Ibid., p. 12.
96 Ibid., p. 2.
97 Ibid., p. 12.
98 Ibid.
99 Thomas, *Collected Poems*, p. 1. 'Out of the Hills' was published in Thomas, *The Stones of the Field* (Carmarthen: The Druid Press, 1946).

[100] Ibid., p. 4. 'A Peasant' was published in *The Stones of the Field.*

[101] Ibid.

[102] *The New Oxford Dictionary of English*, ed. Judy Pearsall (Oxford: Clarendon Press, 1998), p. 1492.

[103] Ibid.

[104] Ibid., p. 90. 'Meet the Family' was published in Thomas, *Poetry for Supper* (London: Rupert Hart-Davis, 1958).

[105] Ibid., p. 112. 'Portrait' was published in Thomas, *Tares* (London: Rupert Hart-Davies, 1961).

[106] Ibid., p. 4.

[107] Ibid., p. 38. 'Valediction' was published in *An Acre of Land* (Carmarthen: The Druid Press).

[108] Scientists such as Cuvier, who dissected Saartje Baartman, and Buffon both claimed physiological similarities between black women and orang-utans and it was believed that orang-utans could be sexually attracted to black women, a 'fact' noted by Thomas Jefferson (see Jefferson, 'Laws', in Eze (ed.), *Race and the Enlightenment*, p. 98; and Buffon [Georges-Louis Leclerc], *A Natural History, General and Particular*, in Eze, *Race and the Enlightenment*, pp. 20–33).

[109] Thomas, *Collected Poems*, p. 13. My italics. 'A Priest to his People' was published in Thomas, *The Stones of the Field.*

[110] Ibid., p. 20. 'The Airy Tomb' was published in Thomas, *The Stones of the Field.*

[111] Ibid., p. 66. 'The Last of the Peasantry' was published in Thomas, *Song at the Year's Turning* (London: Rupert Hart-Davies, 1955).

[112] Ibid., p. 117. 'A Welsh Testament' was published in Thomas, *Tares.*

[113] Ibid.

[114] Ibid., p. 118.

[115] Jennifer DeVere Brody, *Impossible Purities: Blackness, Femininity, and Victorian Culture* (Durham, NC, and London: Duke University Press, 1998), p. 24.

[116] Ibid., p. 92. 'Absolution' was published in Thomas, *Poetry for Supper.*

[117] *The New Oxford Dictionary of English*, p. 1256.

[118] R. S. Thomas, 'Y Llwybrau Gynt 2', *Selected Prose*, ed. Sandra Anstey (Bridgend: Poetry Wales Press, 1983), pp. 137–8.

[119] 'Nativism' refers to movements or people often criticized by postcolonialists, although also recognized by some as a necessary stage of anti-colonial resistance, for seeking to anchor and authenticate the 'true' national character at some arbitrary point in history, usually selected on the basis of being pre-colonial.

[120] Thomas, *Collected Poems*, p. 75. 'On Hearing a Welshman Speak' was published in *Poetry for Supper.*

[121] Ibid., p. 75.

[122] Ibid., p. 111. My translation. 'Those Others' was published in *Tares.*

[123] Ibid., p. 111. The comparison between the *národ/lid* of Bohemia and the *gwerin* of Wales is perhaps more apt than more common comparisons with

the German *Volk*, as the Czech experience included the domination of their towns and cities by a German-speaking upper and middle class, intent on completing the Germanicization of the Czech people. The association between the idealized *lid/národ* and notions of national identity may be seen in the way the words *lid*, meaning 'the people' (in the sense of the ordinary, largely rural population), and *národ*, meaning 'nation', came to be interchangeable. Derek Sayer, in *Coasts of Bohemia: A Czech History* (Princeton: Princeton University Press, 1998), describes how 'Folksongs are interchangeably referred to both as *lidové písne* and as *národní písne* in the titles of nineteenth century Czech collections . . . This says much for what the idea of the *ceský národ* [Czech nation or people] came eventually to convey. It took on class as well as ethnic connotations, and its favoured imagery was sturdily rural. [Thus] . . . social distance from *lid* easily translated into foreignness from *národ*' (p. 119).

[124] Saree Makdisi, *Romantic Imperialism: Universal Empire and the Culture of Modernity* (Cambridge: Cambridge University Press, 1998), p. 56.

[125] Thomas, *Collected Poems*, p. 77. 'Green Categories' was published in *Song at the Year's Turning*.

[126] Thomas, *Collected Poems*, p. 2. 'A Labourer' was published in *The Stones of the Field*.

3 En-gendering a New Wales

[1] Declan Kiberd, in *SPAN*, 41 (1995), p. 40.

[2] I follow Vron Ware in my use of the term 'feminism' here 'to mean the political formation that grew out of the early nineteenth-century demands for women's rights, and which continued to oppose and redefine dominant views of what constituted "womanhood"', *Beyond the Pale: White Women, Racism and History* (London: Verso, 1992), p. xiii.

[3] A contemporary term which referred to the many interlinked issues of suffrage, public life, dress codes, marriage, sexuality and so on.

[4] A detailed discussion of the circumstances leading up to the formal alliance between the Welsh Union of Women's Liberal Associations and Cymru Fydd (as embodied in the Welsh National Federation), which was finally, if briefly, achieved in 1895, as well as of the internal tensions of this alliance, may be found in Ursula Masson's '"Hand in Hand with the Women, Forward We will Go": Welsh Nationalism and Feminism in the 1890s', in *Women's History Review* (forthcoming). This essay also provides a wealth of references for further reading in this area.

[5] Masson, 'Hand in Hand'.

[6] Mrs Wynford Philipps [Nora], 'Notes on the Work of Welsh Liberal Women', *Young Wales*, 1/2 (February 1895), 37–9 (39). *Young Wales* was a Liberal, nationalist, monthly periodical that derived its title from the 'Young Italy' nationalist movement, as well as echoing the Young Ireland movement.

[7] Ibid., 38.

8 This construction could be seen as operating within the wider Victorian discourse of '*Cymru Lân, Cymru Lonydd*' [pure and peaceable Wales]. See Hywel Teifi Edwards, *Codi'r Hen Wlad yn ei Hôl: 1850–1914* (Llandysul: Gomer, 1989).

9 Anon., *Young Wales*, 1/1 (January 1895), 17–19 (19).

10 Anne McClintock, '"No Longer in a Future Heaven": Women and Nationalism in South Africa', in *Transition* , 51 (1991), 104–23 (105).

11 Ursula Masson, 'Nationalism and Feminism: Women Liberals and Cymru Fydd' (unpublished paper given at the Annual Conference of the Archif Menywod Cymru/Women's Archive of Wales, Aberystwyth, National Library of Wales, November 1999), and 'Nationalism and Feminism: Women Liberals and Cymru Fydd' (unpublished paper given at the Mamwlad/Motherland 2000 conference, Trinity College, Carmarthen, April 2000). I am very grateful to Ursula Masson for allowing me to read these papers and for responding to numerous enquiries.

12 For some other discussions of the place of women in colonial (and anti-colonial) discourse, see Partha Chatterjee's chapters on 'The Nation and Its Women' and 'Women and the Nation', in *The Nation and its Fragments: Colonial and Postcolonial Histories* (Chichester: Princeton University Press, 1993), while some more general discussions on women and nation/nationalism include Anne McClintock, '"No Longer in a Future Heaven"', *Transition*, 51, reprinted in Nicki Charles and Helen Hintjens (eds), *Gender, Ethnicity and Political Ideologies* (London: Routledge, 1998); Nira Yuval-Davies and Floya Anthias (eds), *Woman-Nation-State* (London: Macmillan, 1989); Sylvia Walby, 'Woman and Nation', in Gopal Balakrishnan and Benedict Anderson (eds), *Mapping the Nation* (London: Verso, 1996).

13 The title of the periodical means 'Future Wales: The Periodical of the National Party of Wales'.

14 *Cymru Fydd*, 3/6, 335.

15 *Cymru Fydd*, 4/4, 180.

16 Ibid.

17 Ibid., 181.

18 See references in the *Oxford Companion to New Zealand Literature* (1998) (entries on 'Science fiction', 'Utopianism', 'Vogel, Julius' and 'Women's Suffrage'); in Lawrence Jones's chapter 'The Novel', in the *Oxford History of New Zealand Literature in English*, ed. Terry Sturm, 2nd edn, 1998; and in Raewyn Dalziel, *Julius Vogel, Business Politician* (1986). See also Roger Robinson's introductions to Vogel's novel in editions from Exisle Press, Auckland, 2000, and University of Hawai'i, 2002.

19 Julis Vogel, *Anno Domini 2000; or, Woman's Destiny* (Auckland: Exisle Publishing, 2000), p. 140.

20 Ibid., p. 38.

21 Ibid., p. 39.

22 Ibid., p. 140.

23 *Cymru Fydd*, 3/6, 341.

24 *Cymru Fydd*, 3/6, 334.

25 *Cymru Fydd*, 4/3, 181–2.

26 *Cymru Fydd*, 4/3, 179.

27 This is exactly the kind of national institution that the Anglican Church in Wales is criticized for failing to develop, earlier in the story. Lady Gwen suggests that even though the Church of England could never be an adequate substitute for Calvinism – the 'true' religion of Wales and the source of all its strength – a truly national, or Celtic, Anglican Church might have offered something of value to the Welsh nation: 'It [the Church] had the noblest storehouse which an intellectual artist could have craved to build a religious life for the nation. It had stories from almost every century in the Christian era which it might have taught its children' (*Cymru Fydd*, 4/3, 177). Thus the engrafting of Christianity upon India could be viewed, from a Christian perspective at least, as saving souls without necessarily undermining national culture.

28 *Cymru Fydd*, 4/1, 39–40.

29 *Cymru Fydd*, 4/3, 179.

30 Interestingly, Lady Gwen reinforces gender boundaries by retaining military valour as a male domain; thus the Fishguard Invasion is repelled by male Christian soldiers, and the well-known story that it was the local women who scared off the invaders by using their red petticoats or mantles to mimic soldiers' red coats is ignored. I am grateful to Jeni Williams for pointing this out.

31 *Cymru Fydd*, 4/3, 173.

32 *Cymru Fydd*, 4/3, 173–4.

33 *Cymru Fydd*, 3/6, 344.

34 Ibid., my italics.

35 *Cymru Fydd*, 3/7, 385.

36 *Cymru Fydd*, 4/1, 35.

37 *Cymru Fydd*, 4/1, 40.

38 I am grateful to Jeni Williams for highlighting this point.

39 Since we are told at the outset that this story is a romance, it is also worth noting that if our heroine were to marry she would, we are told, have to retire from politics, and so a traditionally happy ending of marriage would be a dubious one in a feminist context. Such a marriage might not be such a disaster in terms of her role as national allegory, however, since – insofar as it is possible to guess the direction of the unfinished story – the most appropriate match for Gwen would appear to be her masculine veteran cousin, and thus the independence of Wales would be perpetuated in this idealized union – although of course there is no way of knowing whether this was to be the outcome of the novel.

40 Ann Heilmann, *New Woman Fiction: Women Writing First-Wave Feminism* (London: Macmillan, 2000), p. 31.

41 Ceridwen Lloyd-Morgan made this point during a discussion following a paper (Kirsti Bohata, 'En-gendering a New Wales') given at the annual

conference of the Association for Welsh Writing in English, at Gregynog, Newtown, in March 2002.

[42] Mallt Williams ('Un o'r ddau Wynne'), 'Patriotism and the Women of Cymru', *Young Wales*, 4/5 (May 1898), 115.

[43] See, for example, Susheila Nasta (ed.), *Motherlands: Black Women's Writing from Africa, the Caribbean and South Asia* (London: The Women's Press, 1991), p. xii.

[44] See bell hooks, *Yearning: Race, Gender and Cultural Politics* (London: Turnaround, 1991).

[45] Matthew Arnold's *On the Study of Celtic Literature* (1868) followed Ernest Renan's *La Poésie des Races Celtiques* (1854) in describing the Celts (referring to the Irish and the Welsh) as 'an essentially feminine race' (see David Cairns and Shaun Richards, *Writing Ireland: Colonialism, Nationalism and Culture* (Manchester: Manchester University Press, 1988), p. 44). The Celts were, according to Arnold, timid, delicate and shy, with a preference for a retired life and an embarrassment at encounters with the great world, possessing quick perceptions and a sensitive disposition. These modest and unassuming 'positive' feminine traits are not without their negative counterparts. The Celts are sentimental and prone to exaggeration, they are irrational, in the full sense of lacking the rationalism upon which post-Enlightenment Europe laid so much value. While they might display genius, their lack of moderation or 'measure' renders them the slaves and not the masters of the creative impulse. When coupled with the lack of the masculine qualities attributed to the Teutonic peoples, the effect is to undermine completely the possibility of the Welsh or Irish ever being *capable* of self-rule, showing them as dependent by necessity on the English for the vital balancing of their feminine characteristics. The 'Celtic people' are described as wanting pragmatism, balance, patience and – significantly – sanity, just as Victorian (middle-class) women were undermined by their supposed tendency towards madness, hysteria and irrationality. In interpreting nationalities in terms of gender, Arnold (and Renan before him) had constructed a picture of the Welsh as *naturally* incapable of independence and *naturally* inferior to England, as women were naturally dependent upon and inferior to men. It was, of course, a familiar portrait of colonized peoples, sketched by the colonizer to justify and normalize the dominance of another country. Interestingly, the increasing prestige of feminism in the second half of this century has allowed Wales to promote an image of ancient Welsh society as egalitarian, using, amongst other evidence, the laws of Hywel Dda, which are seen to champion women's rights in an otherwise misogynistic Europe. In this interpretation of the past, the Welsh are seen as having had a misogynistic culture forced upon them by the institution of English law, and also by the destruction of the Celtic Church. (This is a position adopted by the author of 'Lady Gwen'.) Christopher Meredith's portrayal, in *Griffri* (Bridgend: Seren, 1991), of the Celtic Church as allied with nature and a positive image of sex is in marked contrast to later puritanical religious doctrine. His startling image of the transformation of a beautiful, sexually experienced young woman into a

devil, during a sexual encounter with a young man, might be seen as a graphic portrayal of the demonization of women and sex by the imported religion of the Norman colonizers.

46 Rodanthi Tzanelli, 'Experiments on Puerile Nations, or the Impossibility of Surpassing your Father: The Case of the Anglo-Greek Dialogue' (unpublished paper). I am indebted to the author for generously allowing me to read this essay. See also Tzanelli's unpublished Ph.D. thesis, 'The "'Greece" of Britain and the "Britain" of Greece: Performance, Stereotypes, Expectations and Intermediaries in Victorian and Neo-Hellenic Narratives, 1864–81' (University of Lancaster, 2002).

47 Tzanelli, 'Experiments on Puerile Nations'.

48 Hywel Teifi Edwards, *Codi'r Hen Wlad yn ei Hôl*, p. 17.

49 I am indebted to Rhys Hywyn for kindly providing the translation that appears here.

50 *National Pageant of Wales: Book of the Words* by G. P. Hawtrey, Master of the Pageant and 'Owen Rhoscomyl', 'Historian' (Cardiff: *Western Mail*, 1909, preliminary edn), p. 2.

51 Quoted in Edwards, *Codi'r Hen Wlad yn ei Hôl*, p. 256.

52 The quotation is from *The Theatre* (1907), 17 (no number is given; however, since it was 'short-lived' it may be that only one issue was printed), in Helen Gilbert and Joanne Tompkins, *Post-Colonial Drama: Theory, Practice and Politics* (London: Routledge, 1996), p. 1.

53 *Book of Words*, p. 56.

54 Ibid., p. 54. Gwen's lack of a romantic connection (except, as I have already speculated, for her fondness for her heroic Cymric soldier) saves her from relegation from Parliament and there seems to be no danger of her forming any (inevitably symbolic) union with a non-Welsh man. Whether 'A Welsh Nationalist' intended to follow Vogel in marrying his heroine to an equivalent of the Emperor of Greater Britain, as is the fate of Lady Gwen's New Zealand counterpart, Hilda Fitzherbert, is impossible to tell. Although we know Wales is loyal to the Crown, a similar union would have more problematic implications for the Welsh story, which asserts the need for Welsh independence, albeit one which at the same time advocates a fierce imperial loyalty.

55 Marina Warner, *Monuments and Maidens: The Allegory of the Female Form* (London: Vintage, 1996), p. xx.

56 Ibid.

57 Ibid., p. 66.

58 See Richard Pankhurst, *Sylvia Pankhurst: Artist and Crusader* (London: Paddington Press, 1979), pp. 103–11.

59 I am grateful to Elaine Zinkham for drawing my attention to this Australian example. See also Elaine Zinkham, 'Louisa Albury Lawson: Feminist and Patriot', in Debra Adelaide (ed.), *A Bright and Fiery Troop: Australian Women Writers of the Nineteenth Century* (Ringwood, Victoria: Penguin, 1988).

[60] Margaret Ward, 'National Liberation Movements and the Question of Women's Liberation: The Irish Experience', in Clare Midgley (ed.), *Gender and Imperialism* (Manchester: Manchester University Press, 1998), p. 106.

[61] Ibid.

[62] Ceridwen Lloyd-Morgan, 'From Temperance to Suffrage?', in Angela V. John (ed.), *Our Mother's Land: Chapters in Welsh Women's History 1830–1939* (Cardiff: University of Wales Press, 1991), p. 148.

4 *The Battle for the Hills*

[1] Thomas, *Collected Poems*, p. 194. 'Reservoirs' was published in Thomas, *Not That He Brought Flowers* (London: Rupert Hart-Davies, 1968).

[2] Erica Carter, James Donald and Judith Squires (eds), *Space and Place: Theories of Identity and Location* (London: Lawrence & Wishart, 1993), p. xii.

[3] See, for example, Iwan Bala's exploration of what he describes as 'custodial aesthetics' in visual art in *Custodial Aesthetics*.

[4] Ned Thomas, *The Welsh Extremist*, 1991 edn, p. 31.

[5] Jan Penrose, 'Reification in the Name of Change: The Impact of Nationalism on Social Constructions of Nation, People and Place in Scotland and the United Kingdom', in Peter Jackson and Jan Penrose (eds), *Constructions of Race, Place and Nation* (London: UCL Press, 1993), p. 29.

[6] Pyrs Gruffudd, 'Prospects of Wales: Contested Geographical Imaginations: Perspectives from Wales', in Ralph Fevre and Andrew Thompson (eds), *Nation, Identity and Social Theory* (Cardiff: University of Wales Press, 1999), p. 161.

[7] Aschcroft, Griffiths and Tifffin, *Post-Colonial Studies*, p. 92.

[8] Kitchener Davies, for example, was predicting the widespread exploitation of Welsh resources for the benefit of England in a 1936 essay 'Lle Cymru Yng Nghynllwynion Lloegr' (Wales's Place in England's Conspiracies), in *Heddiw*, 1/3 (October 1936), 90–2. It is also interesting to remember that the story of Tryweryn is uncannily prefigured by the myth of *Cantref y Gwaelod* in which a whole community and a great swathe of territory are lost to Wales in one great catastrophe when the sea breaks through Welsh defences which are decayed or undefended.

[9] Saunders Lewis, 'The Caernarfon Court Speech', in Alun R. Jones and Gwyn Thomas (eds), *Presenting Saunders Lewis* (Cardiff: University of Wales Press, 1973), p. 124.

[10] See Herbert Hughes, *An Uprooted Community: A History of Epynt* (Llandysul: Gomer, 1998), p. 104. Some 219 people and 54 farms and holdings were compulsorily purchased to provide an artillery range for army training.

[11] Cited in Hughes, *An Uprooted Community*, p. 98.

[12] See George Ryle, *Forest Service: The First Forty-five Years of the Forestry*

Commission of Great Britain (Newton Abbot: David & Charles, 1969), and Richard Phillips, 'Y Bugail a'r Coedwigwr', *Gwyddor Gwlad: Cylchgrawn Amaethyddol Cymraeg*, 5 (March 1963), 24–37.

[13] See M. Wynn Thomas's introduction to *Internal Difference: Literature in Twentieth-Century Wales* (Cardiff: University of Wales Press, 1992), or Nigel Jenkins's discussion in Jeremy Moore and Nigel Jenkins, *Wales: The Lie of the Land* (Llandysul: Gomer, 1996), especially p. 97.

[14] While the mass unemployment in south Wales in the inter-war years, as well as the demands for timber in the coal industry, were significant factors in the design and execution of Forestry Commission policy in Wales, by nature of the requirements of afforestation the areas chosen for planting were outside the industrial valleys.

[15] Walter, *Outsiders Inside*, p. 196.

[16] This chapter does not address the contested economics of depopulation and afforestation, concentrating instead on the ideological battles which were waged on both 'sides' of the debate. However, it is worth noting that in many places work for local people was provided by the Forestry Commission's policies of afforestation. Interestingly, however, there is some anecdotal evidence that even then the relationship between the indigenous labourers and the Commission was, at times, rather ambivalent. Steve Tompkins makes a casual reference to the high incidence of forest fires in Wales acting as a disincentive for investment and further planting in the country. 'Afforestation in Wales followed a similar trend to that in England, although private forestry has taken a secondary role, possibly due to the tendency of Welsh plantations to be set on fire, which has a deterrent effect on investors' (Steve Tompkins, *Forestry in Crisis: The Battle for the Hills* (Bromley: Christopher Helm, 1989), p. 16). The suggestion is that the fires were started deliberately in protest at the planting of the land. I have been unable to find any firm evidence of the nature of such fires, but anecdotal evidence from Lampeter alleges that at least some of the arsonists were or had been employed by the Commission to plant the very trees they then burned. To dismiss this as another of the many apocryphal 'Free Wales Army' stories which abound – especially in Lampeter – is to miss the point.

[17] Jim Perrin notes that 'The Welsh language, usefully, has two words to fill the space in its discourse of the English-language word "landscape". The one is geographical: *tirwedd*, the very shape and contours of the land . . . The other word . . . is *tirlun*, the term used for the artistic work, which means quite literally, the picture of the land. *Not the way it looks but the way it is looked at.*' (Jim Perrin, *Spirits of Place: Travels, Encounters and Adventures in and from Wales* (Llandysul: Gomer, 1997), p. 8; my italics).

[18] This has been further complicated by the dual role of the Forestry Commission. It acted as adviser and agent in the forestry sector in Britain, but additional obligations were placed upon it as a public body; for example, ensuring safe public access and, more recently, being required by the government to raise revenue for the Treasury.

[19] Ryle, *Forest Service*, p. 124.
[20] *The Land and the Nation: Rural Report of the Liberal Land Committee 1923–25* (London: Hodder & Stoughton; 2nd edn [n.d.]), pp. 122–31.
[21] Steve Tompkins describes, in *Forestry in Crisis*, the tendency of foresters to 'denigrate the uplands as barren, unproductive, bleak, bare wasteland' as a 'transparent campaigning . . . device adopted to give themselves permission to afforest as much of the uplands as possible' (p. 7).
[22] *The Land and the Nation*, p. 125; my italics.
[23] Ibid., pp. 127–8.
[24] Ibid., pp. 130–1; original italics.
[25] Ibid., p. 127.
[26] Ibid., p. 129.
[27] Ibid.
[28] John Saville, *Rural Depopulation in England and Wales 1851–1951* (London: Routledge & Kegan Paul, 1957), pp. 145–6.
[29] Ibid., p. 146.
[30] Treasury Review of 1972, quoted in Tompkins, *Forestry in Crisis*, p. 171.
[31] Ryle, *Forest Service*, ch. 3.
[32] Ibid., p. 51.
[33] Ibid., pp. 56–7.
[34] William Linnard, *Welsh Woods and Forests: A History* (Llandysul: Gomer, 2000), p. 194.
[35] Ryle, *Forest Service*, p. 57.
[36] Ibid., p. 124. It is interesting that the spectre of Twm Shon Catti should surface here, mentioned in the same sentence as the 'Battle of the Towy', that confrontation between the Commission and widespread local and national popular opposition.
[37] Ryle, *Forest Service*, p. 123.
[38] Ibid., p. 124.
[39] Ibid.
[40] See Philip Lowe, Graham Cox, Malcom MacEwen, Tim O'Riordan and Michael Winter, *Countryside Conflicts: The Politics of Farming, Forestry and Conservation* (Aldershot: Gower Publishing Company, 1986), pp. 209–31.
[41] Phillips, 'Y Bugail a'r Coedwigwr', p. 27.
[42] Ryle, *Forest Service*, p. 126.
[43] Ibid., pp. 180–1.
[44] Gwenallt, *Cerddi Gwenallt: Y Casgliad Cyflawn*, ed. Christine James (Llandysul: Gomer, 2001), p. 149.
[45] J. R. Jones, cited in Phillips, *J. R. Jones*, p. 71.
[46] See, for example, Christopher Meredith's *Shifts* (Bridgend: Seren, 1988), for a study of the relationship between language, social history and place, or Emyr Humphreys's poetic sequence, 'Landscapes', ten poems which explore cultural and historical change through place (Emyr Humphreys, *Collected Poems* (Cardiff: University of Wales Press, 1999), pp. 101–10).
[47] Thomas, *Collected Poems*, p. 130. 'Afforestation' was published in Thomas, *The Bread of Truth* (London: Rupert Hart-Davies, 1963).

48 Tryfan, 'Yr Awdl: Cwm Carnedd', in *Eisteddfod Genedlaethol Cymru, Sir Fôn, 1957: Cyfansoddiadau a Beirniadaethau* (Liverpool: Gwasg y Brython, 1957), p. 41. Diolch o galon i Eddie Morgan, Felinwynt, am gyfieithu'r gerdd hir hon.

49 Ibid., p. 40.

50 Ibid.

51 Waldo Williams, 'Preseli', *The Peacemakers: Selected Poems*, trans. by Tony Conran (Llandysul: Gomer, 1997), pp. 112–13.

52 Tryfan, 'Cwm Carnedd', p. 41.

53 Ibid., p. 42.

54 D. J. Williams, *The Old Farmhouse*, translated from the Welsh by Waldo Williams (London: George G. Harrap & Co., 1961), p. 197.

55 Gwenallt, *Cerddi Gwenallt*, p. 148.

56 Ibid., p. 149.

57 Thomas, *Collected Poems*, p. 194.

58 Islwyn Ffowc Elis, *Wythnos yng Nghymru Fydd* (Caerdydd [Cardiff]: Plaid Cymru, 1957), p. 214.

59 Ned Thomas, *Derek Walcott: Poet of the Islands* (Cardiff: Welsh Arts Council, 1980), p. 15.

60 Christopher Meredith, *Shifts* ([1988], Bridgend: Seren, 1997), p. 45.

61 Williams, *The Old Farmhouse*, p. 61.

62 Gwenallt, *Cerddi Gwenallt*, p. 148.

63 Tryfan, 'Cwm Carnedd', p. 41.

64 Harri Webb, 'Cwmtaf Bridge', *The Green Desert: Collected Poems 1950–1969* ([1969], Llandysul: Gomer, 1976), p. 37.

65 Williams, *The Old Farmhouse*, p. 235. The Lowland Hundred mentioned here is a reference to the story of *Cantref y Gwaelod*.

66 Ibid., p. 79.

67 Thomas, *The Complete Poems*, p. 108. 'Too Late' was published in Thomas, *Tares*.

68 Harri Webb, 'Above Tregaron', *The Green Desert*, p. 36.

69 Walter, *Outsiders Inside*, p. 10.

70 Doreen Massey, *Space, Place and Gender* (Cambridge: Polity Press, 1994), p. 8.

71 Walter, *Outsiders Inside*, p. 196.

72 hooks, *Yearning*, p. 147.

73 Ibid.

5 'Devices of Otherness'?

1 Raja Rao, *Kanthapura* (1938), cited in Dennis Walder, *Post-colonial Literatures in English: History, Language, Theory* (Oxford: Blackwell Publishers, 1998), p. 43.

2 Janet Davies, *The Welsh Language* (Cardiff: University of Wales Press, 1993), p. 56.

[3] Ned Thomas, *Derek Walcott: Poet of the Islands* (Cardiff: Welsh Arts Council, 1980), p. 2.

[4] See, for example, Jane Aaron, 'Echoing the (M)other Tongue: *Cynghanedd* and the English Language Poet', in Belinda Humfrey (ed.), *Fire Green as Grass: Studies of the Creative Impulse in Anglo-Welsh Poetry and Short Stories of the Twentieth Century* (Llandysul: Gomer, 1995).

[5] Bill Ashcroft, 'Is that the Congo? Language as Metonymy in the Post-Colonial Text', in *World Literature in English*, 29/2 (1989), 3–10 (5).

[6] Ibid.

[7] John Harris, 'Introduction' to *My People*, Caradoc Evans ([1915]; Bridgend: Seren, 1987), p. 11.

[8] Elizabeth Gordon and Mark Williams, 'Raids on the Articulate: Code-Switching, Style-Shifting, and Post-Colonial Writing', at (*http://www.engl.canterbury.ac.nz/research/raids.html* (9.04.02), originally published in *Journal of Commonwealth Literature*, 33/2 (September 1998), 75–96. All references are from the electronic version, consequently no page numbers are available.

[9] I use the word 'foreign' (in inverted commas) here simply to denote a language other than the language of the main body of the text, although the other connotations of this word are difficult to overlook.

[10] In some postcolonial writing, including some English-language Welsh texts, the insertion of 'native' words may occur even when the author may not actually speak the 'native' language fluently.

[11] Ashcroft, Griffiths and Tiffin, *The Empire Writes Back*, p. 44.

[12] Ngugi wa Thiong'o, *Writers in Politics: Essays* (London: Heinemann, 1981), pp. 59–60.

[13] Karl Marx, *Pre-capitalist Economic Formations*, tr. from the German by Jack Cohen, ed. and intro. by E. J. Hobsbawm (London: Lawrence & Wishart, 1964), p. 74.

[14] Saunders Lewis, 'The Fate of the Language', in Jones and Thomas (eds), *Presenting Saunders Lewis*, p. 127.

[15] R. Tudur Jones, 'The Welsh Language and Religion', in Meic Stephens (ed.), *The Welsh Language Today* (Llandysul: Gomer, 1973), p. 80.

[16] The first chapter of Dai Smith's *Wales! Wales?* (London: George Allen & Unwin, 1984) is entitled 'A Welcome to Wales', and the author begins by asking whose Wales he is welcoming the reader to. His answer is 'my Wales of course'.

[17] Tim Williams, *The Patriot Game: 1* (Beddau: Tynant Books, 1997), p. 52. My italics.

[18] Ibid., p. 51.

[19] Robyn Lewis, *Second Class Citizen: A Selection of Highly Personal Opinions Concerning the Two Languages of Wales* (Llandysul: Gomer, 1969), p. xv.

[20] See, for example, M. Wynn Thomas, *Corresponding Cultures: The Two Literatures of Wales* (Cardiff: University of Wales Press, 1999).

[21] Ieuan Gwynedd Jones, *Mid Victorian Wales: The Observers and the Observed* (Cardiff: University of Wales Press, 1992), p. 72.

22 Ieuan Gwynedd Jones cited in Janet Davies, *The Welsh Language*, p. 47. Interestingly, in terms of a consideration of the alliance of language with religion in Wales and with the wider question of the essential role of language in culture, Ieuan Gwynedd Jones notes the tendency of some earlier in the nineteenth century to regard Welsh as a *functional* rather than an *essential* aspect of culture and religion. This is revealed in the attempt to assimilate incomers through religion rather than language and a consequent effort to provide English chapels. In part, this devaluation of language must be seen in the light of the increasingly ambivalent relationship to the language which was the result of its less than prestigious position compared with English. It can also be seen in relation to the ideas of Matthew Arnold, which described the supposed mystical and spiritual genius, which was the essence of the Welsh identity, as detached from any relationship of the language (which he maintained was detrimental to the Welsh and to Britain). The emphasis on the cultural significance of language, which has been reiterated through the twentieth century is a result of the historical experience of the consequences of such a functionalist view of language.

23 Jones, *Mid-Victorian Wales*, p. 78.

24 Davies, *The Welsh Language*, p. 117.

25 See R. S. Thomas, 'Abercuawg', in *Selected Prose*. R. S. Thomas's 1978 review of Dee Brown's *Bury My Heart at Wounded Knee* is available in *Selected Prose* and, for a wider discussion of R. S. Thomas's 'alternative Wales', see Graham Davies, 'Resident Aliens: R. S. Thomas and the Anti-Modern Movement', in *Welsh Writing in English: A Yearbook of Critical Essays* 7 (2001–2), 50–77; and Jane Aaron and M. Wynn Thomas, ' "Pulling You through Changes": Welsh Writing in English Before, Between and After Two Referenda', in Thomas (ed.), *A Guide to Welsh Literature, VII.*

26 See Thomas, *Internal Difference* and *Corresponding Cultures.*

27 Jeremy Paxman, *The English: A Portrait of a People* (London: Penguin, 1999), p. 47; my italics.

28 Chinua Achebe, *Morning Yet on Creation Day: Essays* (London: Heinemann, 1975), p. 62. Interestingly, Achebe's statement about having been given a language by his parents of course implies that choices are indeed made over which language to use, that parents and schools make certain limited choices about which language their children will speak and learn in class. In Wales, some parents did 'choose' *not* to pass on the language to their children.

29 Quoted in Wiliam Owen Roberts, 'Writing on the Edge of Catastrophe', in Ian A. Bell (ed.), *Peripheral Visions: Images of Nationhood in Contemporary British Fiction* (Cardiff: University of Wales Press, 1995), p. 78.

30 Ngugi, *Writers in Politics*, p. 51.

31 Achebe, *Morning Yet on Creation Day*, p. 58.

32 Ibid., p. 62.

33 See Ngugi wa Thiong'o, 'Return to the Roots', in *Writers in Politics.*

34 Roberts, 'Writing on the Edge of Catastrophe', p. 77.

35 Siân James, a comment made during an interview at the 'Mamwlad/ Motherlands 2000' conference, Trinity College, Carmarthen (April 2000).

36 M. Drabble (ed.), *Oxford Companion to English Literature* (1985), cited in K. D. M. Snell (ed.), *The Regional Novel in Britain and Ireland: 1800–1990* (New York: Cambridge University Press), p. 2, n. 6; my italics.

37 Gordon and Williams, 'Raids on the Articulate'.

38 Glyn Jones, *Welsh Heirs* (Llandysul: Gomer, 1977), p. 29. Interestingly, the later use of the plural *cymanfaeodd* is not translated.

39 Gordon and Williams, 'Raids on the Articulate'.

40 Ashcroft, 'Is that the Congo?', p. 4.

41 Ibid.

42 See Ashcroft, Griffiths and Tiffin, *The Empire Writes Back*, p. 66.

43 Margiad Evans, *Country Dance* (1932; London: John Calder, 1978), p. 14.

44 Ibid., p. vii.

45 Ibid.

46 Ibid., p. 24.

47 Ibid., p. 36.

48 Clare Morgan, 'Exile and Kingdom: Margiad Evans and the Mythic Landscape of Wales', in *Welsh Writing in English: A Yearbook of Critical Essays*, 6 (2000), 89–118 (106). See this essay for a more detailed discussion of Margiad Evans's relationship to the Welsh language, as well as her use of French phrases in her journal, and for Morgan's study of Evan's use of dialect in her stories of the Welsh Border.

49 Gayatri Chakravorty Spivak, *Outside in the Teaching Machine* (London: Routledge, 1993), p. 91.

50 Ashcroft, 'Is that the Congo?', p. 4. Original italics.

51 Monica Heller (ed.), *Codeswitching: Anthropological and Sociolinguistic Perspectives* (Berlin: Mouton de Gruyter, 1988), cited in Gordon and Williams, 'Raids on the Articulate'.

52 Gordon and Williams, 'Raids on the Articulate'. Gordon and Williams point to the discrepancy between the perception of code-switching when the untranslated language is a dominant (European) one compared with a less prestigious, often colonial or post-colonial one: 'When it [code-switching] is done by lower-class people, less educated people, ethnic minorities, it is frequently condemned as carelessness, an irresponsible jumbling up of languages by people who do no know any better . . . Nevertheless, when it is done by educated people using acceptable Western languages, code-switching is seen as perfectly acceptable and even praiseworthy – a sign of high culture and intelligence.' Reading T. S. Eliot's critical essays, with their large chunks of untranslated Latin, Greek and other European languages, provokes a sense of exclusion for any readers so unfortunate as not to have a solid grounding in the Classics.

53 Donna Landry and Gerald Maclean (eds), *Spivak Reader* (London: Routledge, 1996), p. 304.

54 Graziella Parati, 'Looking through Non-Western Eyes: Immigrant Women's Autobiographical Narratives in Italian', in Giesela Brinker-Gabler and Sidone

Smith (eds), *Writing New Identities: Gender, Nation, and Immigration in Contemporary Europe* (London: University of Minnesota Press, 1997), p. 135.

55 Ibid.

56 Christoper Meredith, *Shifts*, p. 45.

57 In Meredith's own work there are numerous other examples. In *Griffri*, for instance, although a glossary of the Welsh words associated with twelfth-century Welsh culture is provided, it is by no means complete. The humorous names of a host of spirits or demons, for example, remain untranslated, thus forming a rather private joke between author and Welsh-language readers, and – perhaps not insignificantly – a pleasing reward to those who reach for *Y Geiriadur Mawr*.

58 Conversation with the author (Pontypridd, 29 November 2000).

59 Conversation with the author (Pontypridd, 29 November 2000).

60 Meredith, *Shifts*, p. 118.

61 Emyr Humphreys, *Collected Poems* (Cardiff: University of Wales Press, 1999), p. x.

62 Humphreys, *Collected Poems*.

63 Gordon and Williams, 'Raids on the Articulate'.

64 Peter Finch, *Useful* (Bridgend: Seren, 1997), p. 46.

65 It is an interesting comment on the relative 'strengths' of the two languages of Wales that when Peter Finch, working from an English-language base, plays with language like this it is regarded as an exciting, innovative and linguistically enriching experiment. When the controversial writer John Owen, working from a Welsh-language base, made similarly playful use of Welsh and English, albeit in prose rather than poetry, he was accused (although by no means universally) of damaging the language, or promoting the sloppy use of 'Wenglish'.

6 Hybridity and Authenticity

1 Neil ten Kortenaar, 'Beyond Authenticity and Creolization', pp. 40–1.

2 See Ashcroft, Griffiths and Tiffin, *Post-Colonial Studies*, p. 229.

3 Morgan, *The Eighteenth Century Cultural Renaissance*, p. 17.

4 Lenore Keeshing-Tobias, 'Stop Stealing Native Stories', in Bruce Ziff and Pratima V. Rao (eds), *Borrowed Power: Essays on Cultural Appropriation* (New Brunswick, New Jersey: Rutgers University Press, 1997), p. 71, first published in *Globe* (26 January 1990). My thanks to Michelle LaFlamme for alerting me to this article.

5 Williams, *When Was Wales?*, p. 114.

6 Cited in Loomba, *Colonialism/Postcolonialism*, p. 85.

7 Ibid., p. 86.

8 Cited in Ned Thomas, *The Welsh Extremist*, 1991 edn, p. 37.

9 Dorothy Entwistle, 'Children's Reward Books in Nonconformist Sunday Schools, 1870–1914', unpublished Ph.D. thesis (University of Lancaster, 1990).

[10] Archives of Blackie & Son Ltd, Publishers, Glasgow, UGD61, held at Glasgow University library.

[11] One was awarded to Brynmor Davies by Seion Sunday School in Edwardsville, for good attendance, and the other was presented to Glen Edwards, in 1928, for regular attendance and good conduct at Weslyan Methodist Sunday School (there is no location given for this Sunday School, but the book was found in a second-hand bookshop in Powys). The third is in the National Library of Wales and bears no inscription. I have found no copy at the British Library.

[12] Sir Walter Scott, *On the Welsh Marches* (Glasgow: Blackie and Son, 1906), p. 27.

[13] Scott shortened the name of the prince from Gwenwynwyn to Gwenwyn. Andrew Davies explains that Scott 'claim[ed] in the preface [to *The Betrothed*] that it was less obtrusive to his readership. Whether he was a aware of the fact that "gwenwyn" means "poison" in Welsh is not clear. The unsympathetic characterisation of the Welsh prince could imply that he did' (Andrew Davies, 'From Fictional Nation to National Fiction? Reconsidering T. J. Llewelyn Prichard's *The Adventures and Vagaries of Twm Shon Catti*), in *Welsh Writing in English: A Yearbook of Critical Essays*, 8 (2003), 1–28 (24, n. 32)).

[14] Scott, *On the Welsh Marches*, pp. 10–11.

[15] Ibid., pp. 95–6.

[16] Williams, ' "I going away, I going home" ', p. 181.

[17] This novella is Thomas's most explicit study of the experience of Welshness and hybridity, but it also concerns itself with issues of gender, the role of women and the differences between class structures in Wales and England which must, unfortunately, be largely ignored in this discussion. Thomas's concern with the figures of the outsider and the hybrid is also evident elsewhere in her writing. For a fuller treatment of her interest in the figure of the hybrid, see Kirsti Bohata, 'Bertha Thomas: The New Woman and Anglo-Welsh Hybridity', in Ann Heilmann and Margaret Beetham (eds), *New Woman Hybridities: Feminity, Feminism and International Consumer Culture, 1880–1930* (London: Routledge, 2004). See also the introduction to Bertha Thomas, *The Only Girl*, ed. and intro by Kirsti Bohata (Aberystwyth: Honno, forthcoming).

[18] Thomas, *Picture Tales from Welsh Hills*, p. 52.

[19] Ibid., pp. 114–15.

[20] Ibid., p. 56.

[21] Ibid., p. 58.

[22] Ibid., p. 84.

[23] Ibid., p. 56. Bertha Thomas's Llanffelix has been identified as Llandeilo, in Carmarthenshire, and all Thomas's stories with a Welsh setting are located in the Towy valley countryside to the south of this town. A Roman temple and hoards of Roman coins had indeed been discovered in this area of the Towy valley and by the late nineteenth century the Roman gold mines at Dolaucothi had been reopened.

24 Thomas, *Picture Tales from Welsh Hills*, p. 60.

25 Elwyn 'irreverently' criticizes the 'highfalutin' bardic names, which he gives as 'The Peacock of the Platform' or 'The Eagle of Snowdon', 'The Nightingale of the Universe' and so on, imagining himself as 'The Thunderer of Trearavon' or 'The Trothi Twitterer' (p. 60). Interestingly, Elwyn compares these Welsh bardic names as 'Just like the Red Indian chiefs in "The Old Trail", the book Dobson junior lent me, "Big Bear", "Bellowing Bison", "Prairie Warbler"' (ibid.), thus emphasizing, perhaps, his sense of distance from and the exoticism of this Welsh cultural tradition.

26 Thomas, *Picture Tales from Welsh Hills*, p. 60.

27 The Treason of the Long Knives is a powerful motif in Welsh history. Although without any reliable historical substantiation, it refers to a supposed event in the time of Hengist, when the Welsh and Saxons had declared a truce and Welsh princes and nobles went to a Saxon feast in order to seal a peace. During the feast a signal was given by their leader whereupon the Saxons slew all the Welsh. The lack of historical proof for this event does not undermine the significance for the Welsh of a story which, along with acknowledging a great and bloody defeat for the Welsh, paints the Saxon as having overcome the Welsh dishonourably. A similar event, for example, occurs in Christopher Meredith's novel, *Griffri* (see p. 148–9), where the Welsh are slaughtered in the Norman castle at Abergavenny in the twelfth century. Meredith's fictional episode is based on an event recorded as historical fact by Thomas Stephens, in his *Welshmen: A Sketch of their History from Earliest Times to Llewelyn, the Last Welsh Prince* (London: T. F. Spriggs; Cardiff: Western Mail, 1901). Stephens emotively describes the 'dastardly act of treachery on the part of William de Braose' when 'a great feast was made in the castle [at Abergavenny], to which the chieftains of Wales were invited. The chieftains were cruelly assassinated in cold blood by the Norman murderers, and buried within the castle. The same monsters also put to death the wife of Seisyllt and her little child. This act, which for baseness is unmatched in the history of Wales, threatened to upset all the peaceful relations of the Welsh with England' (p. 168). The resonance of the Treason of the Long Knives continued to echo down the centuries, finding a new lease of life when the 1847 Education Report became known as the Treason of the Blue Books (*Brad y Llyfrau Gleision*), as well as in accounts such as Stephens's description of Norman treachery, published over fifty years later.

28 Thomas, *Picture Tales from Welsh Hills*, p. 61.

29 Ibid.

30 Ibid.

31 Ibid., p. 62.

32 Ibid., p. 73.

33 Ibid.

34 Ibid., p. 75.

35 Ibid., p. 58.

36 Elwyn's educational headstart is in part due to his perusal of his English uncle's library, diligently preserved by his mother.

[37] Thomas, *Picture Tales from Welsh Hills*, pp. 57–8.

[38] See Bohata, 'Bertha Thomas'.

[39] Thomas, *Picture Tales from Welsh Hills*, p. 79; original italics.

[40] See, for example, Bertha Thomas, 'The Madness of Winifred Owen', *Picture Tales from Welsh Hills*, repr. in Jane Aaron (ed.), *A View Across the Valley: Short Stories by Women from Wales c.1850–1950* (Dinas Powys: Honno, 1999).

[41] One question which should be considered at this point is why Bertha Thomas chose a male character for her story. She was a strong supporter of female suffrage and, while of an older generation than the fashionable young New Women of the *fin de siècle*, Thomas nevertheless testifies in her writing to a strong belief in the ability of women to excel in any sphere in which they find themselves, including that of the home, and there are plenty of other examples of her using strong and unconventional female characters to explore – amongst other themes – the position of the 'outsider'. The fact that the same routes to university and the Church were not open to women is of course one reason for her choice of a male central character, and it is worth noting the similarities between the biography of Thomas's father and that of the fictional Elwyn. John Thomas lived to be more than seventy years old and excelled in his Church career, but in other ways his origins parallel Elwyn's. He was born at a riverside farmstead called Glanyrafon, won a scholarship to Oxford and married (above him) the daughter of John Bird Sumner – at that time the Bishop of Chester and later Archbishop of Canterbury. Without any surviving papers, we can only speculate on how far Thomas's empathetic narrative may have been inspired by her father's more personal experiences.

[42] Thomas, *Picture Tales from Welsh Hills*, p. 58.

[43] Ibid., p. 67.

[44] Ibid., p. 108.

[45] Ibid., p. 79.

[46] Ibid., p. 145.

[47] Ibid.

[48] Ibid., pp. 126–7.

[49] Ibid., p. 129.

[50] Ibid.

[51] Ibid., p. 130. The unusual name of the father, Pam, is explained as 'a contraction of Padan-aram, a chance word caught from the Book of Genesis and bestowed on him as a luck-bearing appellation' (ibid.).

[52] Ibid., p. 131.

[53] Ibid., p. 132.

[54] Ibid., pp. 132–3.

[55] Ibid., p. 133.

[56] Ibid.

[57] Ibid., p. 137.

[58] Ibid., p. 127.

[59] Ibid., p. 123. Original italics.

60 Ibid.

61 Benedict Anderson, *Imagined Communities: Reflections on the Origin and Spread of Nationalism*, revised edn (London: Verso, 1991), p. 91.

62 Loomba, *Colonialism/Postcolonialism*, p. 173.

63 Fanon, *Black Skin, White Masks*, p. 18.

64 Ibid., p. 25.

65 Dafydd Johnston, 'Making History in Two Languages: Wiliam Owen Roberts's *Y Pla* and Christopher Meredith's *Griffri*', in *Welsh Writing in English: A Yearbook of Critical Essays*, 3 (1997), 118–33 (123).

66 While questioning the possibility of constructing a reliable linear narrative at all, the novel seems to suggest that artists have the ability to offer some sense of identity which historians are unable to achieve: 'How can we put what we are into items on a list? Your chronicle and my recitation of genealogies are so much dust. That's where song of either tongue or instrument can do something real, once in a while anyway. It can tell us what we are. But not too often or the clients get put off' (p. 9). 'Song' here seems to refer to poetry rather than storytelling, and Griffri later laments that he has been 'reduced from song to a kind of storytelling' (p. 154).

67 Meredith, *Griffri* ([1991] Bridgend: Seren, 1994), p. 44.

68 The cauldron referred to here is mentioned in 'Branwen Ferch Llŷr' (Branwen the Daughter of Llŷr) which is one of the four branches of the Mabinogi. It is a gift from Bendigeidfran (or Bendigeid Vran) to Matholwch and has a magical property: 'a man of thine slain to-day, cast him into the cauldron, and by tomorrow he will be as well as he was at the best, save that he will not have the power of speech' (Gwyn Jones and Thomas Jones (tr.), *The Mabinogion*, revised edn (London: Dent, 1993), p. 24). Thus to be a 'cauldron of the people' is metaphorically to re-member, to make whole, to (re)vivify a people.

69 Williams, *When Was Wales?*, p. 62.

70 Ibid.

71 Ibid.

72 Meredith, *Griffri*, p. 223.

73 Williams, *When Was Wales?*, p. 62.

74 Meredith, *Griffri*, p. 39.

75 Ibid., p. 158.

76 Ibid., p. 127.

77 Ibid., p. 205.

78 Ibid., p. 196.

79 Ibid.

80 Ibid., p. 61.

81 Ibid.

82 Ibid., p. 97.

83 Johnston, 'Making History in Two Languages', p. 123.

84 Charlotte Williams, ' "I going away, I going home" ', p. 180.

85 Meredith, *Griffri*, p. 40.

[86] Ashcroft, Griffiths and Tiffin, *The Empire Writes Back*, p. 37.

[87] Johnston, 'Making History in Two Languages', p. 123.

[88] Landscape is privileged over time as a central 'ordering concept of reality' by other Welsh writers to achieve similar ends of authentication. The effect of a poem such as 'Epil y Filiast', by Harri Webb in Meic Stephens (ed.), *Collected Poems* (Llandysul: Gomer, 1995), for example, is to emphasize the Welshness of an area which has become an (Anglicized?) wasteland of modern consumerism and is thus stigmatized in certain quarters as culturally derelict. In the poem, perceived historico-cultural fracture is healed and temporal measurements are rejected in favour of a view which presents place as constituting a unifying Welsh identity/history.

[89] Williams, *When Was Wales?*, p. 62.

[90] Bryan Martin Davies, 'Y Clawdd', *Deuoliaethau* (Llandysul: Gomer, 1976), p. 47.

[91] Cited in Thomas, *Internal Difference*, p. xi.

[92] Williams, ' "I going away, I going home" ', p. 190.

[93] Bhabha borrows the image of the stairwell from Renée Green; see *The Location of Culture*, pp. 3–4.

[94] Meredith, *Griffri*, p. 245.

[95] Ibid.

[96] Alun Lewis, 'The Orange Grove', *In the Green Tree* (London: Allen & Unwin, 1948). For a discussion of this story and interpretations of its transcendental fantasy, see M. Wynn Thomas and Tony Brown, 'Colonial Wales and Fractured Language', and Kirsti Bohata, 'Beyond Authenticity? Hybridity and Assimilation in Welsh Writing in English', in *Nations and Relations: Writing Across the British Isles* (Cardiff: New Welsh Review, 2000).

[97] Meredith, *Shifts*, p. 161.

[98] E. G. Bowen, 'The Geography of Wales as a Background to its History', in I. Hume and W. T. R. Price (eds), *The Welsh and their Country: Selected Readings in the Social Sciences* (Llandysul: Gomer, in association with the Open University, 1986), p. 85.

[99] See 'On Hearing a Welshman Speak', Thomas, *Collected Poems*, p. 75.

[100] See 'Out of the Hills', ibid., p. 1.

[101] See 'A Welshman in St James' Park', ibid., p. 165. This is reminiscent of Waldo Williams's poem 'Preseli' where the mountains are 'Wrth fy nghefn ym mhob annibyniaeth barn' (At my back in all independence of mind) (Williams, *The Peacemakers*, p. 112).

[102] Thomas, *Internal Difference*, p. xiv.

[103] Ibid. This thesis is developed further in *Corresponding Cultures*.

[104] Bhabha, *The Location of Culture*, p. 38; original italics.

Bibliography

ARCHIVES
Blackie and Son Ltd, Publishers, Glasgow, UGD61, held at Glasgow University library.

BOOKS AND ARTICLES
[Anon.], 'Lady Gwen, or the days that are to be, by a Welsh nationalist', *Cymru Fydd*, 3, 4 (1890–1).

Aaron, Jane, 'Finding a voice in two tongues: gender and colonization', in Jane Aaron, Teresa Rees, Sandra Betts and Moira Vincentelli (eds), *Our Sister's Land: The Changing Identities of Women in Wales* (Cardiff: University of Wales Press, 1994).

Aaron, Jane, 'Echoing the (m)other tongue: *Cynghanedd* and the English language poet', in Belinda Humfrey (ed.), *Fire Green as Grass: Studies of the Creative Impulse in Anglo-Welsh Poetry and Short Stories of the Twentieth Century* (Llandysul: Gomer, 1995).

Aaron, Jane, 'Slaughter and salvation: Welsh missionary activity and British imperialism', in Charlotte Williams, Neil Evans and Paul O'Leary (eds), *A Tolerant Nation?: Exploring Ethnic Diversity in Wales* (Cardiff: University of Wales Press, 2003).

Aaron, Jane and Thomas, M. Wynn, ' "Pulling you through changes": Welsh writing in English before, between and after two referenda', in M. Wynn Thomas (ed.), *A Guide to Welsh Literature, Volume VII: Welsh Writing in English* (Cardiff: University of Wales Press, 2003).

Achebe, Chinua, *Morning Yet on Creation Day: Essays* (London: Heinemann, 1975).

Anderson, Benedict, *Imagined Communities: Reflections on the Origin and Spread of Nationalism*, revised edition (London: Verso, 1991).

Arnold, Matthew, *On the Study of Celtic Literature* (1868) in Matthew

Arnold, *The Study of Celtic Literature and Other Essays* (London: Dent, 1910).

Ashcroft, Bill, 'Is that the Congo? Language as metonymy in the post-colonial text', *World Literature in English*, 29/2 (1989), 3–10.

Ashcroft, Bill, Griffiths, Gareth and Tiffin, Helen, *The Empire Writes Back Theory and Practice in Post-Colonial Literatures* (1989; London: Routledge, 1994).

Ashcroft, Bill, Griffiths, Gareth and Tiffin, Helen, *Post-Colonial Theory: The Key Concepts* (2000; London: Routledge, 2003).

Bala, Iwan (ed.), *Certain Welsh Artists: Custodial Aesthetics in Contemporary Welsh Art* (Bridgend: Seren, 1999).

Balsom, Denis, 'The three-Wales model', in John Osmond (ed.), *The National Question Again: Welsh Political Identity in the 1980s* (Llandysul: Gomer, 1985).

Beddoe, John, *The Races of Britain: A Contribution to the Anthropology of Western Europe* (Bristol: J. W. Arrowsmith, 1885).

Bhabha, Homi, *The Location of Culture* (1994; London: Routledge, 1998).

Bohata, Kirsti, 'Apes and cannibals in Cambria: images of the racial and gendered other in Gothic writing in Wales', in *Welsh Writing in English: A Yearbook of Critical Essays*, 6 (Cardiff: New Welsh Review, 2000), 119–43.

Bohata, Kirsti, 'Beyond authenticity? Hybridity and assimilation in Welsh writing in English', in Tony Brown and Russell Stephens (eds), *Nations and Relations: Writing Across the British Isles* (Cardiff: New Welsh Review, 2000).

Bohata, Kirsti, 'Bertha Thomas: the new woman and Anglo-Welsh hybridity', in Ann Heilmann and Margaret Beetham (eds), *New Woman Hybridities: Feminity, Feminism and International Consumer Culture, 1880–1930* (London: Routledge, 2004).

Bowen, E. G., 'The geography of Wales as a background to its history', in I. Hume and W. T. R. Price (eds), *The Welsh and their Country: Selected Readings in the Social Sciences* (Llandysul: Gomer, published in association with the Open University, 1986).

Brown, Tony and Thomas, M. Wynn, 'Alun Lewis and the politics of empire: two replies', in the 'forum' section of *Welsh Writing in English: A Yearbook of Critical Essays*, 8 (Cardiff: New Welsh Review, 2003), 175–9.

Buffon [Georges-Louis Leclerc], *A Natural History, General and Particular*, extracts from Emanuel Chukwudi Eze (ed.), *Race and the Enlightenment: A Reader* (Oxford: Blackwell, 1996).

Cairns, David and Richards, Shaun, *Writing Ireland: Colonialism, Nationalism and Culture* (Manchester: Manchester University Press, 1988).

Carter, Erica, Donald, James and Squires, Judith, (eds), *Space and Place: Theories of Identity and Location* (London: Lawrence & Wishart, 1993).

Chatterjee, Partha, *The Nation and Its Fragments: Colonial and Postcolonial Histories* (Chichester: Princeton University Press, 1993).

Cohen, Jeffrey Jerome, 'Hybrids, monsters, borderlands: the bodies of Gerald of Wales', in Jeffrey Jerome Cohen (ed.), *The Postcolonial Middle-Ages* (New York: St Martin's Press, 2000).

Conran, Tony, *Frontiers in Anglo-Welsh Poetry* (Cardiff: University of Wales Press, 1997).

Craig, Cairns, *The Modern Scottish Novel: Narrative and the National Imagination* (Edinburgh: Edinburgh University Press, 1999).

Crawford, Robert, *Devolving English Literature* (Oxford: Oxford University Press, 1992).

Davies, Andrew, 'From fictional nation to national fiction? Reconsidering T. J. Llywelyn Prichard's *The Adventures and Vagaries of Twm Shon Catti*', in *Welsh Writing in English: A Yearbook of Critical Essays*, 8 (Cardiff: New Welsh Review, 2003), 1–28.

Davies, Bryan Martin, 'Y clawdd', *Deuoliaethau* (Llandysul: Gomer, 1976).

Davies, Graham, 'Resident aliens: R. S. Thomas and the anti-modern movement', in *Welsh Writing in English: A Yearbook of Critical Essays* 7 (Cardiff: New Welsh Review, 2001–2), 50–77.

Davies, Janet, *The Welsh Language* (Cardiff: University of Wales Press, 1993).

Davies, Jonathan Ceredig, *Folk-lore of the West and Mid Wales* (1911; Lampeter: Llannerch, 1992).

Davies, Kitchener, 'Lle Cymru yng nghynllwynion Lloegr' (Wales's place in England's conspiracies), in *Heddiw* 1/3 (Oct 1936), 90–2.

Davies, Norman, *The Isles: A History* (Basingstoke: Macmillan, 1999).

Daniel, Patricia and Môn/Arfon Central America Group, *We Share the Same Struggle: Women in Wales, Women in Nicaragua* ([Bethesda?]: Môn/Arfon Central America Group, 1996/1998).

Davies, R. R., 'Colonial Wales', *Past and Present*, 65 (November 1974), 3–23.

Davies, R. R., 'Race relations in post conquest Wales: confrontation and compromise', *Transactions of the Honourable Society of Cymmrodorion* (1974–5), 32–56.

Davies, R. R., *Domination and Conquest: The Experience of Ireland, Scotland and Wales, 1100–1300* (Cambridge: Cambridge University Press, 1990).

Davies, R. R., *The First English Empire: Power and Identities in the British Isles 1093–1343* (Oxford: Oxford University Press, 2000).

Davies, Rhys, *The Black Venus* (London: Heinemann, 1944).

Davies, Rhys, 'The chosen one', *The Chosen One and Other Stories* (London: Heinemann, 1967).

Davies, Rhys, *Ram with Red Horns* (Bridgend: Seren, 1996).

Dijkstra, Bram, *Evil Sisters: The Threat of Female Sexuality and the Cult of Manhood* (New York: Alfred A. Knopf, 1996).

Drabble, Margaret (ed.), *Oxford Companion to English Literature* (Oxford: Oxford University Press, 1985).

Edwards, Hywel Teifi, *Codi'r Hen Wlad yn ei Hôl: 1850–1914* (Llandysul: Gomer, 1989).

Elis, Islwyn Ffowc, *Wythnos yng Nghymru Fydd* (Caerdydd [Cardiff]: Plaid Cymru, 1957).

Entwistle, Dorothy, 'Children's reward books in Nonconformist Sunday schools, 1870–1914', unpublished Ph.D. thesis (University of Lancaster, 1990).

Evans, Margiad, *Country Dance* (1932; London: John Calder, 1978).

Evans, Margiad, 'A modest adornment', in Jane Aaron (ed.), *A View Across the Valley* (Dinas Powys: Honno, 1999).

Evans, Neil, 'Internal colonialism? Colonization, economic development and political mobilization in Wales, Scotland and Ireland', in Graham Day and Gareth Rees (eds), *Regions, Nations and European Integration: Remaking the Celtic Periphery* (Cardiff: University of Wales Press, 1991).

Eze, Emanuel Chukwudi (ed.), *Race and the Enlightenment: A Reader* (Oxford: Blackwell, 1996).

Fanon, Frantz, *Black Skin, White Masks*, translated from the French by Charles Lam Markham (1967; London: Pluto Press, 1986).

Ferro, Marc, *Colonization: A Global History* (London: Routledge, 1997).

Finch, Peter, *Useful* (Bridgend: Seren, 1997).

Gandhi, Leela, *Postcolonial Theory: A Critical Introduction* (Edinburgh: Edinburgh University Press, 1998).

Gilbert, Helen and Tompkins, Joanne, *Post-Colonial Drama: Theory, Practice and Politics* (London: Routledge, 1996).

Gilman, Sander L., *Difference and Pathology: Stereotypes of Sexuality, Race, and Madness* (London: Cornell University Press, 1985).

Gordon, Elizabeth, and Williams, Mark, 'Raids on the articulate: code-switching, style-shifting, and post-colonial writing', at *http://www.engl. canterbury.ac.nz/research/raids.html* (9.04.02), originally published in *Journal of Commonwealth Literature* 33/2 (September 1998), 75–96.

Grosz, Elizabeth, 'Animal sex: libido as desire and death', in Elizabeth Grosz and Elspeth Probyn, *Sexy Bodies: The Strange Carnalities of Feminism* (London and New York: Routledge, 1995).

Gruffudd, Pyrs, 'Prospects of Wales: contested geographical imaginations', in Ralph Fevre and Andrew Thompson (eds), *Nation, Identity and Social Theory: Perspectives from Wales* (Cardiff: University of Wales Press, 1999).

Gwenallt, *Cerddi Gwenallt: Y Casgliad Cyflawn*, Christine James (ed.), (Llandysul: Gomer, 2001).

Harris, John, 'introduction' to *My People* by Caradoc Evans (1915; Bridgend: Seren, 1987), 11.

Hawtrey, G. P. and Rhoscomyl, Owen, *National Pageant of Wales: Book of the Words* (Cardiff: Western Mail, Preliminary Edition, 1909).

Heaney, Seamus, 'Open Letter', in Seamus Deane (ed.), *Ireland's Field Day* (London: Hutchinson, 1985).

Heilmann, Ann, *New Woman Fiction: Women Writing First-Wave Feminism* (London: Macmillan, 2000).

Heller, Monica (ed.), *Code Switching: Anthropological and Sociolinguistic Perspectives* (Berlin: Mouton de Gruyter, 1988).

Hill, Greg, 'Sisyphus goes to school', *Planet: The Welsh Internationalist*, 161 (October/November 2003), 82–5.

hooks, bell, *Yearning: Race, Gender and Cultural Politics* (London: Turnaround, 1991).

Hughes, Herbert, *An Uprooted Community: A History of Epynt* (Llandysul: Gomer, 1998).

Humphreys, Emyr, *Collected Poems* (Cardiff: University of Wales Press, 1999).

Jefferson, Thomas, 'Laws', in *Notes on the State of Virginia*, cited in Emmanuel Chukwudi Eze (ed.), *Race and the Enlightenment: A Reader* (Oxford: Blackwell, 1997).

John, Angela V. (ed.), *Our Mother's Land: Chapters in Welsh Women's History: 1830–1939* (Cardiff: University of Wales Press, 1991).

Johnston, Dafydd, 'Making history in two languages: William Owen Robert's *Y Pla* and Christopher Meredith's *Griffri*', in *Welsh Writing in English: A Yearbook of Critical Essays*, 3 (Cardiff: New Welsh Review, 1997), 118–33.

Jones, Aled, 'The other internationalism? Missionary activity and Welsh nonconformist perceptions of the world in the nineteenth and twentieth centuries', in Charlotte Williams, Neil Evans and Paul O'Leary (eds), *A Tolerant Nation?: Exploring Ethnic Diversity in Wales* (Cardiff: University of Wales Press, 2003).

Jones, Glyn, *Welsh Heirs* (Llandysul: Gomer, 1977).

Jones, Gwyn and Jones, Thomas (trans.), *The Mabinogion*, revised edition (London: Dent, 1993).

Jones, Ieuan Gwynedd, *Mid Victorian Wales: The Observers and the Observed* (Cardiff: University of Wales Press, 1992).

Jones, Lewis, *Cwmardy: The Story of a Welsh Mining Village* ([1937] London: Lawrence & Wishart, 1978).

Jones, R. Tudur, 'The Welsh language and religion', in Meic Stephens (ed.), *The Welsh Language Today* (Llandysul: Gomer, 1973).

Keeshig-Tobias, Lenore, 'Stop stealing native stories', in Bruce Ziff and Pratima V. Rao (eds), *Borrowed Power: Essays on Cultural Appropriation*

(New Brunswick, New Jersey: Rutgers University Press, 1997). First published in *Globe* (26 January 1990).

Kortenaar, Neil ten, 'Beyond authenticity and creolization: reading Achebe writing culture, *PMLA*, 110, 1 (January 1995), 30–42.

Landry, Donna, and Maclean, Gerald (eds), *Spivak Reader* (London: Routledge, 1996).

Larson, Charles R., *The Ordeal of the African Writer* (London: Zed Books, 2001).

Lawrence, D. H., *Women in Love* ([1920] London: Wordsworth Classics, 1992).

Lewis, Alun, 'The orange grove', *In the Green Tree* (London: Allen & Unwin, 1948).

Lewis, Robyn, *Second Class Citizen: A Selection of Highly Personal Opinions Concerning the Two Languages of Wales* (Llandysul: Gomer, 1969).

Lewis, Saunders, 'The fate of the language', in Alun R. Jones and Gwyn Thomas (eds), *Presenting Saunders Lewis* (Cardiff: University of Wales Press, 1983).

Linnard, William, *Welsh Woods and Forests: A History* (Llandysul: Gomer, 2000).

Lloyd-Morgan, Ceridwen, 'From temperance to suffrage?', in Angela V. John (ed.) *Our Mother's Land: Chapters in Welsh Women's History 1830-1939* (Cardiff: University of Wales Press, 1991).

Llywellyn, Richard, *How Green Was My Valley* ([1939]; London: Penguin, 2001).

Loomba, Ania, *Colonialism/Postcolonialism* (London: Routledge, 1998).

Lovejoy, Arthur O., *The Great Chain of Being: A Study of the History of an Idea* (Cambridge, Massachusetts: Harvard University Press, 1957).

Lowe, Philip, Cox, Graham, MacEwen, Malcom, O'Riordan, Tim and Winter, Michael, *Countryside Conflicts: The Politics of Farming, Forestry and Conservation* (Aldershot: Gower Publishing Company, 1986).

Machen, Arthur, 'The novel of the black seal', *Tales of Horror and the Supernatural* (London: The Richards Press, 1949).

Makdisi, Saree, *Romantic Imperialism: Universal Empire and the Culture of Modernity* (Cambridge: Cambridge University Press, 1998).

Malchow, H. L., *Gothic Images of Race in Nineteenth Century Britain* (Stanford, California: Stanford University Press, 1996).

Marx, Karl, *Pre-capitalist Economic Formations*, translated from the German by Jack Cohen, introduction by E. J. Hobsbawm (ed.), (London: Lawrence & Wishart, 1964).

Massey, Doreen, *Space, Place and Gender* (Cambridge: Polity Press, 1994).

Masson, Ursula, ' "Hand in hand with the women, forward we will go": Welsh nationalism and feminism in the 1890s', *Women's History Review*, 4/12 (2003), 357–86.

Masson, Ursula, 'Nationalism and feminism: women liberals and Cymru Fydd' (unpublished paper given at the annual conference of the Archif Menywod Cymru/Women's Archive of Wales, Aberystwyth, National Library of Wales, November 1999).

Masson, Ursula, 'Nationalism and feminism: women liberals and Cymru Fydd', (Unpublished paper given at the Mamwlad/Motherland 2000 conference, Trinity College Carmarthen, April 2000).

McClintock, Anne, 'The angel of progress: pitfalls of the term "post-colonialism"', in Francis Barker, Peter Hulme and Margaret Iversen (eds), *Colonial Discourse/Postcolonial Theory* (Manchester: Manchester University Press, 1994).

McClintock, Anne, 'No longer in a future heaven', in Nicki Charles and Helen Hintjens (eds), *Gender, Ethnicity and Political Ideologies* (London: Routledge, 1998).

McClintock, Anne, '"No longer in a future heaven": women and nationalism in South Africa', *Transition*, 51 (1991), 104–23.

Memmi, Albert, *The Colonizer and the Colonized*, translated by Howard Greenfeld, original introduction by Jean-Paul Sartre (1965), new introduction by Liam O'Dowd (London: Earthscan Publications, 1990).

Meredith, Christopher, *Shifts* (1988; Bridgend: Seren, 1997).

Meredith, Christopher, *Griffri* ([1991] Bridgend: Seren, 1994).

Moore, Jeremy and Jenkins, Nigel, *Wales: The Lie of the Land* (Llandysul: Gomer, 1996).

Moore, Lisa, '"Something more tender still than friendship": romantic friendship in early-nineteenth century England', *Feminist Studies*, 18, 3 (Fall 1992), 499–520.

Moore, Lisa, 'Teledildonics: virtual lesbians in the fiction of Jeanette Winterson', in Elizabeth Grosz and Elspeth Probyn (eds), *Sexy Bodies: The Strange Carnalities of Feminism* (London and New York: Routledge, 1995).

Morgan, Clare, 'Exile and kingdom: Margiad Evans and the mythic landscape of Wales', in *Welsh Writing in English: A Yearbook of Critical Essays*, 6 (Cardiff: New Welsh Review, 2000), 89–118.

Morgan, Prys, 'From a death to a view: the hunt for the Welsh past in the Romantic period', in Eric Hobsbawm and Terence Ranger (eds), *The Invention of Tradition* (Cambridge: Cambridge University Press, 1983).

Morgan, Prys, 'From Long Knives to Blue Books', in R. R. Davies, Ralph A. Griffiths, Ieuan Gwynedd Jones and Kenneth O. Morgan (eds), *Welsh Society and Nationhood: Historical Essays Presented to Glanmor Williams* (Cardiff: University of Wales Press, 1984).

Morgan, Prys, 'Keeping the legends alive', in Tony Curtis (ed.), *Wales: The Imagined Nation* (Bridgend: Poetry Wales Press, 1986).

Morgan, Prys, *The Eighteenth-Century Renaissance* (Llandybïe: Christopher Davies, 1981).

Murray, Stuart and Riach, Alan (guest eds), *SPAN: Journal of the South Pacific Association for Commonwealth Literature and Language Studies*, 41 (October 1995).

Nasta, Susheila (ed.), *Motherlands: Black Women's Writing from Africa, the Caribbean and South Asia* (London: The Women's Press, 1991).

Ngugi wa Thiong'o, *Writers in Politics: Essays* (London: Heinemann, 1981).

Ngugi wa Thiong'o, *Decolonising the Mind: The Politics of Language in African Literature* (London: James Currey, 1986).

Pankhurst, Richard, *Sylvia Pankhurst: Artist and Crusader* (London: Paddington Press, 1979).

Parati, Graziella, 'Looking through non-Western eyes: immigrant women's autobiographical narratives in Italian', in Giesela Brinker-Gabler and Sidone Smith (eds), *Writing New Identities: Gender, Nation, and Immigration in Contemporary Europe* (Minneapolis: University of Minnesota Press, 1997).

Paxman, Jeremy, *The English: A Portrait of a People* (London: Penguin, 1999).

Penrose, Jan, 'Reification in the name of change: the impact of nationalism on social constructions of nation, people and place in Scotland and the United Kingdom', in Peter Jackson and Jan Penrose (eds), *Constructions of Race, Place and Nation* (London: UCL Press, 1993).

Perrin, Jim, *Spirits of Place: Travels, Encounters and Adventures in and from Wales* (Llandysul: Gomer, 1997).

Philipps, Mrs Wynford [Nora], 'Notes on the work of Welsh liberal women', *Young Wales*, 1/2 (February 1895), 37–9.

Phillips, Dewi Z., *Writers of Wales: J. R. Jones* (Cardiff: University of Wales Press, 1995).

Phillips, Richard, 'Y bugail a'r coedwigwr', *Gwyddor Gwlad: Cylchgrawn Amaethyddol Cymraeg*, 5 (March 1963), 24–37.

Pick, Daniel, *Faces of Degeneration: A European Disorder, c.1848–c.1914* (Cambridge: Cambridge University Press, 1989).

Pikoulis, John, 'Alun Lewis and the politics of empire', in *Welsh Writing in English: A Yearbook of Critical Essays*, 8 (Cardiff: New Welsh Review, 2003), 157–75.

Pratt, Mary Louise, *Imperial Eyes: Travel Writing and Transculturation* (London: Routledge, 1992).

Pritchard, T. J. Llywelyn, *The Adventures and Vagaries of Twm Shon Catti: Descriptive of Life in Wales, interspersed with poems* (Aberystwyth: John Cox, 1828).

Rao, Raja, *Kanthapura* ([1938]; Oxford: Oxford University Press, 1989).

Rees, Alun, 'Anglo-Taffy', in Gwyneth Tyson Roberts, *The Language of the Blue Books: The Perfect Instrument of Empire* (Cardiff: University of Wales Press, 1998).

Renan, Ernest, *La Poésie des Races Celtiques* (1854), translated by William G. Hutchison as *The Poetry of the Celtic Races: And Other Studies* (London: Walter Scott, Ltd, 1896).

Roberts, Gwyneth Tyson, *The Language of the Blue Books: The Perfect Instrument of Empire* (Cardiff: University of Wales Press, 1998).

Roberts, Harri, 'Embodying identity: class, nation and corporeality in the 1847 Blue Books report', *North American Journal of Welsh Studies*, 3, 1 (Winter 2003), 1–22.

Roberts, Wiliam Owen, 'Writing on the edge of catastrophe', in Ian A. Bell (ed.), *Peripheral Visions: Images of Nationhood in Contemporary British Fiction* (Cardiff: University of Wales Press, 1995).

Rothwell, Jerry (ed.), *Creating Meaning: A Book about Culture and Democracy* (Blaengarw: Valley and Vale, 1992).

Ryle, George, *Forest Service: The First Forty-five Years of the Forestry Commission of Great Britain* (Newton Abbot: David and Charles, 1969).

Said, Edward, *Orientalism: Western Conceptions of the Orient* ([1978] London: Penguin, 2003).

Said, Edward, *Out of Place: A Memoir* ([1999] London: Granta Books, 2000).

Saville, John, *Rural Depopulation in England and Wales 1851–1951* (London: Routledge & Kegan Paul, 1957).

Sayer, Derek, *Coasts of Bohemia: A Czech History* (Princeton: Princeton University Press, 1998).

Scott, Walter, *On the Welsh Marches* (Glasgow: Blackie and Son, 1906).

Sharpley-Whiting, T. Denean, *Black Venus: Sexualised Savages, Primal Fears and Primitive Narratives in French* (Durham: Duke University Press, 1999).

Sheers, Owen, *The Blue Book* (Bridgend: Seren, 2000).

Shelley, Mary, *Frankenstein* ([1818] London: Penguin, 1994).

Shome, R., 'Caught in the term "post-colonial": why the "post-colonial" still matters', in Ismail S. Talib, *The Language of Postcolonial Literatures: An Introduction* (London: Routledge, 2002).

Sikes, Wirt, *British Goblins: Welsh Folk-Lore, Fairy Mythology, Legends and Traditions*, illustrations by T. H. Thomas (London: Sampson Low, 1880).

Smith, Dai, *Wales! Wales?* (London: George Allen and Unwin, 1984).

Smith, Eric, *A Dictionary of Classical Reference in English Poetry* (Cambridge: Brewer, 1984)

Snell, K. D. M. (ed.), *The Regional Novel in Britain and Ireland: 1800-1990* (New York: Cambridge University Press, 1998).

Spivak, Gayatri Chakravorty, *Outside in the Teaching Machine* (London: Routledge, 1993).

Spivak, Gayatri Chakravorty, 'Three women's texts and a critique of imperialism', in Bill Ashcroft, Gareth Griffiths, and Helen Tiffin (eds), *The Post-Colonial Studies Reader* (London: Routledge, 1995).

Stepan, Nancy, *The Idea of Race in Science: Great Britain 1800–1960* (London: Macmillan, in association with St Anthony's College, Oxford, 1982).

Stephens, Thomas, *Welshmen: A Sketch of their History from Earliest Times to the Death of Llewelyn, the Last Welsh Prince* (London: J. F. Spriggs; Cardiff: Western Mail, 1901).

Talib, Ismail S., *The Language of Postcolonial Literatures: An Introduction* (London: Routledge, 2002).

The Land and the Nation: Rural Report of the Liberal Land Committee 1923–25 (London: Hodder and Stoughton; Second Edition, [n.d.]).

Thomas, Bertha, 'The madness of Winifred Owen', in Jane Aaron (ed.), *A View Across the Valley: Short Stories by Women from Wales c.1850–1950* (Dinas Powys: Honno, 1999).

Thomas, Bertha, *Picture Tales of Welsh Hills* (London: T. Fisher Unwin, 1912).

Thomas, M. Wynn (ed.), *A Guide to Welsh Literature, Volume VII: Welsh Writing in English* (Cardiff: University of Wales Press, 2003).

Thomas, M. Wynn, *Internal Difference: Literature in Twentieth Century Wales* (Cardiff: University of Wales Press, 1992).

Thomas, M. Wynn, *Corresponding Cultures: The Two Literatures of Wales* (Cardiff: University of Wales Press, 1999).

Thomas, M. Wynn, 'Review of Sam Adams's *Writers of Wales: Roland Mathias*', *Planet*, 117 (June/July 1996), 105–6.

Thomas, M. Wynn, ' "Never seek to tell thy love": Rhys Davies's fiction', in Meic Stephens (ed.), *Rhys Davies: Decoding the Hare* (Cardiff: University of Wales Press, 2001).

Thomas, M. Wynn and Brown, Tony, 'Colonial Wales and fractured language', in Tony Brown and Russell Stephens (eds), *Nations and Relations: Writing Across the British Isles* (Cardiff: New Welsh Review, 2000).

Thomas, Ned, *Derek Walcott: Poet of the Islands* (Cardiff: Welsh Arts Council, 1980).

Thomas, Ned, *The Welsh Extremist: A Culture in Crisis* (London: Gollancz, 1971).

Thomas, Ned, *The Welsh Extremist: Modern Welsh Politics, Literature and Society* (Talybont: Y Lolfa, 1991).

Thomas, R. S., *The Stones of the Field* (Carmarthen: The Druid Press, 1946).

Thomas, R. S., *An Acre of Land* (Carmarthen: The Druid Press, 1952).

Thomas, R. S., *Song at the Year's Turning* (London: Rupert Hart-Davis, 1955).

Thomas, R. S., *Poetry for Supper* (London: Rupert Hart-Davis, 1958).

Thomas, R. S., *Tares* (London: Rupert Hart-Davis, 1961).

Thomas, R. S., *The Bread of Truth* (London: Rupert Hart-Davis, 1963).

Thomas, R. S., *Not That He Brought Flowers* (London: Rupert Hart-Davis, 1968).

Thomas, R. S. *The Collected Poems: 1945–1990* (London: Dent, 1993).

Thomas, R. S., 'Abercuawg', in *Selected Prose*, ed. Sandra Anstey (Bridgend: Poetry Wales Press, 1983).

Thomas, R. S., 'Y llwybrau gynt 2', in *Selected Prose*, ed. Sandra Anstey (Bridgend: Poetry Wales Press, 1983).

Tompkins, Steve, *Forestry in Crisis: The Battle for the Hills* (Bromley: Christopher Helm, 1989).

Tryfan, 'Yr awdl: Cwm Carnedd', in *Eisteddfod Genedlaethol Cymru, Sir Fôn, 1957: Cyfansoddiadau a Beirniadaethau* (Liverpool: Gwasg y Brython, 1957).

Tzanelli, Rodanthi, 'Experiments on puerile nations, or the impossibility of surpassing your father: the case of the Anglo-Greek dialogue' (unpublished paper).

Tzanelli, Rodanthi, 'The "Greece" of Britain and the "Britain" of Greece: performance, stereotypes, expectations and intermediaries in Victorian and Neohellenic narratives, 1864–81' (unpublished Ph.D. thesis, Lancaster 2002).

Usher, Jane M., *Women's Madness: Misogyny or Mental Illness?* (London: Harvester Wheatsheaf, 1991).

Valentine, Mark, *Arthur Machen* (Bridgend: Seren, 1995).

Vogel, Julius, *Anno Domini 2000: or, Woman's Destiny* (Auckland: Exisle Publishing, 2000).

Walby, Sylvia, 'Woman and nation', in Gopal Balakrishnan and Benedict Anderson (eds), *Mapping the Nation* (London: Verso, 1996).

Walder, Dennis, *Post-colonial Literatures in English: History, Language, Theory* (Oxford: Blackwell Publishers, 1998).

Walter, Bronwen, *Outsiders Inside: Whiteness, Place and Irish Women* (London: Routledge, 2001).

Ward, Margaret, 'National liberation movements and the question of women's liberation: the Irish experience', in Clare Midgley (ed.), *Gender and Imperialism* (Manchester: Manchester University Press, 1998).

Ware, Vron, *Beyond the Pale: White Women, Racism and History* (London: Verso, 1992).

Warner, Marina, *Monuments and Maidens: The Allegory of the Female Form* (London: Vintage, 1996).

Webb, Harri, *The Green Desert: Collected Poems 1950–1969* ([1969] Llandysul: Gomer, 1976).

Williams, Charlotte, ' "I going away, I going home" ': mixed-"race", movement, and identity', in Lynne Pearce (ed.), *Devolving Identities: Feminist Readings in Home and Belonging* (Aldershot: Ashgate, 2000).

Williams, Charlotte, Evans, Neil and O'Leary, Paul (eds), *A Tolerant Nation?: Exploring Ethnic Diversity in Wales* (Cardiff: University of Wales Press, 2003).

Williams, Charlotte, *Sugar and Slate* (Aberystwyth: Planet, 2002).

Williams, D. J., *The Old Farmhouse,* translated from the Welsh by Waldo Williams (London: George G. Harrap and Co., 1961).

Williams, Daniel, 'Withered roots: ideas of race in the writings of Rhys Davies and D. H. Lawrence', in Meic Stephens (ed.), *Rhys Davies: Decoding the Hare* (Cardiff: University of Wales Press, 2001).

Williams, Gwyn A., *When Was Wales? A History of the Welsh* ([1985] London: Penguin, 1991).

Williams, Mallt, 'Patriotism and the women of Cymru', *Young Wales*, 4/5 (May 1898), 115.

Williams, Raymond, 'Welsh culture', in Daniel Williams (ed.), *Who Speaks for Wales?: Raymond Williams on Nation and Identity* (Cardiff: University of Wales Press, 2003).

Williams, Sian Rhiannon, 'The true "Cymraes": images of women in women's nineteenth-century Welsh periodicals', in Angela V. John (ed.), *Our Mother's Land: Chapters in Welsh Women's History, 1830–1939* (Cardiff: University of Wales Press, 1991).

Williams, Tim, *The Patriot Game: Volume 1* (Beddau: Tynant Books, 1997).

Williams, Waldo, 'Preseli', *The Peacemakers: Selected Poems*, translated by Tony Conran (Llandysul: Gomer, 1997).

Wohl, Anthony S., 'Racism and anti-Irish prejudice in Victorian England', (*http://www.victorianweb.org/history/race/Racism.html* [28.10.03]).

Young, Robert, *Colonial Desire: Hybridity in Theory, Culture and Race* (London: Routledge, 1995).

Yuval-Davies, Nira and Anthias, Floya (eds), *Woman–Nation–State* (London: Macmillan, 1989).

Zinkham, Elaine, 'Louisa Albury Lawson: feminist and patriot', in Debra Adelaide (ed.), *A Bright and Fiery Troop: Australian Women Writers of the Nineteenth Century* (Victoria: Penguin, 1988).

Index